Facebook™
Application Development

Facebook™
Application Development

Nick Gerakines

WILEY

Wiley Publishing, Inc.

Facebook™ Application Development

Published by
Wiley Publishing, Inc.
10475 Crosspoint Boulevard
Indianapolis, IN 46256
www.wiley.com

To my wife, Carolyn, and my little girl, Vanessa: Thank you for enduring and making this possible.

To my family, friends, co-workers, and editors: Thank you. I would not have been able to do this without your support.

About the Author

Nick Gerakines is a software engineer at Yahoo! in San Francisco, California where he works on del.icio.us and contributes to numerous other projects and Facebook applications. In addition, he has written several Facebook applications of his own, including the popular I Play WoW application. He is an active member of the Facebook developer community and writes frequently on the topic. He lives in Mountain View, California with his wife, Carolyn, and daughter, Vanessa.

Credits

Executive Editor
Chris Webb

Development Editor
Kevin Shafer

Technical Editor
Leslie M. Orchard

Production Editor
Daniel Scribner

Copy Editor
Cate Caffrey

Editorial Manager
Mary Beth Wakefield

Production Manager
Tim Tate

Vice President and Executive Group Publisher
Richard Swadley

Vice President and Executive Publisher
Joseph B. Wikert

Project Coordinator, Cover
Lynsey Stanford

Proofreader
Sossity Smith

Indexer
Robert Swanson

Acknowledgments

This book didn't produce itself. Chris Webb, Kevin Shafer, and Leslie M. Orchard played monumental roles in its preparation and production.

Contents

Contents

Contents

Contents

Contents

Introduction

Developing Facebook applications can be fun and challenging. With that development comes a set of unique problems and possibilities that require a different way of thinking than traditional web site development. *Facebook Application Development* takes you through some of those situations and provides you with the tools and know-how to develop feature-rich Facebook applications.

Who This Book Is For

This book is for software engineers who are new to the Facebook Platform or who have had some experience with it and want to go further. *Facebook Application Development* assumes that you have an understanding of basic web technologies and have some web development experience.

In particular, this book is geared to the following:

❑ Novices to the Facebook Platform will benefit from this book the most because it will take you through several introductory projects and progress to some of the more advanced concepts.

❑ Developers who have some experience with the Facebook Platform will also benefit from this book because it explores many of the seemingly simple technologies powering the Facebook Platform.

❑ Designers and developers focusing on some of the more user-focused aspects of Facebook application development can use this book as a solid reference (especially Chapters 3 and 4).

What This Book Covers

Facebook Application Development covers a variety of topics and theory that can immediately be applied to develop Facebook applications. This includes (but is not limited to) the following:

❑ Working with Facebook Markup Language (FBML)

❑ Using Facebook API requests and responses, and method definitions

❑ Querying Facebook with the Facebook Query Language (FQL)

❑ Using automated and scheduled tasks

Keep in mind that the Facebook Platform is under constant development, and changes occur regularly. Many of the topics of this book will remain immutable, but there are bound to be topics that go out of date.

How This Book Is Structured

This book opens with an introduction to the Facebook Platform and explains what Facebook applications are. It immediately goes into an example application to demonstrate some of the introductory concepts, and gives you a taste at what Facebook application development is like.

The next several chapters introduce the core components of the Facebook Platform and provide examples and common use cases. The last chapters of the book continue to move deeper into the Facebook Platform with more examples and demonstrations of key concepts.

Following is a breakdown of the chapter organization in *Facebook Application Development*:

❑ **Part I: Understanding the Facebook Platform** — This part of the book includes the following chapters:

❑ **Chapter 1: Facebook as a Platform** — This chapter begins by providing background information on where Facebook started, as well as information on the growth and worldwide use of the web site. The chapter then progresses into a discussion about the operations and technology behind Facebook.

❑ **Chapter 2: Building Your First Application** — This chapter provides information you need to create, configure, and develop an application on the Facebook Platform. The Hello World project presented in this chapter is written in PHP and uses the PHP Client Library.

❑ **Chapter 3: Facebook Markup Language (FBML)** — This chapter provides detailed information about available FBML entities, as well as providing important caveats and rules applied to FBML by the rendering engine.

❑ **Chapter 4: Advanced FBML** — This chapter describes advanced features that extend and push FBML beyond a simple markup language. This chapter also looks at Facebook JavaScript (FBJS) and explores FBJS functions and objects that extend the commonly available JavaScript functions and objects.

❑ **Chapter 5: Using the Facebook API** — This chapter examines the Facebook API, including the formats and structures of the requests and responses to the API methods, as well as error handling and some special cases developers may encounter while developing applications.

❑ **Chapter 6: Data Mining with FQL** — This chapter explores FQL by discussing the tables and fields that are available, as well as the common data structures returned by those fields.

❑ **Chapter 7: Authentication** — This chapter takes a close look at authentication and examines how its components are spread throughout the Facebook platform.

❑ **Part II: Building Facebook Applications** — This part of the book includes the following chapters:

❑ **Chapter 8: Resources for Developers** — This chapter reviews the official Developers Application and Developers Web Site, as well as examining the community-supported wiki and bug-tracker provided by Facebook.

❑ **Chapter 9: Doing More with Hello World** — This chapter describes how to enhance the functionality of the Hello World application created in Chapter 2 by adding several staple features.

❑ **Chapter 10: External Application Development** — This chapter discusses how to integrate external application development into your own Facebook application by taking advantage of how Facebook works with a web site or service outside of the Facebook Platform.

❑ **Chapter 11: Best Practices** — This chapter examines several strategies used when approaching specific situations and developing features for your Facebook application.

❑ **Part III: Appendix** — This part of the book includes the following appendix:

❑ **Appendix A: PHP File Reference** — This appendix provides the code listings for three important PHP files.

What You Need to Use This Book

Facebook Application Development assumes that you have a good understanding of web development technologies, including PHP and MySQL. Developers with experience in Perl, Ruby, or Java will also benefit from the practical examples.

Conventions

To help you get the most from the text and keep track of what's happening, we've used a number of conventions throughout the book.

Boxes like this one hold important, not-to-be forgotten information that is directly relevant to the surrounding text.

> **Tips, hints, tricks, and asides to the current discussion are offset and placed in italics like this.**

As for styles in the text:

❑ Important new terms and important words are *highlighted* when we introduce them.

❑ Keyboard strokes are shown like this: Ctrl+A.

❑ URLs and code within the text are shown like this: `persistence.properties`.

❑ Code is presented as follows:

```
\\This is a code example.
```

Source Code

As you work through the examples in this book, you may choose either to type in all the code manually or use the source code files that accompany the book. All of the source code used in this book is available for download at www.wrox.com. Once at the site, simply locate the book's title (either by using the Search box or by using one of the title lists), and click the Download Code link on the book's detail page to obtain all the source code for the book.

> *Because many books have similar titles, you may find it easiest to search by ISBN; for this book the ISBN is 978-0-470-24666-5.*

Once you download the code, just decompress it with your favorite compression tool. Alternately, you can go to the main Wrox code download page at www.wrox.com/dynamic/books/download.aspx to see the code available for this book and all other Wrox books.

Errata

We make every effort to ensure that there are no errors in the text or in the code. However, no one is perfect, and mistakes do occur. If you find an error in one of our books (such as a spelling mistake or faulty piece of code), we would be very grateful for your feedback. By sending in errata, you may save another reader hours of frustration and, at the same time, you will be helping us provide even higher quality information.

To find the errata page for this book, go to www.wrox.com and locate the title using the Search box or one of the title lists. Then, on the book details page, click the Book Errata link. On this page, you can view all errata that have been submitted for this book and posted by Wrox editors. A complete book list including links to each book's errata is also available at www.wrox.com/misc-pages/booklist.shtml.

If you don't spot "your" error on the Book Errata page, go to www.wrox.com/contact/techsupport.shtml and complete the form there to send us the error you have found. We'll check the information and, if appropriate, post a message to the book's errata page and fix the problem in subsequent editions of the book.

p2p.wrox.com

For author and peer discussion, join the P2P forums at p2p.wrox.com. The forums are a web-based system for you to post messages relating to Wrox books and related technologies, and to interact with other readers and technology users. The forums offer a subscription feature to e-mail you topics of interest of your choosing when new posts are made to the forums. Wrox authors, editors, other industry experts, and your fellow readers are present on these forums.

At `http://p2p.wrox.com`, you will find several different forums that will help you not only as you read this book, but also as you develop your own applications. To join the forums, just follow these steps:

1. Go to `p2p.wrox.com` and click the Register link.

2. Read the terms of use and click Agree.

3. Complete the required information to join, as well as any optional information you wish to provide, and click Submit.

4. You will receive an e-mail with information describing how to verify your account and complete the joining process.

You can read messages in the forums without joining P2P, but to post your own messages, you must join.

Once you join, you can post new messages and respond to messages that other users post. You can read messages at any time on the Web. If you would like to have new messages from a particular forum e-mailed to you, click the "Subscribe to this Forum" icon by the forum name in the forum listing.

For more information about how to use the Wrox P2P, be sure to read the P2P FAQs for answers to questions about how the forum software works, as well as many common questions specific to P2P and Wrox books. To read the FAQs, click the FAQ link on any P2P page.

Part I

Understanding the Facebook Platform

Facebook as a Platform

The Internet has plenty of social networks and communal web sites focused on helping those with like interests contact and interact with each other. A *social network* focuses on the building and verifying of online social networks for communities of people who share interests and activities, or who are interested in exploring the interests and activities of others — which necessitates the use of software. A *social platform* goes beyond that, though. In addition to providing its own services and content to its users, it allows other developers and communities to extend its social attributes and reach.

This chapter is split into two parts. In the beginning, I'll give some background information on where Facebook started and some more information on the growth and worldwide use of the web site. After that, I will go into detail about the operations and technology behind Facebook. This chapter will also cover the Facebook Application and describe what it is and how it works and give an overview of Application traits.

Evolution of Facebook

Launched in early February 2004, Facebook is, on its own, a social networking web site. From February 2004 to March 2004, more than half of the students in the undergraduate program at Harvard were members. In seven months, the user base hit its first millionth user. Later that year, it also raised its first round of funding from angel investors.

In May 2005, Facebook raised another round of venture capital from Accel Partners and started to brand itself. The *the* was dropped from the domain, and the domain facebook.com was purchased. Facebook also began its high school initiative, allowing students from various high schools throughout the United States to join. By October 2005, Facebook included the majority of universities and junior colleges in the United States, Canada, and the United Kingdom. The Facebook user base included more than 2,000 colleges and more than 25,000 high schools in the United States, Canada, Mexico, the United Kingdom, Australia, New Zealand, and Ireland, with more than 11 million users worldwide.

In May 2007, Facebook transcended from social network to social platform by opening up its user base to allow applications to extend and deepen the communal reaches. It quickly became one of the top social network web sites with more than 30 million users as of July 2007. It was ranked in the top 20 most-visited web sites in the summer of 2007 and is the top photo-sharing web site in the United States. More than 85 percent of all U.S. college students have Facebook accounts. According to Facebook, more than 50 percent of members log in daily, spending on average 19 minutes a day on the site.

For several reasons, 2007 was a good year for Facebook. The development and release of the *Application Programming Interface (API)* put the growing web site in the spotlight, giving it a chance to shine. In May 2007, the Facebook Platform was officially launched, bringing new ideas and a wealth of buzz to the industry.

According to ComScore, the number of unique monthly visitors almost doubled from 14 million in May 2006 to 26.6 million in May 2007. Total page views increased more than 140 percent during the same time period, from 6.5 billion per month in May 2006 to 15.8 billion per month in May 2007. Most provocatively, average minutes spent on the site per user per month increased 35 percent over the last year, from 138 minutes in May 2006 to 186 minutes per month in May 2007.

Facebook is no longer just for college students. The number of visitors between the ages of 25 and 34 increased 181 percent between May 2006 and May 2007. Visitors over the age of 35 have also increased by 98 percent in that same period.

The launch of the Facebook Platform has received the attention of its competitors, too. Within weeks of the Platform launch, two of Facebook's biggest competitors were making press announcements stating that they would be (or were in the process of) launching something similar.

Facebook Services

Facebook has several basic services that compose its core services available to its users. Through the Facebook Platform, the majority of these and the information contained are available to third parties through Facebook applications.

- ❏ **The Social Graph** — The Facebook *social graph* is made up of users and their direct or indirect relationships. *Direct relationships* include meeting someone at a party or through a business connection. *Indirect relationships* could include a social, educational, or regional network.

- ❏ **User Profiles** — Information about users is available through *user profile* pages. These pages include user-generated content, as well as information derived from the social graph. These pages make this information available to other users. In addition, there are also hints about the users' activities within Facebook, including photos they are in and groups they have joined.

  User profile pages include the different ways to communicate with other users through message links and a profile *Wall* where users can post one-off messages to each other.

- ❑ **Messaging** — *Messaging* includes user-to-user messages, as well as general notifications.

- ❑ **Pages** — *Facebook Pages* are one of the more recent additions to Facebook. Pages are a way to create a sort of profile for a business, band, or product that can be managed and modified by one or more Facebook users. A Facebook Page allows Facebook users to interact with the page's subject by becoming a fan or by using the message board.

- ❑ **Information Aggregates** — With all of the information available on Facebook, sorting out what users are really interested in is a job in and of itself. This is done through *information aggregates* such as the News Feed or Mini-Feed (available on the Facebook home page), or the user profile pages.

The Technology behind Facebook

Facebook is built on open-source software. Some of the open-source technologies used by Facebook include Apache, PHP, MySQL, and memcached. Facebook has also released several projects under open-source licenses, including the following:

- ❑ **Thrift** — This is an open-source package used to create libraries and systems that efficiently communicate with each other. It includes software libraries and code-generation tools to build client/server protocols. It is available in many languages and has been extensively tested. As Facebook says, if you are using Facebook, you are using Thrift. More information can be found at `http://developers.facebook.com/thrift/`.

- ❑ **PhpEmbed** — This is an a open-source software library that allows developers to embed PHP into C++ projects and code. More information can be found at `http://developers.facebook.com/phpembed/`.

Facebook also provides a mirror of the open-source projects and code used at `http://mirror.facebook.com/`.

Introduction to the Core Technologies

Like any other large web service, there are many moving parts and pieces, and it is important to understand how they fit together to create the Facebook Platform. It is the platform model that Facebook has adopted that separates it from just another web site with an API.

At the very highest level, the Facebook Platform has four main duties:

1. Provide uniform and consistent methods to exchange information between itself and third parties.

2. Manage relationships between users.

3. Provide methods to distribute content on different mediums.

4. Provide methods of interaction between users.

From the application developer's point of view, there are three components that create the Platform. Those components are the Application Programming Interface (API), the Facebook Markup Language (FBML), and the Facebook Query Language. These are the Platform Core Technologies that allow developers to create rich applications that interact with Facebook.

From a Facebook application developer's point of view, there are four components to be concerned with:

1. **Application Program Interface (API)** — The Facebook API is a collection of REST methods that allow developers to exchange information with the Facebook Platform.

2. **Facebook Markup Language (FBML)** — This is a markup language designed to provide developers and designers with a quick medium to create clean and uniform interfaces.

3. **Facebook Query Language (FQL)** — This is a SQL-like query language to mine data from the Facebook Platform.

4. **Authentication** — While not a component of its own, the authentication process and model require a certain amount of understanding, and no other component can be used without first understanding authentication.

There are other technologies that make up the Facebook Core Technologies, which the Platform Core Technologies access and use indirectly. These are authentication, user management, user relationship management, and message handling.

At a very high level, Facebook itself is a modular content management system (CMS) with authentication. It manages the high-level user functionality and system-wide authentication, as well as subsystems like caching and message handling. Facebook uses callbacks and hooks to allow more feature-rich applications and maintains an API-to-API protocol for the Facebook-supplied applications such as Photos and Groups.

Role of the Application

Applications on Facebook are the key pieces that turn Facebook into a social platform. They have a direct impact on the users and, as the Platform continues to grow, they will play a pivotal role in the growth of Facebook as a whole. More and more, entrepreneurs are discovering that instead of creating an independent social networking site, it's easier and more effective to just plug in to an existing platform like Facebook. The applications available help transition users from using *web sites* into using *web operating systems*.

Within weeks of the Platform launch, there were more than half a dozen applications available with a million users. One of them crossed the 10-million-user threshold in late July 2007.

The real shift is the total cost of building, releasing, and maintaining your web applications versus creating a Facebook application. More and more, developers and companies are looking at what it takes to create a full web application, acquire users, and add new features, instead of creating a Facebook application that can be just as feature-rich, as well as offering a reliable user base and platform to build upon. Facebook provides the building blocks and the users.

Anatomy of an Application

The term *Facebook application* is a bit misleading in that a Facebook application doesn't really live on Facebook or any of its servers. A Facebook application, in its strictest sense, is a web application that is viewed and used by Facebook users through Facebook by means of *callbacks*.

This model works very well and gives the developers everything they need to create unique, feature-rich applications without affecting the core functionality of Facebook. Through the use of callbacks, Facebook enables applications to integrate very tightly with Facebook.

Facebook applications have two types of components. The first type is what the application renders data onto. The second type is those that the application shares with other applications and Facebook itself.

An application can interface with the users and Facebook as a whole. Following are the areas that the application directly draws onto:

- ❑ The Application Canvas
- ❑ The Application Profile Box
- ❑ The Application About page
- ❑ The News Feed and Mini-Feed
- ❑ The Application Directory
- ❑ Application Alerts and Notifications
- ❑ Facebook Pages
- ❑ Message attachments

Application Canvas

The *Application Canvas* (Figure 1-1) is the area where the application can directly render content, and is considered the Application Home. More information about the markup provided by the application is provided later in this chapter in the section, "Application Request Process."

Figure 1-1: Application Canvas.

The FBML provides a toolset of common elements for applications to use to create the user interface. The FBML generated by the application is taken by Facebook and rendered on the Application Canvas with several caveats. Facebook does heavy filtering of possible dangerous content and prevents it from being accessed. The Facebook Platform also parses those FBML elements and replaces them with structured content and HTML widgets.

Application Profile Box

The *Application Profile Box* (Figure 1-2) is the area on the user's profile through which applications can display content. There are two forms of the profile box: the wide and narrow. The wide form is displayed on the right-hand side of the user profile, and the narrow form of the profile box is displayed on the left. The content of each version of the profile box is set explicitly by the application developer.

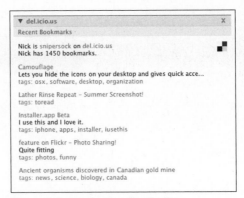

Figure 1-2: Application Profile Box.

The Application Profile Box has several restrictions in place on the types of FBML entities that can be used. This is to prevent private or otherwise sensitive information from being displayed to users. Chapter 3 provides more detail on FBML and contains a full listing of the FBML entities available on user profiles.

Application About Page

The *Application About page* (Figure 1-3) is one of the most trafficked areas of an application when the application has not been installed by the user. This is where users go to see what the application is about, which and how many of their friends have it installed, who made the application, and how often it is updated. The Application About page also includes a Wall where users can post quick one-off comments or messages, as well as a Discussion Board.

Once your application is alive and users start coming in, be sure to watch the Wall posts and Discussion Board for feedback. These provide users with a means of communicating how they feel about the application, and what issues they may have. If the Discussion Board is active, be sure to keep up with what your users are saying, and watch any messages and comments that could get lost in the activity.

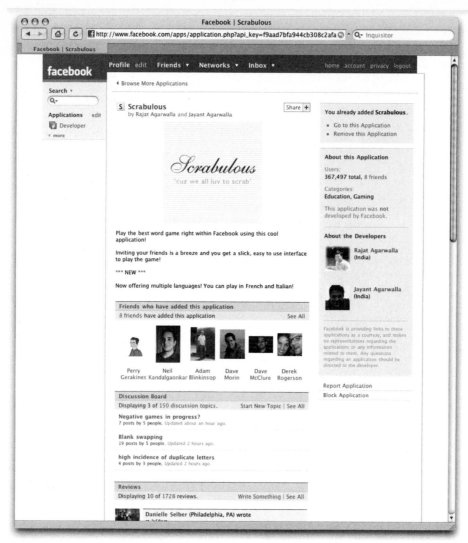

Figure 1-3: Application About page.

News Feed and Mini-Feed

The *News Feed* and *Mini-Feed* are shared Platform components used to broadcast actions of the user. Some examples include a user in your network adding an application, uploading or adding a new photo, or one or more of your friends adding the same person as a friend.

The difference between the News Feed (Figure 1-4) and the Mini-Feed (Figure 1-5) can be confusing. The News Feed is the main component of the home page and is a live stream showing the activity of your friends. The Mini Feed is a compact view of events specific to a single user and is displayed on the user's Facebook profile page.

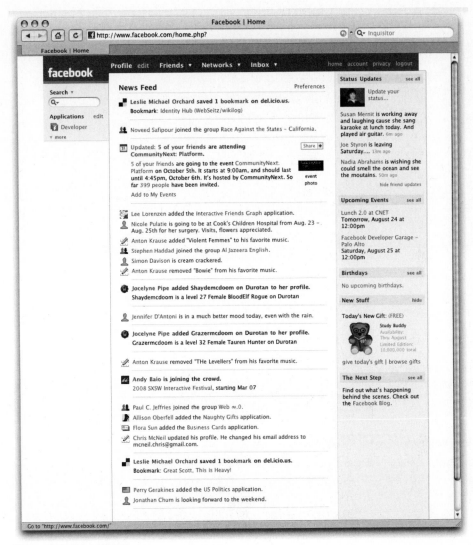

Figure 1-4: News Feed.

Facebook has imposed several restrictions on how often an application can send content to be included in the News Feed and Mini-Feed. Users also have a decent amount of control regarding the types of updates they see, and whom the updates are about. Users can also opt to see more information about certain users or block feed updates from a list of users.

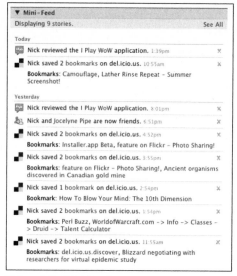

Figure 1-5: Mini-Feed.

From the developer's point of view, the feeds are an excellent way to broadcast messages. However, given the level of customization involved, it is not the most reliable way to get your message out. The Facebook Platform ranks and organizes the data available to be displayed in the News Feed and weeds out content that it determines shouldn't be displayed. There is no way to guarantee that a particular story will be displayed to a user's friends.

Application Directory

The *Application Directory* (Figure 1-6) is where applications are categorized and listed for users to look through. Users can search through the applications listed in the directory and get some basic information, including a description and the number of users who have added it.

> *There is an approval process that an application must go through to be listed in the Directory. At a minimum, the application must have an icon, description, and at least five users.*

A developer's application need not be added to the Directory for it to be used, or even widely accepted. Being listed just means that someone in authority at Facebook has approved the application.

> *Be prepared for a wait when submitting your application to the Directory. All applications are viewed and examined by a human before being approved.*

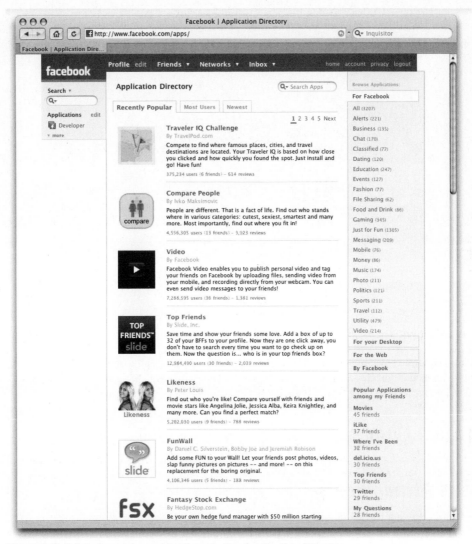

Figure 1-6: A list of popular applications in the Application Directory.

Notifications and Requests

Within Facebook, one of the nicer features is the internal messaging systems for messages and shared content. Applications have the capability to do the same thing with notifications and requests.

Notifications are a way of letting users know about an invitation or action. Notifications range from a small notice that a user has sent you a message (and it is in your Inbox) to a notice about it being your turn in a game of Scrabble.

Requests include things such as friend detail confirmations and requests, group and event invitations, and so forth. Unlike a notification, a request requires some sort of action before something can be done. Figure 1-7 shows an example of approving a Friend Request before being able to view the profile of the user.

Figure 1-7: A request.

Facebook Pages

The *Facebook Pages* component was introduced in late 2007 and provides a way to create a Facebook profile for a celebrity, organization, band, product, and so on. Facebook Pages were designed to allow those entities to connect with Facebook users to engage and promote themselves.

Facebook users who are considered owners of one or more Facebook Pages have access to the demographics of the users considered fans of the page. They can also send broadcast messages to Facebook Page fans.

Message Attachments

One often overlooked feature is the capability of an application to include attachments in messages between users (Figure 1-8). This is displayed as a button below the body area of a message. When a user selects the application action to include an attachment, the application renders whatever form or body is necessary for it to include the content in question. Figure 1-8 shows an Add Music button under the message window. Clicking that button displays the window shown in Figure 1-9.

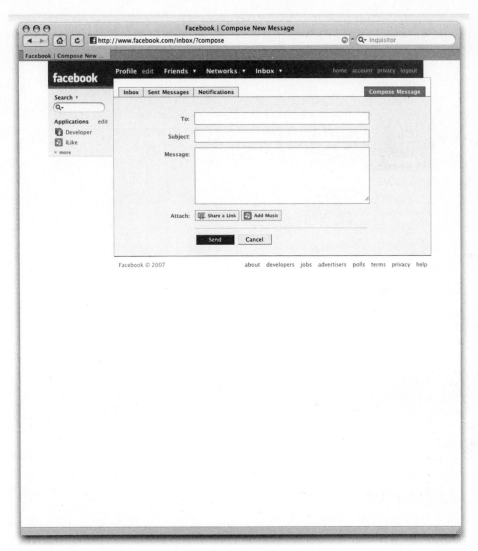

Figure 1-8: Add a link or attachment to your message.

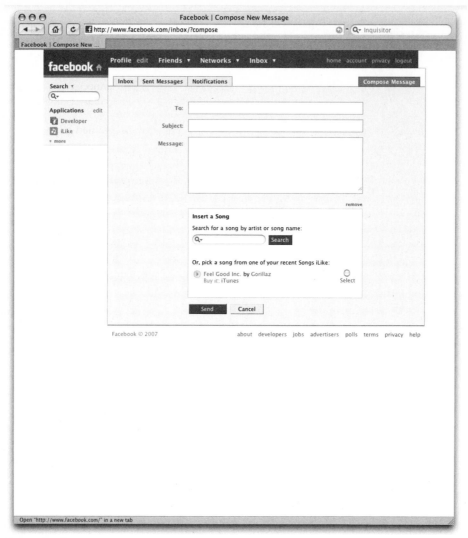

Figure 1-9: Browse for the file to attach.

Application Request Process

Facebook treats all applications as modular plug-ins that Facebook interacts with. Facebook does not host the applications, nor do the applications live on the Facebook network. Therefore, there is a strict request process that all applications must conform to.

1. The user accesses the Application ExampleApp at `http://apps.facebook.com/exampleapp`.

2. Facebook sends a `POST` request to a URL based on the Callback URL provided in the Application configuration.

3. The application parses the POST body and validates the POST signature.

4. The application performs its actions and generates markup for Facebook to display.

5. Facebook analyzes the markup (FBML) provided and renders it to the user's browser.

At first, the steps involved to display an application may look complex and unnecessary, but with closer examination, there is much reason behind this process. Following are the two main things accomplished:

❑ All of the business logic and data storage and management can be handled by the applications.

❑ Facebook can force applications to conform to certain display patterns through the use of FBML.

As stated above, every application request contains several parameters. These POST parameters vary depending on use and application request type. When a user accesses the application through the Application Canvas, the following parameters will always be included:

❑ fb_sig_in_canvas — With a value of 0 or 1, this indicates that the request was made through the Facebook Canvas.

❑ fb_sig_added — With a value of 0 or 1, this indicates that the requesting user has added the application.

❑ fb_sig_time — This is the current time in seconds since UNIX Epoch.

❑ fb_sig_api_key — This is the API key of the application.

❑ fb_sig — This parameter is used to verify that the request came from Facebook. See the section, "Validating the Request Signature," below in this chapter for more information on validating this parameter.

Users who have already granted access to your application trigger the following POST parameters to be sent in addition to those already mentioned:

❑ fb_sig_user — The numeric ID for the requesting user

❑ fb_sig_friends — A comma-separated list of user IDs (UIDs) that the requesting user has as friends

❑ fb_sig_session_key — The current session key tied to the application and requesting user

❑ fb_sig_profile_update_time — The time in seconds since the last update that the requesting user made to the user's profile

The different combinations of request arguments lead to four different Canvas page request types:

❑ Requests where the user is logged into Facebook, but the requesting user has not granted access to the application. This is represented by the absence of a fb_sig_user parameter.

❑ Requests where the user is logged into Facebook and has granted access to the application but has not added the application. This is indicated when the fb_sig_added parameter is set to 0.

❑ Requests where the user is logged into Facebook, has granted access to the application, and has added the application. This is indicated when the fb_sig_added parameter is set to 1.

Validating the Request Signature

Verifying the signature of a Facebook application is very simple. As per the Facebook documentation, take the POST arguments in key=value pairs. Sort that list alphabetically by the key. Concatenate the sorted list and append the secret key for your application. The signature is the Message Digest 5 (MD5) encryption of that concatenated string.

Client Libraries

Facebook has released official *client libraries* and links to *unofficial libraries* (created and made available by third parties). The two supported languages are PHP (4 and 5) and Java. Both official client libraries contain relevant classes, as well as an example application.

The unofficial libraries support the following languages:

- ❑ ActionScript
- ❑ Cocoa
- ❑ ColdFusion
- ❑ .NET
- ❑ Perl
- ❑ PHP4
- ❑ Python
- ❑ Ruby
- ❑ VB.NET

> *Be aware that Facebook does not support these libraries, and links to them are provided only as a courtesy.*

It should also be noted that Microsoft and Facebook have partnered to make it easier to develop Facebook Applications in Visual Studio. Visit the Visual Studio Express Showcase for more information: http://msdn2.microsoft.com/en-us/express/bb510381.aspx.

The Developer Center and Developer Application

Facebook has provided two places for developers to get more information about the Facebook Platform, as well as documentation, client libraries, and community support.

The first is the official *Facebook Developer Application*. This Facebook Application is the central destination for creating applications and configuring them. It is also the best place to get up-to-date information on the status of the Facebook Platform and news. The developer discussion board is also available here: www.facebook.com/developers.

The *Facebook Development Center* is where you will find the official documentation, client libraries, and several online tools that can be used to debug your application. The official wiki is also available here. It contains a wealth of information across many subjects.

```
http://developers.facebook.com/
http://wiki.developers.facebook.com/index.php/Main_Page
```

Application Traits

There are many types of applications that do many different things. Some build on new features, some extend existing functionality, and others are just for fun. This section gives an overview of 11 applications, each with one or more notable traits that are worth mentioning. Some of these applications have crossed the million-user milestone, and others have only thousands.

Top Friends

The *Top Friends* application by Slide Inc. has almost 11 million users. This application allows users to display and rank a list of other users on their profiles. This plays into the "top 8" concept that MySpace started, and has worked very well for this application. You can display up to 32 of your friends.

This application has done very well for two main reasons. On social actions such as changing the place of a friend within your ranked list, it notifies that user of the action. If the user hasn't added the application, the user is prompted to do so. On large networks, this could lead to "spammy" behavior, but generally it is very sound. Top Friends also heavily encourages its users to invite and accumulate more users within the Application Canvas.

The second reason this application does so well is because it plays off user popularity. By allowing users to rank and list other users according to relationship status, it makes for a "Who's Who" within the social network. It also computes popularity and provides a hard number that users can display. Users can try to increase the number by inviting other users and increasing their own rank with other users.

Following is some key information about Top Friends:

❑ **Notable Feature** — This application has excelled at viral marketing. Because of its viral nature, it has grown extremely fast and has become a huge success.

❑ **URL** — www.facebook.com/apps/application.php?id=2425101550.

Viral marketing *is a marketing phenomenon that facilitates and encourages people to advertise a product or service voluntarily.*

iLike

The application *iLike* by iLike Inc. currently has more than 4 million users and was one of the first large Facebook applications. This application allows users to enter favorite music genres and artists. With that information, you can find similar music and present songs/artists on your profiles for other users to listen to.

iLike has much more utility than many of the other Facebook applications. Its main purpose is to allow users to discover and share musical interests in a variety of ways. The application provides links to songs in the iTunes Music Store, allowing users to quickly purchase music and videos. iLike also has several secondary features that build on top of it. Users can connect through concerts, dedicate songs to each other, and customize the content that is display within the profile.

Following is some key information about iLike:

❑ **Notable Feature** — This application allows users to create and strengthen social relationships through musical connections and like interests.

❑ **URL** — www.facebook.com/apps/application.php?id=2413267546.

Extended Info

The *Extended Info* application is a profile enhancer written by Trey Philips. This application allows you to add custom content to your profile similar to the Facebook-provided profile information.

In addition to being one of the earlier applications available, it was also one of the first application acquisitions. Sidestep, creators of the Tips application, purchased the Extended Info application for an undisclosed sum.

This application is a perfect example of Facebook applications that extend current functionality of Facebook. With it, you can add and display more relevant information to your profile visitors.

Following is some key information about Extended Info:

❑ **Notable Feature** — This application implements a single really good idea very well.

❑ **URL** — www.facebook.com/apps/application.php?id=2374336051.

Art

The *Art* application is purely cosmetic from the user's perspective. The application, written by Matt Kraft and Phil Edwards, has more than 53,000 users. It allows Facebook users to display a piece of art on their profiles. It is one of the smaller applications, but definitely one of the nicer ones.

Once the application is installed, you are presented with a library of more than 160,000 works of art to add to your profile. You can also sift through other types of images depicting such things as bands, movies, sports, and so on. This application provides links to purchase pieces through allposters.com, which makes it very easy to display your favorite piece that you have hanging in your Facebook profile as well.

Following is some key information about Art:

❑ **Notable Feature** — This application is noteworthy because it doesn't attempt to be a social application. It is nothing more than a profile decorator, and a nice one at that.

❑ **URL** — www.facebook.com/apps/application.php?id=3021260327.

Fortune Cookie

The *Fortune Cookie* application, with more than 4.7 million users, is another content-oriented application. It presents a themed fortune on the user's profile for other users to see and provides links to add the application for visitors who have not already done so.

The Application Canvas is very simple, providing a preview of the fortune, a button to cycle to the next fortune, and an interface to send the current fortune to one or more friends. Unlike other applications, it has a very passive viral strategy.

Following is some key information about Fortune Cookie:

❑ **Notable Feature** — This application focuses on small content. The only user input available is to skip to the next fortune. Because of this, the application is incredibly simple.

❑ **URL** — `www.facebook.com/apps/application.php?id=2355237624`.

Honesty Box

The *Honesty Box* application allows users to comment anonymously on other users. At first, this could sound like a very bad idea, but it has proven quite the opposite. With more than 2.5 million users, this application has opened up a refreshing alternative to the traditional Wall application that Facebook provides, which allows users to post notes and comments on your profile.

After you have added the application, you are presented with a seed question on which profile visitors are supposed to remark. Within the Application Canvas, you can configure e-mail notifications, view comment history, and block users (anonymously, of course).

Following is some key information about Honesty Box:

❑ **Notable Feature** — This application takes full advantage of the capability to be anonymous. Given that most social networks are made to expose users, this application is refreshing in that it allows anonymous (and semi-anonymous) actions.

❑ **URL** — `www.facebook.com/apps/application.php?id=2552096927`.

Causes

The *Causes* application allows Facebook users to contribute financially to some of the causes they care about. It has more than 2.2 million users and has had a steady stream of application add-ons and buzz since its launch. The Help section describes its goal very well:

> Facebook Platform presents an unprecedented opportunity to engage our generation, most of whom are on Facebook, in seizing the future and making a difference in the world around us. Our generation cares deeply, but the current system has alienated us. Causes on Facebook provides the tools so that any Facebook user can leverage their network of real friends to affect positive change.

This application creates profiles for causes that users can either join or create. Users can donate money to one or more causes and display on their profiles the causes they have joined. Each "cause" has an area for users to discuss the cause, as well as information about the cause. There is also an area available to include statistics and other information. Each cause includes a low- and high-level description and information on how to join and help.

Following is some key information about Causes:

❑ **Notable Features** — This is one of the first of few altruistic applications. It provides a medium for doing good in the world in a very organized and thought-out way.

❑ **URL** — www.facebook.com/apps/application.php?id=2318966938.

del.icio.us

The *del.icio.us* application allows users to display the bookmarks they have saved on del.icio.us. It is listed here because it is one of the few applications that is almost completely external from the user's point of view. del.icio.us, being a social utility, allows users to save content for themselves as well as other users and expand communal knowledge through knowledge sharing. This fits very well with the tight social networks formed within Facebook.

When users first add this application, they are brought to the del.icio.us Settings page, where they associate their del.icio.us and Facebook accounts, as well as configure how they want the application to work. The application itself does not have any presence within Facebook, other than items in the News Feed and content within the user profile.

Following is some key information about del.icio.us:

❑ **Notable Features** — This application is passive compared to others. It updates the user's feed and profile based on activity on an outside web site. It shifts from an application that is part of Facebook to an application with a presence in Facebook, putting more of a focus on the user's bookmarks, content, and activity, rather than social relationships and Facebook.

❑ **URL** — www.facebook.com/apps/application.php?id=2411052087.

Pirates vs. Ninjas

Pirates vs. Ninjas is a fun application that lets you recruit your friends to become either a ninja or a pirate. It has more than 650,000 users and makes it very easy to recruit other ninjas or pirates to increase the ranks.

This is one of a growing number of competitive applications. It is composed of one or more groups that will "defeat" the other groups based on the number of users and/or points.

Following is some key information about Pirates vs. Ninjas:

❑ **Notable Features** — This class of Facebook application is very viral because of its competitive "help a friend out" nature.

❑ **URL** — www.facebook.com/apps/application.php?id=2400559068.

Election '08

The *Election '08* application is one of a growing number of politically focused Facebook applications. In particular, this application presents the user with several 2008 presidential election candidates (there is an option for independent, green, and none, as well) and allows the user to select one and record his or her vote.

This application serves multiple purposes. The first is to allow users to display their political views and 2008 presidential candidate of choice on their profiles. Facebook allows you to select a political view to display, but this application takes it a step further.

The second role of this application is to collect data. This application, created by NewsVine, has the capability to collect a huge amount of data regarding the political views and candidate preferences of the Facebook user base.

Following is some key information about Election '08:

❑ **Notable Features** — The first is the politically charged theme and purpose. The second is the capability to collect valuable data.

❑ **URL** — www.facebook.com/apps/application.php?id=2360172394.

Scrabulous

This Facebook application is multi-user game within Facebook. It allows you to invite up to three other users to play the turn-based game Scrabble. Because the game does not require all users to be present during each other's turns, it makes playing very easy, and games can take as long as the users wish.

The idea of using Facebook as a gaming platform is very interesting. Turn-based games, multi-user games, and single-player flash games are ideal.

Following is some key information about Scrabulous:

❑ **Notable Features** — Its lax restrictions on user presence during turns makes it easy to start and continue games between friends where it might not be normally feasible. It also allows users who have not added the application to join games.

❑ **URL** — www.facebook.com/apps/application.php?id=3052170175.

Application Trait Overview

Now, let's review the application traits noted here and examine them further. It is a combination of these traits mixed with marketing, audience targeting, utility, and luck that plays a part in the application's success.

Advertising and Marketing

One of the most common things done to promote an application is marketing and/or advertising. A viral application isn't one that installs itself but is promoted by the users with or without their consent. There are many applications that are considered "viral" for just this reason.

There are various tactics used by application developers to make their applications more viral. Following are just a few of the most popular:

❑ **Forced Invited** — Some applications have aggressive policies requiring users who have added the application already to invite other users before they can take full advantage of its features. Sometimes this is done by having an Invite screen displayed after an action. Other times it is done by tracking the number of invites the user has sent with reminders displayed until the target number of invites is met. This is reminiscent of the old shareware days. In some ways, this is a necessary evil, although I don't advocate it. There have been many applications that have done very well with such aggressive behavior. If the users really objected to them, they wouldn't use the application in the first place.

❑ **Application Partnerships** — A growing trend in Facebook applications is to partner with other applications and advertise for each other. This takes several forms, such as a small blurb, series of text links, or larger visual advertisement on a confirmation page. This can work very well, depending on the situation. If you have multiple applications with the same target audience, it could be very beneficial. It also makes for a great way to spread the word about an application and get people to notice.

❑ **User Profiles and Feeds** — User profile real estate is very valuable. At the core of all of this is a social network where users visit the profiles of other users. Having an eye-pleasing profile block for other users to see can go a long way. The same holds true for feeds. Several very successful applications attribute the News Feed and Mini-Feed to much of their success. Good messaging and clarity provide non-application users a feeling of what the application is about.

❑ **Word of Mouth** — There is nothing an application can do that is better than a friend's recommendation. Having the application users spread the good word is the most effective way of getting new users. It also follows that having good feedback and positive comments in the application Forum and Wall is also helpful.

❑ **Building Relationships** — Some applications serve no other purpose than creating, building, and strengthening the relationships between users. Sometimes the application may come across as a popularity contest (such as Top Friends), but what it boils down to is users profiling the relationships they have with their friends.

Perfecting a Single Idea

Applications often do best when taking a single idea and perfecting it. Within the Facebook Platform, it is easy to create multiple applications and have them all serve a specific purpose. Splitting out applications provides the chance to have more of an impact on how the user perceives Facebook and the tools they use.

Adding New Functionality and Extending Functionality

Not all systems are complete. With the launch of the Facebook Platform and the introduction of Applications, Facebook acknowledges that fact. Facebook Applications are a great way to add new functionality to Facebook. What better way to increase the usefulness of the Platform for its users than by allowing the users to do it themselves? The capability to add new functionality to Facebook is the number one purpose of the Platform.

The second purpose of the Platform is to extend and enhance existing functionality. In addition to stating that not all systems are complete, it can also be said that the first revision of a system is not as good as the second. With a Facebook Application, a developer can take an existing application or feature, examine it, take feedback from those who use it, and create a better application from that knowledge.

This has been shown to be true by looking at the usage of countless applications that clone and extend the features built into Facebook.

Cosmetic Enhancements

Whether it is with an image, a list of all of the places you've been, or even a picture of your pet, users like to show things off and cosmetically enhance what is theirs. Profile enhancement comes in many forms, which fits with the many ways that this is accomplished.

Business Relationships

Facebook is making it easier to identify and separate professional networks and social networks. There are applications out there that build on the idea that the line between work life and the home is blurring. They offer various features that appeal to business networking, rather than social networking.

Facebook Beacons

The *Facebook Beacon* service was added in late 2007 and serves as a bridge between actions taken on third-party sites and how they are represented on Facebook. In a nutshell, when a user on a third-party site takes an action such as adding a movie to his or her favorites list or saving a bookmark, that third party sends a small amount of information to Facebook. Facebook then correlates that information with a Facebook account, and, depending on that user's privacy settings, the information is then displayed on the user's News Feed or Mini-Feed.

Summary

This chapter has examined the history of Facebook and taken a look at where it is going. The discussion touched the core components of Facebook and the Facebook Platform. You learned what an Application is and how the underlying structure of requests and components fit together. Finally, this chapter took a deep look at several applications, and defined the notable traits that make them unique.

Chapter 2 dives right into application development and takes a more hands-on approach to the Facebook Platform. Chapter 2 complements this chapter by taking what you have learned and putting it into action with a small application that uses the Facebook Canvas page, the PHP Client Library, and several API methods.

2

Building Your First Application

Chapter 1 discussed the origins and technology of Facebook and the Facebook Platform. In this chapter, you dive right into your first Facebook application to learn a more technical and practical approach to the Facebook Platform.

This chapter has everything you need to create, configure, and develop an application on the Facebook Platform. The opening project is written in PHP and uses the officially supported PHP Client Library. The ideas and concepts are easily transferable to any Web development language.

What You Need

Before you begin, you will need the following things:

❑   A Facebook account

❑   A shared or dedicated server with PHP and MySQL

You also need to have the official Facebook Developer Application installed, but that will be discussed when we create and configure the application as this chapter progresses.

Outlining the Functionality and Features

Every project starts on the drawing board, and this one is no different. Let's spend a few minutes to outline the application's features and capabilities.

The Hello World application is a social application that enables a user to send greetings to other users in that user's network. Greetings are defined by the application and consist of a simple "hello." The application will return Facebook Markup Language (FBML) to be rendered through the Facebook Canvas, and will use several of the entities provided by Facebook.

When an application user sends a greeting to another user, the application will store the sending user, target user, and time. The application will also update the sending user's profile and, if the target user has added the application, update the target user's profile as well.

Creating the Application

The first step in developing an application on the Facebook Platform is creating and configuring it within the Developer Application.

Before you create the application, be sure you know the Web address and location of where the project will be located. As an example, the example project described in this chapter will be accessed by the Facebook Platform at `http://fbexample.socklabs.com/`.

Introducing the Facebook Developer Application

The Developer Application is the center of the application development world in Facebook. There you will find the latest news and updates from the Facebook Platform Team, as well as the discussion board and application control panel known as *My Applications*. Following is the URL: `www.facebook.com/developers/`.

If you have not already done so, visit the Developer Application and add it immediately. Without it, developing on the Facebook Platform is extremely difficult (if not impossible).

Creating the 'Hello World' Application

Inside the Developer Application, click on the "My Applications" control panel. At first, you will see a blank list and a link titled "Apply for another key." Next, you will be presented with a simple form, with the only required field initially being the application name (Figure 2-1). To stay in theme with this project, choose a name similar to *Hello World* or *Friend Greetings*. Enter the application name, and, if you agree to the terms of service, submit the form.

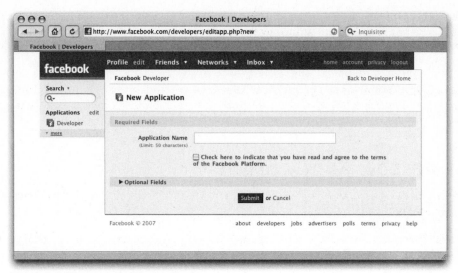

Figure 2-1: The New Application form.

The Hello World application has now been created, and you should have been returned to the My Applications page, where the newly created application should be displayed along with the API Key, Secret Key, and relevant links to the About Page and configuration page (Figure 2-2).

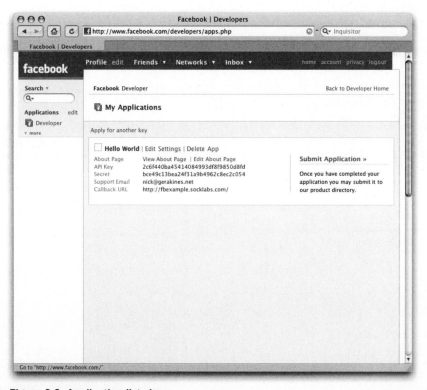

Figure 2-2: Application list view.

Now that the application has been created, you must fill in some more information. Figures 2-3 and 2-4 show the Optional Fields for configuring the Application. Before the application will work, you must supply the Callback URL and the Canvas URL, as shown toward the middle of Figure 2-3.

❑ The Callback URL should point to the htdocs/index.php file; in this example, the full URL is `http://fbexample.socklabs.com/index.php`.

❑ The Canvas URL should be a unique name relative to the project name. This project uses *nghelloworld*.

Figure 2-3: Editing the application's configuration.

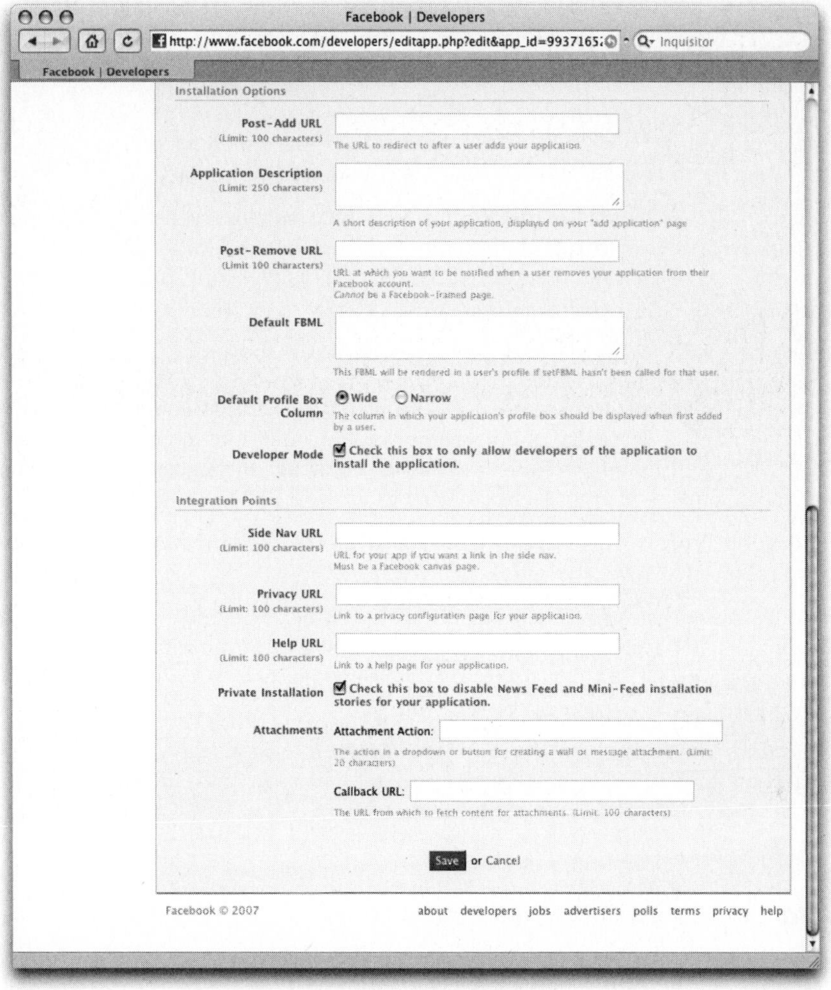

Figure 2-4: The Installation Options and Integration Points fields.

As you can see, the Optional Fields are grouped together into three types:

❑ **Base Options** — These are the core options that describe the type and behavior of the application.

❑ **Installation Options** — These describe the installation process and mechanics of the application.

❑ **Integration Points** — These configure how the application interacts with the different Facebook interfaces and components.

Base Options

Following are descriptions of the fields appearing in this section:

- ❑ **Support E-mail** — This is the e-mail address that Facebook will use to contact you regarding support requests for the application. By default, it is the e-mail address you registered with. Depending on your application's growth, it would be wise to change this.

- ❑ **Callback URL** — Remember that the application doesn't live on the Facebook servers; it lives on your own machine. This URL should point to the default location that will be displayed through the Application Canvas page. Consider this as the Application home page or landing page.

- ❑ **Canvas Page URL** — Facebook applications live under the `apps.facebook.com` domain, thus a unique URL must be provided here. To keep the space clean, I suggest using your initials followed by **helloworld**. Underneath the textbox, you will see two radio buttons: "Use FBML" and "Use iframe." These two options allow you to render your application through Facebook using FBML, or to simply include the Callback URL page through an iframe. By default, and in most cases, it makes the most sense to use FBML.

- ❑ **Application Type** — This is pretty straightforward. If this were a Desktop application, you would set this. However, leave this set at "Website."

- ❑ **IP Addresses of Servers Making Requests** — This option allows you to set the IP addresses of servers that will be making API requests and to restrict API requests to those servers alone. For larger applications, this is a good security measure. For now, you can leave it blank.

- ❑ **Can Your Application Be Added on Facebook?** — This should be set to "Yes." This allows the application to be added by other users and enables it to be displayed in the side navigation bar. This option is not set when creating external applications. This option and the development of external applications are discussed in Chapter 10.

Installation Options

Following are the options appearing in this section:

- ❑ **Post-Add URL** — When users first add the application, they are sent to this URL.

- ❑ **Application Description** — The application description is displayed in the Application About page.

- ❑ **Post-Remove URL** — When users remove the application, they are sent to this URL. Note that this URL must not be a Facebook-Canvased page.

- ❑ **Default FBML** — With this option, you can set some markup to be displayed in the User Profile Box for the application. This will be displayed if the `facebook.profile.setFBML` method has not been called for that user.

- ❑ **Default Profile Box Column** — This option specifies the profile column that will be used when a user first adds the application.

- ❑ **Developer Mode** — This option prevents the application from being used by non-developers.

Integration Points

Following are the options appearing in this section:

- **Side Nav URL** — The side navigation bar is one of the core user interface (UI) elements within Facebook. The URL provided for this option is the link that appears in the side navigation bar.

- **Privacy URL** — The URL given for this option is the link that users are taken to when configuring the privacy options for the application.

- **Help URL** — This is the Help page for the application.

- **Private Installation** — When this option is selected, entries will not be made in the News Feed or Mini-Feed when the application is added.

- **Attachments** — This option and the subsequent Attachment Callback URL are used to configure attachments in the application. The Attachment Action is a label for the attachment action, and the Callback URL is called to render FBML to the attachment portion of creating a new message.

Writing the Application

Once the application is created and configured in Facebook, you can get started with filling in the features and functionality of the application.

Preparing the Application Environment

This application uses a single table to store the greeting information sent to and from users. Be sure to have a table created with the given schema (Listing 2-1) in a MySQL database that this application will have access to.

Listing 2-1: The Greetings table schema (MySQL).

```
CREATE TABLE greetings (
  user_from BIGINT NOT NULL,
  user_to BIGINT NOT NULL,
  row_created BIGINT NOT NULL
);
```

The `user_from` column is the numeric Facebook user ID (UID) of the user who sent the greeting. The `user_to` column is the numeric Facebook user ID of the user who is receiving the greeting. The `row_created` column is a UNIX time stamp of the date and time that the greeting was sent.

> The Facebook Platform developer team has made it clear that the UIDs representing Facebook users can be 64-bit integers. For this reason, the MySQL `BIGINT` type has been used.

Application Layout and Structure

This project has two types of PHP files:

❑   Those that are publicly accessed (such as the index page)

❑   Those that are included as project libraries

The configuration library, PHP5 Client Library, and project classes fall under the second category.

> *Note that the* `facebook_desktop.php` *class is not included in this project.*

Class Overview

The `lib` directory includes several .class.php files that contain much of the logic for this project. Listing 2-2 shows the `AppConfig` class.

Listing 2-2: The AppConfig.class.php file (PHP).

```php
class AppConfig {
  // Facebook specific configuration variables
  public static $app_name = 'HelloWorld';
  public static $app_id = '9937165273';
  public static $api_key = '2c6f440ba45414084993df8f9850d8fd';
  public static $secret  = 'bce49c13bea24f31a9b4962c8ec2c054';
  // Application specific configuration variables
  public static $db_ip = '127.0.0.1';
  public static $db_user = 'dbuser';
  public static $db_pass = 'dbpassword';
  public static $db_name = 'nghelloworld';
}
```

This class contains all of the configuration for the example application. Within the class, there are also two distinct types of configuration variables:

❑   **Variables Specific to the Application within Facebook** — These are the `app_id`, `api_key`, and `secret` key.

❑   **Configuration Variables That Are Used by the Application outside the Realm of Facebook —** These include database configuration, cache configuration, and so on.

This class is abstracted to make it easier to change the values set for use in example projects.

Listing 2-3 shows the `HelloWorld` class.

Listing 2-3: The HelloWorld class constructor (PHP).

```php
public $fbclient;

public function __construct($fbclient) {
  // On creation, set the facebook client
  $this->fbclient = $fbclient;
}
```

When instantiating a new `HelloWorld` object, you must pass in a valid `Facebook` object. The `HelloWorld` class stores the `Facebook` object internally and uses it throughout the class.

Listing 2-4 shows the `wave_hello` method, which takes two arguments: the user sending the greeting and the user receiving the greeting. The method is composed of two `try` blocks. The first tries to catch any exceptions when writing action to the database. The second tries to catch any exceptions when writing to the user profiles.

Listing 2-4: The `HelloWorld` `wave_hello` method (PHP).

```php
function wave_hello($user_from, $user_to) {
    try {
        $conn = $this->get_db_conn();
        $sql = "INSERT INTO greetings SET user_from = $user_from, user_to = $user_to,
row_created = UNIX_TIMESTAMP(NOW())";
        mysql_query($sql, $conn);
    } catch (Exception $e) {
        error_log($e->getMessage());
        return 0;
    }
    try {
        $this->update_profile($user_from);
        $this->update_profile($user_to);
    } catch (Exception $e) {
        error_log($e->getMessage());
        return 0;
    }
    return 1;

}
```

Listing 2-5 shows the class method `get_greetings($type = 'user_from', $user, $limit = 5)`. This is a simple helper method that returns the greetings either to or from a given user. The method `get_greeting_count($type = 'user_from', $user)` is a close relative that returns the count of greetings to or from the specified user.

Listing 2-5: The `HelloWorld` `get_greetings` method (PHP).

```php
function get_greetings($type = 'user_from', $user, $limit = 5) {
    $conn = $this->get_db_conn();
    $res = mysql_query("SELECT user_to, user_from, row_created FROM greetings WHERE
$type = $user ORDER BY row_created DESC LIMIT $limit", $conn);
    $greetings = array();
    while ($row = mysql_fetch_assoc($res)) {
        $greetings[] = $row;
    }
    return $greetings;

}
```

The `update_profile($user)` method shown in Listing 2-6 is one of the larger class methods that, for a given user, builds the profile box consisting of the most recent greetings to and from that user, and submits the profile FBML to Facebook.

Listing 2-6: The HelloWorld `update_profile` method (PHP).

```php
function update_profile($user) {
    $greetings_from = $self->get_greetings('user_from', $user);
    $gfromcount = count($greetings_from);
    $greetings_to = $self->get_greetings('user_to', $user);
    $gtocount = count($greetings_to);
    $fbml = $tomessage = $frommessage = '';
    $gf_str = $gt_str = '';
    if ($gtocount) {
        $tomessage = "<p><fb:name uid=\"$user\" firstnameonly=\"true\" useyou=
\"false\" />
has been waved to $gtocount times.</p>";
    } else {
        $tomessage = "<p>No one has waved hello to <fb:name uid=\"$user\"
firstnameonly=\"true\" useyou=\"false\" />!</p>";
    }
    if ($gfromcount) {
        $frommessage = "<p><fb:name uid=\"$user\" firstnameonly=\"true\" useyou=
\"false\" />
has waved hello to $gfromcount people.</p>";
    } else {
        $frommessage = "<p><fb:name uid=\"$user\" firstnameonly=\"true\" useyou=
\"false\" />
has not waved to anyone.</p>";
    }
    foreach ($greetings_from as $greeting) {
        $gf_str .= "<fb:if-can-see uid=\"$user\">";
        $gf_str .= '<li><fb:name uid="' . $greeting['to'] . '" useyou="false" /></li>';
        $gf_str .= '</fb:if-can-see>';
    }
    foreach ($greetings_to as $greeting) {
        $gt_str .= "<fb:if-can-see uid=\"$user\">";
        $gt_str .= '<li><fb:name uid="' . $greeting['from'] . '" useyou="false" /></li>';
        $gt_str .= '</fb:if-can-see>';
    }
    $fbml .= '<fb:wide>';
    $fbml .= "$frommessage\n<ul>$gf_str</ul>";
    $fbml .= "$tomessage<ul>$gt_str</ul>";
    $fbml .= '<fb:/wide>';
    $fbml .= '<fb:narrow>';
    $fbml .= "$frommessage\n<ul>$gf_str</ul>";
    $fbml .= "$tomessage<ul>$gt_str</ul>";
    $fbml .= '<fb:/narrow>';
    $this->fbclient->api_client->profile_setFBML($fbml, $user);
    return 1;
}
```

The Facebook class that is part of the Facebook PHP5 Client Library contains several method calls and functions that interact and manipulate Facebook. It takes a lot of the work out of submitting and parsing API method calls by creating methods to do much of the work for you. This method calls profile_setFBML, which sets the content displayed in an application block on a user's profile.

The `update_profile` method introduces the FBML and the Facebook API. The FBML is a strict XML markup language that Facebook makes available to developers. FBML has a number of very useful features including linking UIDs to usernames, markup to define different types of content, Ajax utilities, and more.

It also uses the `Facebook` object method `api_client->profile_setFBML(...)` that is used to submit the markup generated by this method to Facebook to update the user's profile. The use of API calls in this project is minimal but effective. The only API method used is the `facebook.profile.setFBML` method that sets the application content on a user's profile. More information on how API methods calls are handled, the different response formats available, and API error handling will be explained in Chapter 5.

The `facebook.profile.setFBML` method accepts the following nine arguments:

❑ `api_key, string,` — The API key of the application making this request

❑ `session_key, string,` — A valid session key used on behalf of the sending user

❑ `call_id, int,` — The requests sequence number

❑ `sig, string,` — The signature of the request

❑ `v, string,` — The version of the API to use

❑ `format, string,` — The desired response format type

❑ `callback, string,` — If the format selected is JavaScript Object Notation (JSON), wrap the response inside a function call specified by this argument.

❑ `markup, string,` — The FBML that will render the profile box

❑ `uid, string,` — The user whose profile is going to be updated

The last method in this class is `get_db_conn()`. It takes the database connection information provided in the `AppConfig` class, attempts to connect to the database server, and then selects the database. General exceptions are thrown if this operation fails.

Canvas Pages

Setting up the Application Canvas pages entails the following:

❑ The Application home page

❑ The Action Canvas page

This project consists of two Canvas pages. The first is the index page and the second the Action page.

The Application Home Page

The first and main page displayed through the Facebook Canvas is htdocs/index.php. This page is considered the application home page and must not only be functional but also easy on the eyes. A quick run through the code shows that it does the following things:

❑ Creates new `Facebook` and `HelloWorld` objects.

❑ Verifies the incoming request, confirming that it is viewed through the Canvas and that the requesting user has added the application.

❑ Retrieves the list of greetings sent to and received by the requesting user.

❑ Creates the FBML to be processed by Facebook.

The main page, like most, contains several of the special FBML helper entities as well. These make it easier to create links to user profiles and make assertions against a user.

When building the application home page, it is important to remember that this page is going to get the majority of your application's traffic. In most cases, it serves as the only destination available to its users and ends up as a kitchen sink of features and functionality. Removing heavy operations and slow queries from this Canvas page will give a good impression to its users.

Consider the following code:

```
include_once '../lib/client/facebook.php';
include_once '../lib/AppConfig.class.php';
include_once '../lib/HelloWorld.class.php';

$facebook = new Facebook(AppConfig::$api_key, AppConfig::$secret);

$facebook->require_frame();

$user = $facebook->require_login();

$facebook->require_add();

$app = new HelloWorld($facebook);

$greetings_from = $app->get_greetings('user_from', $user, 5);
$greetings_to = $app->get_greetings('user_to', $user, 5);

$greetings_from_count = get_greeting_count('user_from', $user);
$greetings_to_count = get_greeting_count('user_to', $user);
```

As you can see, this application makes three calls on the `Facebook` object and four calls on the `HelloWorld` object. Immediately after instantiating a `Facebook` object, you assert that the request is valid by ensuring that the request has been made through the Facebook Canvas, as well as that the requesting user is valid and has added the application. This way, anyone who hasn't added the application before will be asked to add it. This also verifies the signature of the parameters sent by Facebook to weed out any potential false or disruptive requests.

Once the chore work is taken care of, you can continue with feature functionality. On the main page of the application, you want to display some general information about the greetings sent by the user, the greetings that the user has received, and so on.

Just below the PHP block, you display the markup that Facebook will render through the Canvas, as shown here:

```
<fb:dashboard>
<fb:action href="<?php echo AppConfig::$app_url ?>">View My Greetings</fb:action>
<fb:action href="<?php echo AppConfig::$app_url ?>wave.php">Send a greeting</fb:action>
</fb:dashboard>

<div style="padding: 10px;">
  <h2>Hello <fb:name firstnameonly="true" uid="<?= $user ?>" useyou="false"/>!</h2>
  <fb:if-is-app-user uid="<?= $user ?>">
<? if ($greetings_to_count) { ?>
<p>You have received <?= $greetings_from_count ?> greetings from your friends.</p>
<ul>
<? foreach ($greetings_to as $greeting) { ?>
  <li><fb:name uid="<?= $greeting['user_from'] ?>" useyou="false" /></li>
<? } ?>
</ul>
<? } else { ?>
<p>You have not received any greetings</p>
<? } ?>
<? if ($greetings_from_count) { ?>
<p>You have sent <?= $greetings_from_count ?> greetings.</p>
<ul>
<? foreach ($greetings_from as $greeting) { ?>
  <li><fb:name uid="<?= $greeting['user_to'] ?>" useyou="false" /></li>
<? } ?>
</ul>
<? } else { ?>
<p>You have not sent any greetings</p>
<? } ?>
  <fb:else>
    <p>You need to <a href="<?= $facebook->get_add_url() ?>">add <?=
AppConfig::$app_name ?></a> to use it!</p>
  </fb:else>
</fb:if-is-app-user>

</div>
```

The FBML Test Console

On the Facebook Developers web site there are several tools that can be used to preview and debug your code. One tool in particular, the FBML Test Console (Figure 2-5), is especially useful for previewing and debugging the FBML used in the Facebook Application Canvas, News/Mini-Feed, and User Profile pages. You can find it at the following URL: http://developers.facebook.com/tools.php?fbml.

Figure 2-5: The FBML Test Console.

The `fb:dashboard` entity is used to construct a dashboard. It is primarily used in the Application Canvas and can contain `fb:action`, `fb:help`, and `fb:create-button` FBML entities. The following example FBML renders the dashboard shown in Figure 2-6.

```
<fb:dashboard>
     <fb:action href="users.php">Users</fb:action>
     <fb:action href="settings.php">Settings</fb:action>
     <fb:help href="help.php">Help</fb:help>
     <fb:create-button href="add.php">Add something</fb:create-button>
</fb:dashboard>
```

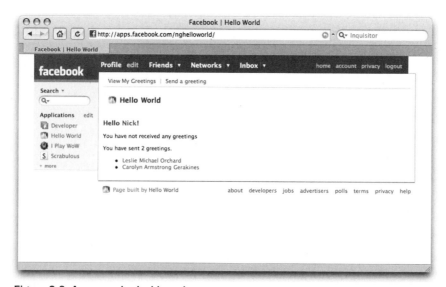

Figure 2-6: An example dashboard.

In the sample project, the `fb:dashboard` entity is used to display a small header at the top of the Canvas section on the application page. Here you draw two links to the index page and then to the Action page.

The `fb:name` entity is easily one of the most used FBML entities. It translates a UID, a username, and, by default, links to that user's profile. It has the capability to display the possessive and reflexive, as well as the first name and last name only. By default, there is only one required attribute, the `uid`. The following code renders the screen shown in Figure 2-7.

```
When logged in as user 500025891:
<fb:name uid="500025891" />
<fb:name uid="500025891" useyou="false" />
<fb:name uid="500025891" useyou="false" linked="true" />
```

```
When logged in as user 500025891:
you
Nick Gerakines
Nick Gerakines
```

Figure 2-7: An example of `fb:name`.

The next FBML entities used, `fb:if-is-app-user` and `fb:else` (shown in the following code), are in some ways, the most important. Content contained inside of the `fb:if-is-app-user` entity is only displayed to viewing users who have granted full permission to the application. The only modifier to this entity is the `uid` attribute, which represents the UID of the user to apply this entity to.

```
<fb:if-is-app-user>
  Hello Application User!
  <fb:else>
     You must sign up to use this application.
  </fb:else>
</fb:if-is-app-user>
```

The Action Canvas Page

The Action page does the work of sending a greeting from one user to another. Its markup has the `fb:editor` entity that is used for the form and also contains the `fb:explanation` entity that is displayed on the form action.

The first section of code is very similar to `index.php`. You create a `Facebook` client object and call several of the provided methods to verify the incoming signature, and also verify that the page is being viewed through the Facebook Canvas.

```
$facebook = new Facebook(AppConfig::$api_key, AppConfig::$secret);
app.facebook.com/appname/
$facebook->require_frame();
$facebook->require_add();
$user = $facebook->require_login();

$app = new HelloWorld($facebook);

$target_user = null;
if (isset($_POST['friend_sel'])) {
  $target_user = (int) $_POST['friend_sel'];
}

$wave_success = false;
$action_wave = false;
$show_form = true;
if ($target_user) {
  $action_wave = true;
  $show_form = false;
  $wave_success = $app->wave_hello($user, $target_user);
}
```

The notable difference here is immediately below the creation of the `HelloWorld` object. The first thing you check is the presence of the `friend_sel` POST parameter. If this is set, then you know that it is the result of a form action. If the value of that POST parameter is a valid `int`, you set the variables `wave_success`, `action_wave`, and `show_form` that control what content you display for Facebook to render.

As in `index.php`, just below the PHP block, you use the `fb:dashboard` element and have an enclosed `fb:if-is-app-user` element to prevent the application from being used by users who have not added the application.

Just below the PHP block, you display the markup that Facebook will render through the Canvas, as shown here:

```
<fb:dashboard>
<fb:action href="<?php echo AppConfig::$app_url ?>">View My Greetings</fb:action>
<fb:action href="<?php echo AppConfig::$app_url ?>wave.php">Send a greeting
</fb:action>
</fb:dashboard>

<div style="padding: 10px;">
  <h2>Hello <fb:name firstnameonly="true" uid="<?= $user ?>" useyou="false"/>!</h2><br/>
  <fb:if-is-app-user uid="<?= $user ?>">
<?
if ($action_wave) {
  if ($wave_success) {
?>
 <fb:explanation>
      <fb:message><fb:name uid="<?= $target_user ?>" /></fb:message>
      You have sent a greeting to <fb:name uid="<?= $target_user ?>" />.
 </fb:explanation>
<?
  }
}
?>
<? if ($show_form) { ?>
    <p>Give someone a smile, send them a greeting. To send someone a greeting start
typing in their name and click on the Send button.</p>
    <fb:editor action="" labelwidth="100">
      <fb:editor-custom label="Tell us who:">
        <fb:friend-selector name="uid" idname="friend_sel" />
      </fb:editor-custom>
      <fb:editor-buttonset>
        <fb:editor-button value="Send"/>
        <fb:editor-cancel />
      </fb:editor-buttonset>
    </fb:editor>
<? } ?>
  <fb:else>
    <p>You need to <a href="<?= $facebook->get_add_url() ?>">add <?=
AppConfig::$app_name ?></a> to use it!</p>
  </fb:else>
</fb:if-is-app-user>

</div>
```

The result is shown in Figure 2-8.

Figure 2-8: The Application Action page.

As determined in the first PHP code block, you want to display the status of the sent greeting if the `friend_sel` POST argument was provided. If it was, you set the `action_wave` variable to `true`. If the wave was successfully sent, you use the `fb:explanation` and `fb:message` entities to display a small status message, as shown here:

```php
<?php
if ($action_wave) {
  if ($wave_success) {
?>
    <fb:explanation>
        <fb:message>Greeting sent to <fb:name uid="<?= $target_user ?>" />
</fb:message>
        You have sent a greeting to <fb:name uid="<?= $target_user ?>" />.
    </fb:explanation>
<?php
  }
}
?>
```

The `fb:explanation` and `fb:message` FBML entities are used for messaging and content organization. Actions have events, and when events happen, Facebook has provided several FBML entities to better organize and display that information. Those FBML entities also conform to the messaging patterns that Facebook uses, giving your application users consistent behavior throughout Facebook. The following code renders the screen shown in Figure 2-9.

```
<fb:explanation>
<fb:message>Read this title!</fb:message>
It contains important information that you should pay attention to.

</fb:explanation>
```

Read this title!

It contains important information that you should pay attention to.

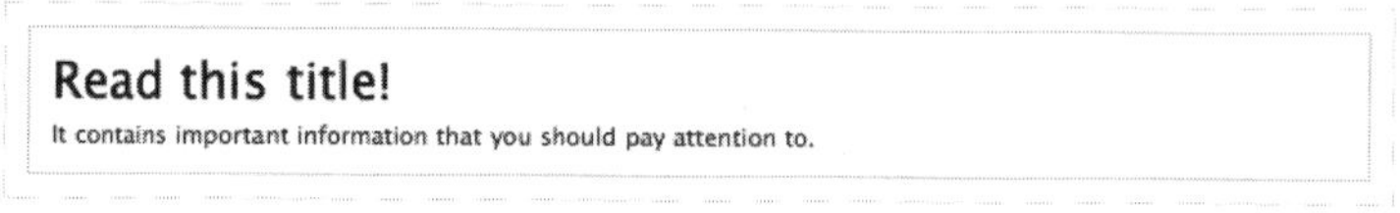

Figure 2-9: An example of `fb:explanation` and `fb:message`.

If the `friend_sel` POST variable is not present, you want to display the form used to select the user to send a greeting to. Facebook provides several FBML entities that make creating forms very easy. More detailed information on creating forms is provided in Chapter 3.

As shown in the following code, you define the form by using the `fb:editor` FBML entity. Inside, you can set various form elements, but the `fb:editor-custom` entity is used to add custom form elements. Inside of the `fb:editor-custom` entity, you wrap the `fb:friend-selector` and include it in the form.

```php
<?php
if ($show_form) {
?>
    <p>Give someone a smile, send them a greeting. To send someone a greeting start
typing in their name and click on the Send button.</p>
    <fb:editor action="" labelwidth="100">
      <fb:editor-custom label="Tell us who:">
        <fb:friend-selector name="uid" idname="friend_sel" />
      </fb:editor-custom>
      <fb:editor-buttonset>
        <fb:editor-button value="Send"/>
        <fb:editor-cancel />
      </fb:editor-buttonset>
    </fb:editor>
<?php
}
?>
```

When a user enters the name of a friend and submits the form, the sending user's profile page is updated with the recent information. The target user's profile is also updated if the target user has added the application. As shown above, the `HelloWorld::wave_hello` method is called, which writes the greeting information to the database and makes the two API method calls to update the users' profiles. As shown in Figure 2-10, the end result is a simple message describing what has happened.

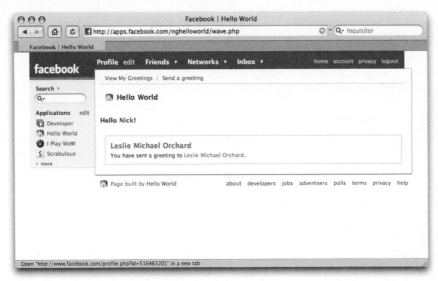

Figure 2-10: The Action Confirmation page.

The last series of FBML entities used in this project is part of the fb:editor set. They control the display and use of HTML forms in Facebook applications. Forms are covered in Chapter 3, but here's a quick look into how they are handled.

By using the fb:editor FBML entity, you can outline the area that contains the form elements. In this project, you want to use the fb:friend-selector FBML entity to quickly select a user to send a greeting to. The fb:friend-selector element is an Ajax auto-complete form element for your friends.

The fb:editor-custom FBML entity is used to wrap the fb:friend-selector and give it a label. You can also use the fb:editor-button and fb:editor-cancel entities to display the Submit button and provide a way to cancel the action.

The fb:editor-custom entity is very useful for adding form elements that do not have FBML. Dropdown menus, images, and raw text can easily be wrapped inside of an fb:editor-custom element to style non-form content and include it in a form.

Evaluating the Status

The sample project may be complete, but there is still a lot to do. You have seen the steps to create the application and configure it using the Facebook Developer Application, and you've written and installed the code that runs the Facebook application. However, there are many things left uncovered.

Now that it's built, let's look at what is wrong and/or missing. First (and most important) is the lack of error handling. The PHP Client library has several methods that can be used to verify that the request is valid and is being viewed properly, but Facebook is in no way a correcting force when it comes to your application code. The Action page has no error handling to check for invalid form data, nor does it verify that, at any point, Facebook returned a failure. You also do not display any messages indicating that the action failed.

Following are a few things that you should act on:

❑ **Error Handling** — You must add error handling and better messaging on the Action page. If an API method call fails, or even if you can't write to the database, you must let the user know that the action failed and why.

❑ **Notifications** — When a user sends a greeting to another user who has not received a greeting from that user before, you should send a notification using the `$facebook->api_client->notifications_send($to_ids, $notification, $email='')` method.

Summary

This chapter took a very hands-on approach to the Facebook Platform by diving in and creating a Facebook Application. You started by creating and configuring the application using the Facebook Developer Application, and continued by breaking down the application step-by-step to expose how it works.

I can't stress enough the usefulness of the FBML and how much time it saves application developers. With it, you created an interface that conforms to the overall Facebook style.

Chapter 3 focuses more on the FBML and how some of the more complex entities are used in real-world applications.

Facebook Markup Language (FBML)

Facebook applications post content to user profiles, send notifications, display content through the application Canvas, and post to the News Feed and Mini-Feed. None of this would be possible without Facebook Markup Language (FBML), the special markup language used by the Facebook Platform to parse, render, and enhance the content that has a direct impact on a user's experience on Facebook and your application.

Chapter 2 walked you through the development of a Facebook application and used several of the Facebook Platform components — one of which was FBML and some of the entities provided. This chapter continues discussing the idea and steps you through the plethora of available FBML entities.

This chapter also walks you through some of the caveats and rules applied to your FBML by the rendering engine and provides a base of understanding for some of the more advanced concepts.

Understanding FBML

In brief, FBML is a strict markup language that is made up of XML entities to deliver a rich experience to Facebook users. FBML is a hybrid markup language deeply rooted in HTML. In fact, the majority of the entities available are taken directly from HTML with several special exceptions. Following is an example of FBML:

```
<fb:name uid="12345"> is <strong>slick</strong>.
```

FBML was released with the Facebook Platform on its launch day, but has gone through several revisions since then. The notable changes include the entities made available to stem user profile content abuse and protect user privacy. This chapter does not include any of the deprecated entities from previous FBML versions. Nor does it include the FBML entities that are considered "beta" by the Facebook Platform.

Entities

An FBML *entity* is nothing more than an XML element within the fb namespace. The fb XML namespace is defined at http://apps.facebook.com/ns/1.0. Entities are used to display and set information, but also act as operators to control the flow and organization of content.

The next several sections cover each of the major groups that define the different types of FBML entities. As you read through the discussions demonstrating some of the uses of these entities, you will probably notice that in some cases there are multiple usage cases for the same entities.

HTML

Almost all HTML entities are available. Those listed here have a modified behavior. Following is a list of the HTML entities acknowledged by Facebook:

Abbr	del	h6	pre	td
acronym	dfn	hr	q	textarea
address	div	i	s	tfoot
b	dl	input	samp	th
bdo	dt	ins	select	thread
big	em	kbd	small span	tr
blockquote	fieldset	label	strike	tt
br	font	legend	strong	u
caption	h1	li	style	ul
center	h2	ol	sub	var
cite	h3	optgroup	sup	a
code	h4	option	table	form
dd	h5	p	tbody	img

Within this list, there are several special cases. The a, form, img, and script HTML entities have processing rules that developers should be aware of.

a

While the application Canvas allows relative and absolute URLs, other FBML instances require absolute URLs. You should use absolute URLs whenever using this HTML entity.

form

Forms are expanded and treated differently. See the section, "Forms," later in this chapter.

img

The img HTML entity is processed before being rendered to the browser. When the FBML rendering engine encounters an image URL, the image is filtered, validated, and cached by the Facebook Platform. The end result is that the URL given is rewritten with the location of the cached content.

The Facebook Platform takes these steps to ensure the protection of its users and information. This prevents animated or large images from degrading the experience of Facebook's users. It also mitigates load away from the applications and onto the Facebook Platform.

All img HTML entities must have absolute URLs.

script

Traditional JavaScript is not allowed. Instead, the Facebook Platform has released FBJS, a JavaScript parser and rendering system that allows developers to enhance their Facebook applications. The FBJS entity and its related concepts are discussed in Chapter 4.

Operators

Operators control the flow, structure, and organization of your FBML. These include the fb:if, fb:else, fb:switch, fb:default, fb:random, and fb:random-option FBML entities.

fb:if

Following is a required attribute:

❑ value — The true or false value to base the check on

The fb:if element is your standard if/then block. At render time, the FBML engine will determine if the value of the value attribute is true, and if so, display the contents of the entity. The default value is false. It should be noted that a very quick and efficient way to comment out sections of FBML is by using fb:if entities.

```
<fb:if value="true">
Candy is dandy but liquor is quicker.
</fb:if>
```

fb:else

The fb:else entity is the other half of the fb:if entity. It handles the else case, displaying its contents. There are no attributes for this entity.

```
The truth is
<fb:if value="true">
absolute
<fb:else>relative</fb:else>
</fb:if>.
```

The `fb:else` entity also applies to several other entities, including all of the `fb:if-*` entities, as well as the `fb:is-in-network` entity.

fb:switch

The `fb:switch` contains several FBML entities and will return the first one that resolves to a non-empty string.

```
<fb:switch>
   <fb:photo pid="12345" />
   <fb:profile-pic uid="54321" />
</fb:switch>
```

fb:default

The `fb:default` entity is used in the `fb:switch` entity to provide a default resolution if one is not found.

```
<fb:switch>
   <fb:photo pid="12345" />
   <fb:profile-pic uid="54321" />
   <fb:default>You can't see either the photo or the profile pic</fb:default>
</fb:switch>
```

fb:random

Following are optional attributes:

❑   `pick` — A number indicating the maximum number of selections to make. The default value is 1.

❑   `unique` — A `true` or `false` value that forces uniqueness among the selections returned. This option is disregarded if the `pick` attribute is less than 2. The default value is `true`.

The `fb:random` entity is a container of `fb:random-option` entities that are returned at random.

```
<fb:random>
  <fb:random-option>Bounjour</fb:random-option>
  <fb:random-option>Hello</fb:random-option>
</fb:random>
```

fb:random-option

Following is an optional attribute:

❑   `weight` — A numeric value associated with an option

The `fb:random-option` entity is used in the `fb:random` entity to provide the options that can be made and returned. Selection of these options is made at random. However, an option weight is factored in.

```
<fb:random>
  <fb:random-option weight="50">You are a winner!</fb:random-option>
  <fb:random-option weight="1">Please try again.</fb:random-option>
</fb:random>
```

The weight of an available option is relative to the total number of options available if more than one selection is being made, and all selections must be unique.

Navigation

The navigational FBML entities allow developers to show a consistent look and feel to their applications with multiple sections and areas. Chapter 10 provides a full comparison of these entities, as well as ideal use cases and more information.

This includes the following FBML entities:

- ❏   fb:dashboard
- ❏   fb:create-button
- ❏   fb:help
- ❏   fb:action
- ❏   fb:header
- ❏   fb:tabs
- ❏   fb:tab-item
- ❏   fb:mediaheader
- ❏   fb:header-title
- ❏   fb:owner-action

fb:dashboard

The fb:dashboard entity is used to create the default Facebook dashboard. The header text displayed is the application name. This cannot be changed or configured. There are no attributes available for this entity. This entity may contain any number of fb:action entities, one fb:create-button entity, and one fb:help entity.

```
<fb:dashboard></fb:dashboard>
```

For applications with icons, the icon will be displayed to the immediate left of the application name.

fb:create-button

Following is a required attribute:

- ❏   href — The destination URL. This must be a Canvas URL.

Following is an optional attribute:

- ❏   title — The title displayed in the tooltip

The `fb:create-button` entity displays the default "Create" button on the right-hand side of the dashboard. It is used to imply that user-generated content can be added through this link. The `fb:dashboard` will only recognize one of these entities. The text inside of the entity is directly displayed. However, the "+" symbol in the display text cannot be removed or styled.

```
<fb:dashboard>
  <fb:create-button href="create.php">Add a meal</fb:create-button>
</fb:dashboard>
```

fb:help

Following is a required attribute:

❑ `href` — The destination URL. This must be a Canvas URL.

Following is an optional attribute:

❑ `title` — The title displayed in the tooltip

The `fb:help` entity will create a right-aligned link within a dashboard widget.

```
<fb:dashboard>
  <fb:help href="help.php">Help</fb:help>
</fb:dashboard>
```

The link text and tooltip will always display "Help." This is not configurable and cannot be styled.

fb:action

Following is a required attribute:

❑ `href` — The destination URL. This must be a Canvas URL.

Following is an optional attribute:

❑ `title` — The title displayed in the tooltip

The `fb:action` entity can be used in two places. The first is within a `fb:dashboard` entity. In this case, it renders a left-aligned link in the dashboard.

```
<fb:dashboard>
  <fb:action href="search.php">Search</fb:action>
</fb:dashboard>
```

This entity can also be used in the context of an `fb:subtitle` entity. In this case, it creates a right-aligned link within the subtitle to the URL provided.

```
<fb:subtitle>
  <fb:action href="http://apps.facebook.com/cowbell/more">More cowbell</fb:action>
  There have been 3 rings.
</fb:subtitle>
```

fb:header

Following are optional attributes:

❑ icon — This `true` or `false` value toggles the display of the application icon next to the header text. The default is `true`.

❑ decoration — This attribute is used to customize the appearance of the header and text. The value of this attribute may be one of the following:

    ❑ add_border — Adds a 1-pixel solid black style to the header.

    ❑ no_padding — Removes the 20-pixel padding from the header style.

    ❑ shorten — Removes 20 pixels from the bottom of the header.

The `fb:header` entity renders a standard Facebook header. By default, the icon of the application is displayed to the left of the header text. Developers can customize the style of the header by setting one of the three available options in the `decoration` attribute.

```
<fb:header>Hello World</fb:header>
```

fb:tabs

The `fb:tabs` entity renders a set of navigational tabs. There are no direct options for this entity. It contains several `fb:tab-item` entities.

```
<fb:tabs></fb:tabs>
```

fb:tab-item

Following are required attributes:

❑ href — The destination URL of the tab. This must be an absolute URL.

❑ title — The text displayed in the tab tooltip

Following are optional attributes:

❑ align — Specify the alignment of the item. The available options are `left` and `right`. The default value is `left`.

❑ selected — A `true` or `false` value that highlights the tab, indicating that it has been selected.

The `fb:tab-item` entity is used to populate an `fb:tabs` entity with one or more tabs.

```
<fb:tabs>
  <fb:tab-item href="/exampleapp/home.php" href="My Home">Home</fb:tab-item>
  <fb:tab-item href="/exampleapp/search.php" href="Find other users">Search
</fb:tab-item>
  <fb:tab-item href="/exampleapp/help.php" href="Help" align="right">Help</fb:tab-
item>
</fb:tabs>
```

fb:mediaheader

Following is a required attribute:

❑   uid — The Facebook user ID of the user the header is displayed for

This fb:mediaheader FBML entity renders a standard media header. Its use is intended for displaying content provided by a Facebook user. There are two different behaviors associated with this entity. When the viewing user is not the user specified by the uid attribute, several links are displayed to contact the user, view the user's profile, and "poke" the user. These links are not present when the viewing user is the user specified.

```
<fb:mediaheader uid="500025891"></fb:mediaheader>
```

fb:header-title

This fb:header-title FBML entity is used within an fb:mediaheader entity to set the header text displayed on a media header widget.

```
<fb:mediaheader uid="500025891">
  <fb:header-title>Nick's Photos</fb:header-title>
</fb:mediaheader>
```

fb:owner-action

Following is a required attribute:

❑   href — The destination of the action

The fb:owner-action FBML entity is used to display an action link when the viewing user is the user specified in the fb:mediaheader parent FBML entity.

```
<fb:mediaheader uid="500025891">
 <fb:header-title>Nick's stuff</fb:header-title>
 <fb:owner-action href="?edit=1">Edit</fb:owner-action>
</fb:mediaheader>
```

Informational

Informational FBML entities are used to display messages and notices to users. This group includes the fb:error, fb:explanation, fb:success, and fb:message FBML entities.

fb:error

Following is a required attribute:

❑   message — The message title to display

Following is an optional attribute:

❑   `decoration` — Customize the appearance of the error box using one of two options:

    ❑   `no_padding` — Removes 20 pixels in padding.

    ❑   `shorten` — Removes 20 pixels from the bottom.

The `fb:error` entity is used to convey a warning or error to the user. It renders a large red box with the title and body specified by the message attribute and entity contents. The display of the error message can be customized using the optional `decoration` attribute.

```
<fb:error message="You already invited that user.">
Do not try to invite users more than once. You have 10 invites left.
</fb:error>
```

fb:explanation

Following is a required attribute:

❑   `message` — The message title to display

Following is an optional attribute:

❑   `decoration` — Customize the appearance of the explanation box using one of two options:

    ❑   `no_padding` — Removes the 20-pixel padding.

    ❑   `shorten` — Removes 20 pixels from the bottom.

The `fb:explanation` entity is used to convey a message or notice. It renders a large white box with the title and body specified by the `message` attribute and entity contents. The display of the message can be customized using the optional `decoration` attribute.

```
<fb:explanation message="Someone attacked your base">
You lost 20 men but thwarted the attack. Morale has increased slightly.
</fb:explanation>
```

fb:success

Following is a required attribute:

❑   `message` — The message title to display

Following is an optional attribute:

❑   `decoration` — Customize the appearance of the success box using one of two options:

    ❑   `no_padding` — Removes the 20-pixel padding.

    ❑   `shorten` — Removes 20 pixels from the bottom.

The fb:success entity is used to convey a success message or notice. It renders a large yellow box with the title and body specified by the message attribute and entity contents. The display of the message can be customized using the optional decoration attribute.

```
<fb:success message="A friend of yours added the application">
Chris has added the application and is now in your application network. Hurray.
</fb:success>
```

fb:message

The fb:message entity is used inside of the fb:error, fb:explanation, and fb:success entities as a drop-in replacement for the message attribute. There are no configuration options or attributes available.

```
<fb:success>
  <fb:message>A friend of yours added the application</fb:message>
  Chris has added the application and is now in your application network. Hurray.
</fb:success>
```

User and Group

The user and group FBML entities are used to display information about users or groups. This group includes the fb:name, fb:grouplink, fb:user, fb:pronoun, and fb:profile-pic FBML entities.

fb:name

Following is a required attribute:

❑   uid — This numeric value represents the Facebook user ID of the user whose name will be displayed. The value loggedinuser can also be given.

Following are optional attributes:

❑   firstnameonly — A Boolean value indicating that only the user's first name should be displayed. The default value for this attribute is false.

❑   lastnameonly — A Boolean value indicating that only the user's last name should be displayed. The default value for this attribute is false.

❑   linked — A Boolean value that controls whether the displayed text will link to the user's profile. The default value for this attribute is true.

❑   possessive — A Boolean value that sets the user's name possessive (e.g., *Joe's* instead of *Joe*). The default value for this attribute is false.

❑   reflexive — A Boolean value that displays the reflexive form of the user's name (e.g., *yourself* or *himself*). The default value for this attribute is false.

❑   useyou — A Boolean value that displays *you* if the uid given is the uid of the viewing user. The default value for this attribute is true. When used in conjunction with the reflexive attribute, the text *yourself* is displayed.

❑   ifcantsee — A string that is displayed as alternate text if the viewing user does not have permission to view the user. The default is an empty string.

❑   capitalize — A Boolean value that capitalizes the displayed text. The default value for this attribute is false.

❑   subjectid — The Facebook user ID of the subject of the sentence where the name is the object of the verb of the sentence. The reflexive form will be used when appropriate.

The fb:name entity at a very basic level provides a drop-in replacement to display the name of a user specified by Facebook user ID. Through several attributes, it is possible to customize how the name is displayed and used.

```
Is <fb:name uid="12345" /> the same as <fb:name uid="loggedinuser"/>?
```

fb:grouplink

Following is a required attribute:

❑   gid — The Facebook Group ID to link to

The fb:grouplink FBML entity links to a Facebook Group. The only option available is the gid attribute, the value being the numeric ID of the Facebook Group you want to link to.

```
<fb:grouplink gid="2204910717" />
```

fb:user

Following is a required attribute:

❑   uid — A numeric value representing the Facebook user ID of the user

The fb:user FBML entity is a user-centric control element. It accepts one option, the uid attribute, with the value being a valid Facebook user ID. If the viewing user is the user represented by the user ID given to the FBML entity, the content is displayed.

```
<fb:user uid="12345">
This is for 12345's eyes only.
</fb:user>
```

fb:pronoun

Following is a required attribute:

❑   uid — A numeric value representing the Facebook user whose name will be generated/displayed.

Following are optional attributes:

❑   objective — A Boolean value that sets the displayed name to the objective form (*him/her/you/them*). The default value for this attribute is false.

❑   usethey — A Boolean value that sets the displayed text to *they* if the gender of the user is not specified. The default value for this attribute is true.

❑   reflexive — A Boolean value that displays the reflexive form of the user's name (e.g., *yourself* or *himself*). The default value for this attribute is false.

❏ useyou — A Boolean value that displays *you* if the uid given is the uid of the viewing user. The default value for this attribute is true. When used in conjunction with the reflexive attribute, the text *yourself* is displayed.

❏ ifcantsee — A string that is displayed as alternate text if the viewing user does not have permission to view the user. The default is an empty string.

❏ capitalize — A Boolean value that capitalizes the displayed text. The default value for this attribute is false.

The fb:pronoun FBML entity returns a pronoun for a user. The uid attribute must be a valid Facebook user ID.

```
<fb:pronoun uid="12345" usethey="true" useyou="false" />
```

fb:profile-pic

Following is a required attribute:

❏ uid — A numeric value representing the Facebook user ID of the user whose profile picture is displayed

Following are optional attributes:

❏ size — The size of the image to display. It must be one of the following values, the default value being thumb:

  ❏ thumb or t — 50 pixels wide

  ❏ small or s — 100 pixels wide

  ❏ normal or n — 200 pixels wide

  ❏ square or q — 50 pixels by 50 pixels

❏ linked — Link the image to the profile of the user. The default is true.

The fb:profile-pic FBML entity takes the uid attribute and returns a valid img HTML entity with the profile picture for that user.

```
<fb:profile-pic uid="12345" size="thumb" linked="true" />
```

Information Control

The Facebook Platform also provides entities that can be used to control the flow and display of information. These can be used to enforce privacy and viewing permissions when displaying content of and about other users to other users.

This group includes the fb:is-in-network, fb:if-can-see, fb:if-can-see-photo, fb:if-is-app-user, fb:if-is-friends-with-viewer, fb:if-is-group-member, fb:if-is-own-profile, fb:if-is-user, and fb:if-user-has-added-app FBML entities.

fb:is-in-network

Following is a required attribute:

❑   network — The numeric ID representing the Facebook network for the membership check

Following is an optional attribute:

❑   uid — The numeric value representing the Facebook user to check the network membership of. If no value is provided, this defaults to the user the FBML was rendered for.

The contents of this entity will render if the user supplied in the uid attribute is in the network supplied in the network attribute.

```
<fb:is-in-network network="67108896">
You are in the Silicon Valley, CA network.
</fb:is-in-network>
```

*This is one of the few non-*fb:if *entities that recognizes the* fb:else *entity.*

fb:if-can-see

Following is a required attribute:

❑   uid — A numeric value representing the Facebook user to validate

Following is an optional attribute:

❑   what — The policy name to validate. Valid values include the following:

    ❑   profile

    ❑   friends

    ❑   not_limited

    ❑   online

    ❑   statusupdates

    ❑   wall

    ❑   groups

    ❑   courses

    ❑   photosofme

    ❑   notes

    ❑   feed

    ❑   contact

    ❑   email

    ❑   aim

- ❑ cell
- ❑ phone
- ❑ mailbox
- ❑ address
- ❑ basic
- ❑ education
- ❑ professional
- ❑ personal
- ❑ seasonal
- ❑ search

The default value is search.

```
<fb:if-can-see uid="12345" what="education">
  Did you go to school with <fb:name uid="12345" linked="true" />?
  <fb:else>Move on, nothing to see here.</fb:else>
</fb:if-can-see>
```

fb:if-can-see-photo

Following is a required attribute:

- ❑ pid — A numeric value provided by the Facebook Platform representing the photo

Following is an optional attribute:

- ❑ uid — A numeric value representing the Facebook user to validate

The fb:if-can-see-photo entity is used to verify that a user can view a photo.

```
<fb:if-can-see-photo uid="12345" pid="555123">
  <a href="/photos/555123">Check out this photo</a>.
</fb:if-can-see>
```

fb:if-is-app-user

Following is an optional attribute:

- ❑ uid — The numeric value representing the Facebook user to check. If no value is provided, this defaults to the user the FBML was rendered for.

The fb:if-is-app-user entity will display the content of the entity only if the user has granted full permission to the application.

Granting an application permission is not the same as adding an application.

```
<fb:if-is-app-user>
  <a href="/myapp/someaction">
  <fb:else>
    You must grant this application permission to access your information before you
can use the advanced features provided.
  </fb:else>
</fb:if-is-app-user>
```

fb:if-is-friends-with-viewer

Following are required attributes:

❑   uid — A numeric value representing the Facebook user

❑   includeself — A Boolean value indicating that the evaluation will return true if the viewing user is the user as per the uid attribute

The fb:if-is-friends-with-viewer FBML entity will display the content of the entity only if the viewing user is friends with the user as specified by the uid attribute.

```
<fb:if-is-friends-with-viewer uid="12345">
  Hey compadre.
  <fb:else>
    Do you want to add <fb:name uid="12345" /> as a friend?
  </fb:else>
</fb:if-is-friends-with-viewer>
```

fb:if-is-group-member

Following is a required attribute:

❑   gid — A numeric value representing a Facebook group

Following are optional attributes:

❑   uid — A numeric value representing a Facebook user

❑   role — The role to check for. The default value is member. Other valid values are officer and admin.

The fb:if-is-group-member entity will display the content of the entity only if the user meets the role requirement for the given group.

```
<fb:if-is-group-member uid="12345" gid="5555123" role="officer">
  This is an officer only message.
  <fb:else>
    Sorry, this message is for officers only.
  </fb:else>
</fb:if-is-group-member>
```

fb:if-is-own-profile

The `fb:if-is-own-profile` FBML entity will display the content of the entity only if the viewing user is the owner of the profile.

```
<fb:if-is-own-profile>
  This is your profile
  <fb:else>
    This is not your profile.
  </fb:else>
</fb:if-is-own-profile>
```

fb:if-is-user

Following is a required attribute:

❑ uid — A list of numeric values representing Facebook users

The `fb:if-is-user` FBML entity will display the content of the entity only if the viewing user is one of the specified users in the `uid` attribute.

```
<fb:if-is-user uid="12345,55512">
  Keep this a secret.
  <fb:else>
    DO NOT WANT KTHNXBAI.
  </fb:else>
</fb:if-is-own-profile>
```

fb:if-user-has-added-app

Following is a required attribute:

❑ uid — A numeric value representing a Facebook user

The `fb:if-user-has-added-app` FBML entity will display the content of the entity only if the user in the `uid` attribute has added the application to the account.

```
<fb:if-user-has-added-app uid="12345">
  Have a feature. No really. Have it.
  <fb:else>
    You must add this application to use this feature.
  </fb:else>
</fb:if-user-has-added-app>
```

Profile

The content displayed on a user's profile is controlled by several FBML entities specific to user profiles. This group includes the `fb:wide`, `fb:narrow`, `fb:profile-action`, `fb:subtitle`, `fb:user-table`, and `fb:user-item` FBML entities. These entities can only be used to display User Profile page content.

fb:wide

The `fb:wide` entity will display the entity contents only when the application profile box is in the wide column of the user profile.

```
<fb:wide>
This is wide content. It has 10 items.
</fb:wide>
```

fb:narrow

The `fb:narrow` entity will display the entity contents only when the application profile box is in the narrow column of the user profile.

```
<fb:narrow>
This is narrow content. It has 6 items.
</fb:narrow>
```

fb:profile-action

Following is a required attribute:

❑   `url` — The destination that the user is taken to. This value must be an absolute URL.

The `fb:profile-action` entity renders a link under the user's profile photo. Each application can set one profile action link. The FBML is set through the `Facebook.profile.setFBML` API method.

```
<fb:profile-action url="http://example.com/books">See all books</fb:profile-action>
```

Conditions may be applied to the `fb:profile-action` based on the user viewing the profile.

```
<fb:if-is-own-profile>
  <fb:profile-action url="http://example.com/user?uid=12345">View my challenges
</fb:profile-action>
  <fb:else>
    <fb:if-is-app-user>
<profile-action url="http://example.com/challenge?uid=12345">Challenge this user
</fb:profile-action>
      <fb:else>
<fb:profile-action url="http://example.com/add?from=12345">Add this application
</fb:profile-action>
      </fb:else>
    </fb:if-is-app-user>
  </fb:else>
</fb:if-is-own-profile>
```

fb:subtitle

Following is an optional attribute:

❑   seeallurl — An absolute application Canvas page URL that displays a "See all" link

The `fb:subtitle` entity defines the subtitle for a profile application box. This FBML entity may have a single `fb:action` entity that is used to render an action link on the right-hand side of the profile box subtitle.

```
<fb:subtitle seeallurl="http://apps.facebook.com/gifts?user=12345">
Displaying 3 recently given gifts.
</fb:subtitle>
```

fb:user-table

Following is an optional attribute:

❑   cols — The number of columns to display

The `fb:user-table` FBML entity prepares a grid of users to display.

```
<fb:user-table cols="4">
  <fb:user-item uid="12345" />
  <fb:user-item uid="23456" />
  <fb:user-item uid="34567" />
  <fb:user-item uid="45678" />
  <fb:user-item uid="56789" />
</fb:user-table>
```

fb:user-item

Following is a required attribute:

❑   uid — A numeric value representing a Facebook user

The `fb:user-item` FBML entity adds a user to a `fb:user-table` grid.

```
<fb:user-table cols="3">
  <fb:user-item uid="123456" />
</fb:user-table>
```

Profile Visibility

These entities control the visibility of information of content displayed on user profile pages. As of FBML 1.2, all content sent to a User Profile page is sent to the browser, but hidden based on the rules applied by these entities. Therefore, it is not safe (nor a good idea) to send any content that could be sensitive or private to a user's profile.

This group includes the `fb:visible-to-owner`, `fb:visible-to-friends`, `fb:visible-to-user`, `fb:visible-to-apps-users`, and `fb:visible-to-added-app-users` FBML entities.

fb:visible-to-owner

The fb:visible-to-owner entity defines content that is only visible if the user viewing a profile is the profile owner. This entity should not be used to display private or sensitive content. This entity can only be used once in a profile entity (fb:wide and fb:narrow).

```
<fb:wide>
<fb:visible-to-owner>
35 people have tagged you. 10 of those tags were private.
</fb:visible-to-owner>
</fb:wide>
```

fb:visible-to-friends

The fb:visible-to-friends entity defines content that is only visible if the user viewing a profile is a friend of the profile owner. This entity should not be used to display private or sensitive content. This entity can only be used once in a profile entity (fb:wide and fb:narrow).

```
<fb:wide>
<fb:visible-to-friend>
You lived with John in a bungalo in '67.
</fb:visible-to-friend>
</fb:wide>
```

fb:visible-to-user

Following is a required attribute:

❑ uid — A numeric value representing a Facebook user

The fb:visible-to-user entity defines content that is only visible if the user viewing a profile is designated to see the enclosed content as per the uid attribute. This entity should not be used to display private or sensitive content. This entity can only be used once in a profile entity (fb:wide and fb:narrow).

```
<fb:wide>
<fb:visible-to-user uid="12345">
You rock my world.
</fb:visible-to-user>
</fb:wide>
```

fb:visible-to-apps-users

The fb:visible-to-apps-users entity defines content that is only visible if the user viewing a profile has given full permission to the application that created that profile box. This entity should not be used to display private or sensitive content. This entity can only be used once in a profile entity (fb:wide and fb:narrow).

```
<fb:wide>
<fb:visible-to-apps-users>
Challenge John to a deul!
</fb:visible-to-apps-users>
</fb:wide>
```

fb:visible-to-added-app-users

The `fb:visible-to-apps-users` entity defines content that is only visible if the user viewing a profile has added the application that created that profile box. This entity should not be used to display private or sensitive content. This entity can only be used once in a profile entity (`fb:wide` and `fb:narrow`).

```
<fb:wide>
<fb:visible-to-added-app-users>
Challenge John to a deul!
</fb:visible-to-added-app-users>
</fb:wide>
```

Media and External Content

The media and external content FBML entities allow developers to include different types of content in their applications to be displayed on application Canvas pages and User Profile pages.

This group includes the `fb:iframe`, `fb:photo`, `fb:mp3`, `fb:swf`, `fb:flv`, and `fb:silverlight` FBML entities.

fb:iframe

Following is a required attribute:

- ❑ `src` — The source URL to display in the IFrame

Following are optional attributes:

- ❑ `smartsize` — A Boolean value directs the rendered `iframe` entity to expand to consume whatever renaming space is available and disables the outer scroll bars.
- ❑ `frameborder` — A Boolean value that shows or hides the frame border
- ❑ `scrolling` — A Boolean value that shows or hides the scroll bars
- ❑ `style` — The standard style attribute used to style the element
- ❑ `width` — The width of the IFrame rendered
- ❑ `height` — The height of the IFrame rendered

The `fb:iframe` FBML entity is used to create an IFrame HTML element for use within the application Canvas. When creating an IFrame, the URL defined by the `src` attribute is rewritten to include several query string parameters indicating that the request was validly made from the Facebook Platform. The `fb_sig_in_iframe` query string parameter is also included accordingly.

```
<fb:iframe src="http://search.yahoo.com/" smartsize="0" frameborder="0"
scrolling="0" width="320" height="45" />
```

fb:photo

Following is a required attribute:

- ❑ `pid` — A numeric ID representing either the API-given ID, or the ID found in the query string in conjunction with a user ID

Following are optional attributes:

❑   uid — The uid found in the query string in conjunction with a non-API-supplied pid

❑   size — The size of the image to display. It must be one of the following values, the default value being thumb:

  ❑   thumb or t — 50 pixels wide

  ❑   small or s — 100 pixels wide

  ❑   normal or n — 200 pixels wide

  ❑   square or q — 50 pixels by 50 pixels

❑   align — This attribute can be set to either left or right to indicate the alignment of the photo on the application Canvas. The default value for this attribute is left.

The fb:photo FBML entity is used to display a photo uploaded to Facebook.

```
<fb:photo pid="12345" />
```

fb:mp3

Following is a required attribute:

❑   src — An absolute URL to the MP3 file to play

Following are optional attributes:

❑   title — The title of the song

❑   artist — The artist of the song

❑   album — The album containing the song

❑   width — The width of the player. The default value is 300.

❑   height — The height of the player. The default value is 29.

The fb:mp3 FBML entity renders a Flash MP3 player.

```
<fb:mp3 src="http://example.com/mp3" title="The Legendary Hero" />
```

fb:swf

Following is a required attribute:

❑   swfsrc — An absolute URL to the SWF object

Following are optional attributes:

❑   imgsrc — The location of a preview image. This must be an absolute URL. If this attribute is not set, the default value is the URL of a transparent image.

❑   width — The width of the image and Flash object

- ❑ `height` — The height of the image and Flash object

- ❑ `imgstyle` — A valid style attribute that applies CSS to the image defined by `imgsrc`

- ❑ `imgclass` — A valid CSS class identifier used to style the image defined by `imgsrc`

- ❑ `flashvars` — The URL encoded Flash variables. This will also include the `fb_sig_` variables described in the "Forms" section below in this chapter.

- ❑ `swfbgcolor` — The background color of the SWF object

- ❑ `waitforclick` — A Boolean indicating that the SWF object should start playing only when the user clicks on the SWF object. This attribute is automatically set to `true` when rendering Flash on a user profile page.

- ❑ `salign` — The `salign` value as per the embedded HTML entity

- ❑ `loop` — A Boolean value indicating that the SWF object should loop continuously

- ❑ `quality` — The scale to apply to the SWF object

- ❑ `align` — A value indicating how the browser should align the SWF object. Valid values include `left`, `right`, and `center`.

- ❑ `wmode` — Indicates the opacity setting for the SWF object. Valid values include `transparent`, `opaque`, or `window`. If this attribute is not specified, the default value is `transparent`.

The `fb:swf` FBML entity renders an SWF object.

```
<fb:swf
  swfsrc="http://example.com/flash/myflash.swf"
  imgsrc="http://example.com/flash/myflash-thumb.jpg"
  width="480"
  height="320"
/>
```

When the SWF object is included, the following variables are also passed:

- ❑ `allowScriptAccess` — A string that is always set to `never`

- ❑ `fb_sig_profile` — The Facebook user ID of the user whose profile the SWF object is being displayed on. If the SWF object is not displayed on a user's profile page, this parameter is blank.

- ❑ `fb_sig_time` — The time the signature was generated

- ❑ `fb_sig_user` — The Facebook user ID of the currently logged-in user

- ❑ `fb_sig_session_key` — The session key of the currently logged-in user

- ❑ `fb_sig_expires` — The UNIX time stamp representing when the session key as defined by `fb_sig_session_key` expires

- ❑ `fb_sig_api_key` — Your application's API key

- ❑ `fb_sig_added` — A Boolean value indicating whether the currently logged-in user has added the application.

- ❑ `fb_sig` — A valid Facebook Platform signature

> **Facebook requires Flash version 9.0.0 for all `fb:swf` FBML entities.**

fb:flv

Following is a required attribute:

- ❑   `src` — An absolute URL to the FLV file

Following are optional attributes:

- ❑   `width` — The width in pixels of the video container
- ❑   `height` — The height in pixels of the video container
- ❑   `title` — The title of the video

The `fb:flv` FBML entity renders a flash FLV media player that allows application developers to display streaming video/audio files.

```
<fb:flv
  src="http://example.com/video/aqd.flv"
  width="480"
  height="320"
  title="A quiet day"
/>
```

The source video must already be an FLV-encoded file. Developers must not pass raw AVI or MPEG video to be encoded on-the-fly. Also, there is a known bug whereby on Internet Explorer, if a height and width are not passed, the video container will render the file as a gray 1 × 1 square pixel. It is considered good practice to always specify the height, weight, and title of videos displayed.

fb:silverlight

Following is a required attribute:

- ❑   `silverlightsrc` — An absolute URL to the Silverlight control

Following are optional attributes:

- ❑   `width` — The width in pixels of the video container
- ❑   `height` — The height in pixels of the video container
- ❑   `imgsrc` — An absolute URL to control the preview image. This must be a .GIF or .JPEG image. If this attribute is left blank, the image used is a transparent 1 × 1 pixel image that effectively renders the FBML entity useless.
- ❑   `imgstyle` — The style attribute applied to the image
- ❑   `imgclass` — The class attributed applied to the image
- ❑   `swfbgcolor` — The default background applied to the Silverlight control. This must be a hex-encoded value (e.g., #006400).

The fb:silverlight FBML entity renders a Microsoft Silverlight control.

```
<fb:silverlight
  silverlightsrc="http://example.com/ms/silverlight/demo"
  width="400"
  height="200"
/>
```

When rendering Silverlight controls on non-application Canvas pages, the image specified as the imgsrc attribute will appear first. The user must click on the image to display the Silverlight control.

Notifications and Requests

When sending notifications or requests through the Facebook Platform, the content of such notifications or requests extends to several additional FBML entities. This group includes the fb:notif-subject, fb:notif-page, fb:notif-email, fb:req-choice, fb:multi-friend-input, fb:request-form, and fb:request-form-submit FBML entities.

fb:notif-subject

The fb:notif-subject entity defines the subject line for a notification through FBML, as opposed to an additional argument.

```
<fb:notif-subject>
<fb:name uid="12345" linked="false" /> sent you a gift.
</fb:notif-subject>
```

fb:notif-page

The fb:notif-page entity defines the content that is displayed on the notification page when a user receives a notice.

```
<fb:notif-page>
<fb:name uid="12345" linked="false" /> sent you a gift. Add the gifts application
to receive the gift and display it on your profile.
</fb:notif-page>
```

fb:notif-email

The fb:notif-email entity is used to define the content displayed in the e-mail sent for a notification.

```
<fb:notif-email>
Facebook user <fb:name uid="12345" linked="false" /> sent you a gift. Log into
Facebook and add the gifts application to receive this gift and display it on your
profile.
</fb:notif-email>
```

fb:req-choice

Following are required attributes:

- ❑ url — The destination the user is taken to when clicked

- ❑ label — The title of the request choice

The `fb:req-choice` entity is used to define one or more options that a user may select when viewing a notification/request. These choices are displayed at the bottom of the request, regardless of where the FBML entities are in the body.

```
<fb:req-choice url="http://apps.facebook.com/example/confirm?" label="Confirm"/>
<fb:req-choice url="http://example.com/about" label="More about this app"/>
<fb:req-choice url="http://example.com/block?uid=1234" label="Do not send me any
more notifications or requests" />
```

fb:multi-friend-input

Following are optional attributes:

❑   `width` — The width of the input box. The default value for this attribute is 350 pixels.

❑   `border_color` — This attribute sets the border color of the input box. The default value for this attribute is #8496ba.

❑   `include_me` — A Boolean value that tells the Facebook Platform to include the viewing user as an option. The default value for this attribute is `false`.

❑   `max` — The maximum number of users that can be selected. The default value for this attribute is 20.

❑   `exclude_ids` — A comma-separate list of users to exclude from the selections

The `fb:multi-friend-input` element is much like the `fb:friend-selector` entity. It renders an input box that, as you type, predicts the friends that you are selecting, and makes those predictions available to quick selection. The major difference is that with this entity, you can select more than one friend. Facebook users who have been selected cannot be selected again and appear as widgets within the input box that can be removed.

```
<fb:multi-friend-input max="10" />
```

When this entity is rendered to the Facebook Canvas, the output is a hidden input field. Upon Form submission, the values are sent as a comma-separated list in the POST argument `ids[]`.

```
<input type="hidden" value="334455" name="ids[]"/>
```

fb:request-form

Following are required attributes:

❑   `type` — A string indicating the type of request or invitation to generate. This corresponds to the word displayed on the home page and notification page. Commonly `invitation`, `request`, and `event` are used.

❑   `content` — The body of the request or invitation. This body should be HTML/FBML formatted, but may only contain links and the `fb:req-choice` FBML entity. Be sure to HTML-encode this string when rendering the request form.

Following are optional attributes:

❑   `invite` — A Boolean value indicating that the request is an invitation

❑   `action` — The URL that the user is taken to when submitting the form after the confirmation step. If a value to this attribute is not specified, the default action is the current page.

❑   `method` — The HTTP Form method (can be `POST` or `GET`)

The `fb:request-form` FBML entity creates a structured form that allows Facebook users to send requests and invitations to other users. Primarily, it uses the `fb:multi-friend-selector` to create a simple interface that allows users to select multiple people in their friends list to receive the enveloped content.

When using the `fb:multi-friend-selector` FBML entity, the rendered form takes up an entire page and is presented in a way that encourages the user to select a large number of friends.

```
<fb:request-form
  type="Hug Me"
  action="invite/"
  content="Come use Hug Me!"
  invite="true"
>
  <fb:multi-friend-selector
    max="20"
    actiontext="Invite up to twenty of your friends."
    showborder="true"
    rows="5"
    exclude_ids="1234,2345,3456">
</fb:request-form>
```

This FBML entity can also be used with the `fb:multi-friend-input`, `fb:friend-selector`, and `fb:request-form-submit` FBML entities to customize the request interface.

When using the `fb:request-form` FBML entity without the `fb:multi-friend-selector`, be sure to use the `fb:request-form-submit` FBML entity to submit the form. Otherwise, nothing will happen.

```
<fb:request-form
  type="Hug Me"
  action="invite/"
  content="Come use Hug Me!"
  invite="true"
>
  <fb:multi-friend-input
    width="350px"
    border_color="#8496ba"
    exclude_ids="1234,2345,3456" />
  <fb:request-form-submit />
</fb:request-form>
```

When submitting the `request-form`, the user is presented with a confirmation step, and after continuing, the specified message is delivered to the selected Facebook users.

After a user has gone through the `request-form` invitation/notification process, there are two variables passed back to the Facebook application:

❑   `typeahead` — This variable is whatever text was typed into the input box used in the `fb:request-form` FBML entity.

❑   `ids` — This variable is a zero-based array of all of the user IDs that were selected by the user to receive the notification or request.

Developers building applications through an IFrame cannot take advantage of the `fb:request-form` FBML entity. Instead, they must use a work-around such as the `fb_force_mode` parameter to render a particular page through the FBML rendering engine.

fb:request-form-submit

Following are optional attributes:

❑   `uid` — A Facebook user ID representing a single person to receive the invitation or notification

❑   `label` — The label displayed on the Submit button. The text must include `%n` or `%N`, which gets replaced with the first name or full name for the user ID, respectively.

The `fb:request-formsubmit` FBML entity renders a Submit button that is used to submit a `fb:request-form` FBML entity. It can be used with any combination of `fb:multi-friend-input` or `fb:friend-selector` FBML entities, or on its own if the `uid` attribute is specified. When the button is clicked, the `request-form` confirmation dialog is displayed, allowing the user to continue sending the invitation or notification.

```
<fb:request-form-submit />
```

When using this entity with the `uid` attribute specified, the label may allow for displaying the first name or full name of the user specified by the `uid` attribute.

```
<fb:request-form-submit
  uid="1234"
  label="Invite %n to the party." />
```

Facebook Widgets

The Facebook Platform also includes several FBML entities that provide complete and full functionality for several widgets used on Facebook. These include message boards and helper entities for including Google Analytics code in your application. The FBML entities include `fb:comments` and `fb:google-analytics`.

fb:comments

Following are required attributes:

❑   `xid` — The unique identifier for the comment handler

❑   `canpost` — A Boolean flag defining the posting permission for the viewing user

- ❑ candelete — A Boolean flag that sets the ability to delete posts

- ❑ numposts — The maximum number of posts to show

Following are optional attributes:

- ❑ callbackurl — The URL to refresh this configuration. If not defined, this value defaults to the current URL.

- ❑ backurl — The URL to allow users to return via a "go back" link. If not defined, this defaults to the current URL.

The fb:comments entity will allow the developer to show comments for an entity defined by the developer. Facebook takes care of the post creation, maintenance, and display of the comments and comment form.

This entity is essentially a Wall framework, making it very easy for developers to create non-threaded discussions for an entity within the developer's scope of objects. There are some restrictions for this entity:

- ❑ Every page load for posting and viewing comments will refresh the configuration via the callbackurl attribute.

- ❑ These pages will pass back the fb_sig_xid parameter, which is the unique identifier supplied by the developer.

- ❑ When an action occurs, the fb_sig_xid_action parameter will additionally be passed. Currently, this can be post or delete. This can be used by the developer to determine if an action was made, and if so, to adjust the FBML accordingly.

- ❑ The refresh will be in the form of a POST request to the callbackurl. This will mimic the behavior of the application Canvas.

This entity may have a single fb:title entity to set the title of the Wall.

```
<fb:comments xid="uuid-ax3-aad-12345" canpost="true" candelete="false"
returnurl="http://apps.facebook.com/example" />
```

fb:google-analytics

Following is a required attribute:

- ❑ uacct — The Google Analytics account ID

Following is an optional attribute:

- ❑ page — The page or virtual page passed to urchin()

The fb:google-analytics FBML entity is a helper entity provided by Facebook to make it easier for developers to track application usage and traffic. When setting the page attribute, remember that it is considered absolute.

```
<fb:google-analytics uacct="nkg01123-01" page="/example/home" />
```

Editor and Forms

These are the entities that define the structured forms displayed on Facebook. They piece together very easily and allow for customizations and tweaks in their usage.

This group includes the following FBML entities:

❏ fb:friend-selector

❏ fb:editor

❏ fb:editor-text

❏ fb:editor-textarea

❏ fb:editor-time

❏ fb:editor-month

❏ fb:editor-date

❏ fb:editor-divider

❏ fb:editor-buttonset

❏ fb:editor-button

❏ fb:submit

❏ fb:editor-cancel

fb:friend-selector

Following are optional attributes:

❏ uid — The Facebook user ID of the user whose friends you can select. This defaults to the currently logged-in user.

❏ idname — The name of the form element that contains the Facebook user ID of the selected friend. The default value for this attribute is `friend_selector_id`.

❏ include_me — A Boolean value indicating that the viewing user is to be included in the list of available users

❏ exclude_ids — A comma-separated list of Facebook user IDs to exclude from the list of available users

❏ name — The name of the form element. The default value for this attribute is `friend_selector_name`.

The `fb:friend-selector` FBML entity renders a form input field that allows Facebook users to auto-complete friend names based on form input.

```
<fb:friend-selector />
```

If the entered text does not match any of the available friends, the hidden form input `idname` is set to an empty string, and the hidden form input `name` is set to the entered text. Also, if no value is entered, the hidden form input `idname` is not added to the `POST` variables upon Form submission.

fb:editor

Following is a required attribute:

❑ `action` — The URL that the data are posted to. This URL does not have to be absolute, nor is it required to be on the application Canvas page.

Following are optional attributes:

❑ `width` — The width of the form and table in pixels. If this attribute is not included, the default width of the form is 425 pixels.

❑ `labelwidth` — The width of the first column of the form/table in pixels. If this attribute is not included, the default value for the label column is 75 pixels. Values set to 0 will be ignored.

The `fb:editor` entity wraps 0 or more form-related FBML entities. This entity creates a table with two columns — the left for element labels and the right for form fields.

```
<fb:editor action="submit.php" width="100">
</fb:editor>
```

fb:editor-text

Following are optional attributes:

❑ `label` — The displayed label on the left side

❑ `name` — The name for the control

❑ `value` — The default value for this field

❑ `maxlength` — The maximum length for the user's input

The `fb:editor-text` entity renders a standard input box within a form.

```
<fb:editor action="submit.php" width="100">
  <fb:editor-text label="Name" name="myname" value="John Smith" />
</fb:editor>
```

fb:editor-textarea

Following are optional attributes:

❑ `label` — The displayed label on the left side

❑ `name` — The name for the control

❑ `rows` — The height of the `textarea` based on the number of lines

The `fb:editor-textarea` entity renders a standard input box within a form. It is also possible to define the content of the `textarea` element by setting the text of the FBML entity.

```
<fb:editor action="submit.php" width="100">
  <fb:editor-textarea label="message" name="mymessage">
    I couldn't believe what John did!
  </fb:editor-textarea>
</fb:editor>
```

fb:editor-time

Following are optional attributes:

❑   `name` — The name of the form element. If this attribute is not defined, the name of the form entity is `time`.

❑   `label` — The label displayed for the entity. If this attribute is not defined, no label is displayed.

❑   `value` — The time (in UNIX epoch) to select.

The `fb:editor-time` entity creates a form element that allows users to choose a time (hour, minute, and AM or PM) by creating three select form elements. It is possible to preset the time using the `value` attribute.

```
<fb:editor action="submit.php" width="100">
  <fb:editor-time name="aniversaire" value="1189135953" />
</fb:editor>
```

This response from this entity contains three values (named `hour`, `min`, and `ampm`), with the `name` attribute specified earlier prepended to the variable name. For example, setting the `name` attribute to `aniversaire` will result in `aniversaire_hour`, `aniversaire_min`, and `aniversaire_ampm`.

> **Developers should also be aware that the time value specified is rounded to the nearest 15-minute interval.**

fb:editor-month

Following are optional attributes:

❑   `name` — The name of the form element. The default is `month`.

❑   `value` — This attribute allows you set the value of the form entity. The value is the number of a month.

The `fb:editor-month` entity creates a form element that allows users to choose a month of the Gregorian calendar year by creating a select form element. It is possible to pre-set the month using the `value` attribute.

```
<fb:editor action="submit.php" width="100">
  <fb:editor-month name="themonth" value="10" />
</fb:editor>
```

fb:editor-date

Following is a required attribute:

❑   `label` — The label displayed to the left of the controls

Following is an optional attribute:

❑   `value` — The UNIX time stamp of the date to be displayed

The `fb:editor-date` entity creates two dropdown menus to allow users to select a date (month and day). Only one of these FBML entities can be used per Canvas page. Upon Form submission, the two POST form variables sent are `date_month` and `date_day`.

When using this entity, it is advised to validate the data. This entity does not do any correcting to verify that users are selecting valid dates. It is possible for a user to choose February 31 when submitting the form. To have multiple date selectors, you should create one or more `fb:editor-custom` entities and create the HTML manually.

```
<fb:editor action="submit.php" width="100">
  <fb:editor-date label="aniversaire" />
</fb:editor>
```

fb:editor-divider

This entity creates a horizontal divider.

```
<fb:editor action="submit.php" width="100">
  <fb:editor-text name="name" label="Name" />
  <fb:editor-divider />
  <fb:editor-text name="City" label="City" />
</fb:editor>
```

fb:editor-buttonset

The `fb:editor-buttonset` entity wraps one or more `fb:editor-button` FBML entities.

```
<fb:editor action="submit.php" width="100">
  <fb:editor-date label="aniversaire" />
  <fb:editor-buttonset>
    <fb:editor-button value="Submit" />
  </fb:editor-buttonset>
</fb:editor>
```

fb:editor-button

Following is a required attribute:

❑   value — The label displayed on the button

Following is an optional attribute:

❑   name — The key for the value sent in the POST

The fb:editor-button entity renders a large blue button used to submit the form.

```
<fb:editor-buttonset>
  <fb:editor-button value="Add" name="add"/>
  <fb:editor-button value="Recommend" name="recommend"/>
 </fb:editor-buttonset>
</fb:editor>
```

fb:submit

Following is an optional attribute:

❑   form_id — The ID of a form this button applies to

This entity is not specific to the fb:editor and its related entities. It can be used as a generic mechanism of Form submission.

The fb:submit FBML entity creates a JavaScript Form submission mechanism. The content wrapped by this entity triggers a submit onclick event that submits either the parent form or the form specified by the associated form_id attribute.

```
<fb:submit><img src="http://example.com/image.jpg" title="submit" /></fb:submit>
```

fb:editor-cancel

Following are optional attributes:

❑   value — The caption for the link. The default is Cancel.

❑   href — The URL the user is taken to. If this attribute is not declared, the default value is #.

The fb:editor-cancel entity renders a cancel link within an fb:editor-butonset entity.

```
<fb:editor-buttonset>
  <fb:editor-cancel value="Cancel This" href="http://www.yahoo.com/" />
</fb:editor-buttonset>
```

System

This section examines FBML system entities, including `fb:fbml`, `fb:fbmlversion`, `fb:redirect`, `fb:attachment-preview`, `fb:user-agent`, and `fb:mobile`.

fb:fbml

Following is an optional attribute:

❑   `version` — The FBML version to render the enclosed FBML as

The `fb:fbml` FBML entity takes the enclosed FBML and renders it through a specific version of the FBML rendering engine. The default version used maps to the current production-ready version of the FBML rendering engine.

```
<fb:fbml version="1.0">
  <fb:name uid="12345" />
</fb:fbml>
```

Specifying an invalid FBML version or using an FBML that is not supported in a particular version will result in a rendering error.

```
<fb:fbml version="11.13.33">
  You won't see this, version <fb:fbmlversion /> doesn't exist... yet.
</fb:fbml>
```

fb:fbmlversion

This entity draws the version of the currently scoped FBML rendering engine.

```
<fb:fbmlversion /> wants to destroy my sweater.
```

fb:redirect

Following is a required attribute:

❑   `url` — The URL to direct to

The `fb:redirect` FBML entity is used to redirect the user's browser to a different URL within the application Canvas.

```
<fb:redirect url="http://apps.facebook.com/example/?invalid_id=1" />
```

fb:attachment-preview

The `fb:attachment-preview` FBML entity is used to render an attachment preview used when creating an application attachment.

```
<fb:attachment-preview>Click here to preview attachment</fb:attachment-preview>
```

fb:user-agent

At least one of the following attributes must be given:

❑   `includes` — A comma-separated list of browsers to display the enclosed content to

❑   `excludes` — A comma-separated list of browsers to hide the enclosed content from

The `fb:user-agent` FBML entity renders the content enclosed in this entity to requests that match the exclusion and inclusion rules that apply to the request user agent. When both attributes are given, the order is inclusion first and then exclusion. An example would be to display a block of content to views using the Firefox versions other than Firefox 2.0.1.

```
<fb:user-agent includes="firefox">
  Spread the word!
</fb:user-agent>
<fb:user-agent excludes="safari">
  Not bad
</fb:user-agent>
<fb:user-agent includes="ie">
  You seem to have been assimilated.
</fb:user-agent>
```

fb:mobile

Content enclosed in the `fb:mobile` FBML entity is displayed on mobile application Canvas pages.

```
<fb:mobile>Hey ho, lets go!</fb:mobile>
```

Miscellaneous

This section examines miscellaneous FBML entities, including `fb:share-button`, `fb:time`, `fb:title`, `fb:friend-selector`, and `fb:ref`.

fb:share-button

Following is a required attribute:

❑   `class` — The type of object being shared

The `fb:share-button` FBML entity renders the "share | +" button used throughout Facebook. In its most simple form, it is used to share simple URLs, but can also be configured to share more complex objects such as images or videos.

When the `class` attribute is set to `url`, the required options include the following:

❑   `href` — The URL to share

```
<fb:share-button class="url" href="http://apps.facebook.com/example" />
```

When the `class` attribute is set to `meta`, the following rules apply:

❑ There are no further direct attributes required, but several child FBML entities can be specified. These include the `meta` and `link` entities.

❑ The `meta` entities are composed of `name` and `content` attributes that describe the object being shared. The valid `name` values include the following:

  ❑ `title` — The title of the object

  ❑ `description` — A short description of the object

  ❑ `medium` — An attribute used to define the type of object being described. Valid values include `audio`, `image`, `video`, `news`, `blog`, and `mult`.

  ❑ `audio_type` — The content type of the audio file described

  ❑ `audio_title` — The name of the audio piece described

  ❑ `audio_artist` — The name of the artist

  ❑ `audio_album` — The name of the album

  ❑ `video_height` — The height of the video

  ❑ `video_width` — The width of the video

  ❑ `video_type` — The content type of the video

❑ The `link` entities are composed of `rel` and `href` attributes that link to the actual object being shared.

  ❑ `image_src` — The source file of the image. When used with the `audio_src` attribute, this is the album cover of the track. When used with the `video_src` attribute, this is the preview of the video.

  ❑ `audio_src` — The source file of the audio track

  ❑ `video_src` — The source file of the video

  ❑ `target_url` — The location that the media lives at

```
<fb:share-button class="meta">
  <meta name="medium" content="audio"/>
  <meta name="title" content="The legendary Hero"/>
  <meta name="audio_type" content="application/mp3"/>
  <meta name="description" content="Zro strikes again."/>
  <link rel="image_src" href="http://www.zreomusic.com/covers/Flash_Card_WW.jpg"/>
  <link rel="audio_src" href="http://www.zreomusic.com/music/8-ww/03-
TheLegendaryHeroRedux.mp3"/>
  <link rel="target_url" href="http://www.zreomusic.com/listen"/>
</fb:share-button>
```

fb:time

Following is the required parameter:

❑ `t` — The time to display in Epoch seconds

Following are optional parameters:

❑ `tz` — The time zone in which to display `t`. Acceptable formats include the available PHP supported time zones, as well as the `-/+` formats. The default is the logged-in user's time zone.

❑ `preposition` — This Boolean value directs the FBML rendering engine to include prepositions as appropriate. This includes "on" and "at." The default value is `false`.

The `fb:time` FBML entity draws a human-friendly time stamp, including the hour and minutes, and possibly the year, month, and day. The year, month, and day values expand as needed. The time is on the current day; then the year, month, and day are hidden, with only the hour and minutes displayed.

```
<fb:time t="1196313823" />
<fb:time t="1196313823" tz="America/Los_Angeles"/>
```

fb:title

The `fb:title` FBML entity sets its container's title to the contents of the entity. When used on the application Canvas page, the window title is set. This entity can also be used to set the title when rendering a Wall using the `fb:comments` FBML entity.

```
<fb:title>Settings</fb:title>
```

The end result is `"Facebook | " + - the application's name +" |"` + title.

fb:friend-selector

Following are optional attributes:

❑ `uid` — The numeric Facebook user ID whose friends are selectable. This attribute defaults to the currently logged-in user.

❑ `name` — The key of the value in the POST variables. This defaults to `friend_selector_name`.

❑ `idname` — The ID of the form element. This defaults to `friend_selector_id`.

❑ `include_me` — A Boolean flag indicating that the user using the form should be included. The default value for this option is `false`.

❑ `exclude_ids` — A comma-separated list of user IDs to not include in the selector.

The `fb:friend-selector` entity creates a predictive friend selector for a user. This entity is very useful when the application allows users to interact with each other. This FBML entity is also discussed in the "Editor and Forms" section above.

> If the user enters a name that is not recognized in that user's social graph, the `uid` is represented as `undefined`.

fb:ref

One of the following two attributes is required:

❑   `url` — A URL that is called and the content thereof included

❑   `handle` — The key associated with a piece of data stored by the Facebook Platform

The `fb:ref` FBML entity is used to dynamically include data within a block of FBML. This can be done in one of two ways. The first uses the `facebook.fbml.setRefHandle` API method to explicitly set a value for a given key that is stored by the Facebook Platform. The second sets a URL that the Facebook Platform fetches and caches locally, and is included when appropriate.

```
<fb:ref handle="profileHeader" />
<fb:ref url="http://example.com/fbapp/unframed/profile?user=1234" />
```

When caching or storing content using the `fb:ref` FBML entity, there are a couple of rules and caveats that apply:

❑   When caching the contents of a URL, that content is stored indefinitely. Developers and application owners are strongly encouraged not to rely on this and maintain the original content.

❑   This FBML entity and practice was made to distribute the same content for many users or uses. You should consider using a variation of this FBML entity when performing operations that include the same content for many users.

> Currently it is possible to nest `fb:ref` FBML entities. *Do not do this.*

Dynamic FBML Attributes

This section discusses dynamic FBML attributes, including those dealing with visibility, mock-Ajax, and forms.

Visibility

Although JavaScript is not allowed in its direct form, there are several things allowed that simulate some of the common use cases. This includes several attributes available on entities to manipulate the visibility of other entities.

❑   `clicktoshow` — This attribute is used to show another entity.

❑   `clicktohide` — This attribute is used to hide another entity.

❑   `clicktotoggle` — This attribute maintains a visibility state for one or more entities and toggles that state when clicked.

❑ clickthrough — This attribute is used to send the click action down to the enclosed elements. This is used when the clicktohide, clicktoshow, or clicktotoggle attributes are used on form elements.

❑ requirelogin — This attribute can be applied to anchor tags to set a requirement that the user clicking the entity must be logged in as a valid Facebook user.

When using these attributes, the values are the entities to manipulate.

```
<a href="#" id="showlabel" clicktohide="showlabel"
clicktoshow="entryamore,hidelabel">Show More</a>
<a href="#" id="hidelabel" clicktohide="entryamore,hidelabel"
clicktoshow="showlabel" style="display:none">Show Less</a>
<div id="entryamore" style="display:none">
More data ...
</div>
```

In this example, there are three HTML entities listed. An a entity is used to display some sample text. Another a entity used to hide the sample text. A div contains the sample text. Each of these contains a unique ID. The two a entities have the clicktoshow and clicktohide attributes that show or hide the other in association with the sample text.

```
<input type="checkbox" clicktotoggle="moreoptions" clickthrough="true"
name="moreoptions" />
<div id="moreoptions" style="display:none;">
<p>More complex options ...</p>
</div>
```

In this example, you can see the clickthrough and clicktotoggle attributes in action. The use case may be simple, but it provides a lot of functionality. Consider the FBML to be enclosed in a form that provides several options. To allow your application users to access some of the advanced functionality, you enclose them in a div that is initially hidden, and use a checkbox to toggle the visibility of those options.

```
<a href="http://apps.facebook.com/myapp/settings" requirelogin="1">Settings</a>
```

With this example, the requirelogin attribute can help greatly with making applications available to users who have and have not added the application, but keeping some sections available only to users who have.

Mock-Ajax

As with the attributes used to manipulate the visibility of objects, there are several attributes that allow Facebook application developers to simulate some of the very basic functionality provided by more traditional Ajax libraries.

❑ clickrewriteid — The ID of the entity replaced by the returned data

❑ clickrewriteurl — The URL from which the data will be fetched

❑ clickrewriteform — The ID of the form we want to submit when the entity is clicked

Consider the following example. In it, you have a form with a simple HTML entity that contains the `clickrewriteurl`, `clickrewriteid`, `clickrewriteform`, and `clicktoshow` mock-Ajax attributes. When the a entity is clicked, you submit the `pokeform` to the URL designated by the `clickrewriteurl` attribute and specify the `pokeresponsediv` entity to receive the contents. You also use the `clicktoshow` attribute to display response from the action.

```
<form id="pokeform">
<a href="#" clickrewriteurl="http://example.com/fbapp/unframed/poke/?user=12345"
clickrewriteid="pokeresponse" clickrewriteform="pokeform"
clicktoshow="pokeresponse">Poke <fb:name uid="12345" /></a>
</form>
<div id="pokeresponse" style="display:none;"></div>
```

Forms

There are also several mock-Ajax FBML entity attributes that can be used to manipulate form elements. These include the following:

❑   `clicktoenable` — This attribute will set the target entity as enabled when clicked.

❑   `clicktodisable` — This attribute will set the target entity as disabled when clicked.

Both of these attributes allow developers to specify multiple entity IDs by separating them with a comma in the attribute value. The special thing to note is that disabled form entities do not submit values. This can be especially useful when using forms that have entity dependencies. The most basic example involves using this attribute in conjunction with the `clickthrough` and `clicktohide` attributes to hide a Form Submit button once it is clicked.

```
<form>
  <input type="text" id="firstname" name="firstname" />
  <input id="sendbutton" type="submit" value="Submit"
    clicktodisable="firstname" clicktohide="sendbutton" clickthrough="true" />
</form>
```

Images

Facebook is definitely a multimedia-friendly platform. There are dozens of applications that take advantage of this and allow users to use and manipulate audio files, video files, and image files.

Although the `img` tag isn't technically an FBML entity, it gets special treatment in the FBML render engine. When processing an `img` tag, the `src` attribute is processed and cached, hosting the content and target of the image on the Facebook servers. If the content is not available, the image served is a blank image. Facebook has provided the `facebook.fbml.refreshImgSrc('imgURL')` API method to allow developers to refresh the image URLs that have been cached.

Forms

Forms get very special treatment by the Facebook Platform. Without exception, all form entities are expanded to include several hidden input entities that include information about the user and application.

```
<form>
    <input type="hidden" name="fb_sig_profile" value="12345"/>
    <input type="hidden" name="fb_sig_user" value="12345"/>
    <input type="hidden" name="fb_sig_session_key" value="abcd-1234"/>
    <input type="hidden" name="fb_sig_time" value="1176705186"/>
    <input type="hidden" name="fb_sig" value="hashof values"/>
</form>
```

As listed above, there are also several FBML entities available to create consistent, user-friendly forms. They include the standard input elements usually available, but also go so far as to include date/time input entities and a way to include structured custom content.

```
<fb:editor>
  <fb:editor-custom label="Selection">
    <select>
      <option value="1">San Francisco, CA</option>
      <option value="1">Los Angeles, CA</option>
      <option value="1">New York, NY</option>
    </select>
  </fb:editor-custom>
</fb:editor>
```

CSS and the DOM

The FBML rendering engine processes all input fed to it. This includes the FBML entities that you include in your applications, as well as the HTML entities. When identifying specific entities, those IDs are rewritten throughout the response. There are several reasons for doing this, the main being to prevent styling and entity-specific actions from colliding with those of Facebook Application Canvas frame and other applications.

Summary

By now, you should have a better understanding of FBML and how it can be used in almost every aspect of your Facebook applications. This chapter stepped you through all of the entities available to developers, and surfaced some of the more complex options available to them.

Chapter 4 moves through some of the advanced FBML topics that this chapter hints at. It will include using the Facebook JavaScript parser (FBJS) and rendering engine to enhance your applications with rich client-side scripting.

Advanced FBML

As described in Chapter 3 and demonstrated in Chapter 2, FBML is a powerful markup language. Within it, however, are advanced features that extend and push FBML beyond a simple markup language and widget system.

Many of these features exist within Facebook JavaScript (FBJS), a subsystem of FBML that parses and renders JavaScript. FBJS also provides a series of functions and objects that extend the commonly available JavaScript functions and objects.

This chapter describes FBJS and its merits. Without FBJS, it is very difficult to create some of the more advanced client-side effects and features that are common in everyday web applications. Within this chapter are some example projects that demonstrate how FBJS is used and what can be done with it.

FBML and FBJS

When the Facebook Platform first launched, it offered very little in terms of dynamic client-side scripting. There are several mock-Ajax features that give developers some room to work with, but they don't compare to the flexibility and features provided in modern-day Ajax and widget libraries.

To accommodate the demands of the community and application developers, Facebook launched FBJS. FBJS is composed of the JavaScript processing and rendering component, as well as various helper functions, object methods, best practices, and FBML entities.

The Basics

The syntax and structure of traditional JavaScript and FBJS are identical. Most developers will have very little to learn and adapt to in order to develop FBJS in their own Facebook applications. However, there are certain rules that apply when manipulating the document object model (DOM), handling events, and so on.

Consider the following FBML example:

```
<p>Hi <span id="myname"><fb:name uid="loggedinuser" useyou="false" /></span>.</p>
```

Now, consider the following first JavaScript example:

```
<script>
<!--
function underline_object(obj) {
  obj.style.borderBottom = 'red';
}

underline_object(document.getElementById('myname'));
//-->
</script>
```

Now, look at the following second JavaScript example:

```
<script>
<!--
function underline_object(obj) {
  obj.setStyle('borderBottom', 'red');
}

underline_object(document.getElementById('myname'));
//-->
</script>
```

There is little difference between the two JavaScript code blocks. Both examples create a function that sets the style of a given object and then call that function, passing the response from `document.getElementById`. Notice in the second JavaScript example that you can't set the object style directly. Instead, you use the `setStyle(...)` method provided in FBJS.

When integrating FBJS into your code, just do as you would with the traditional `script` HTML entity, as shown here:

```
<div id="contentroot" style="margin: 5px;">
  <p>Hello <span id="myname">
      <fb:name uid="loggedinuser" firstnameonly="true" useyou="false" />
    </span>.
  </p>
</div>
<script>
<!--
function underline_object(obj) {
  obj.setStyle('border-bottom', '1px dashed red');
}
underline_object(document.getElementById('myname'));
//-->
</script>
```

Element Creation

Because FBML entities are parsed before the content is rendered and displayed to the user on the FBML Canvas, it isn't possible to create FBML entities with the traditional JavaScript methods. To do this, you must use the `document.createElement(...)` method provided by FBJS, as shown here:

```
<div id="bodycontent" style="margin: 5px;">
</div>
<script>
<!--
function show_swfobj(parent) {
    var newSwf = document.createElement('fb:swf');
    parent.appendChild(newSwf);
}
show_swfobj(document.getElementById('bodycontent'));
//-->
</script>
```

Currently, this is limited to create `fb:swf` FBML entities.

Setting Element Content

It is also not possible to set element content in the traditional fashion because of security concerns. To do so, the `setTextValue` and `setInnerFBML` methods are available. The `setInnerFBML` method uses the `fb:js-string` FBML entity to create a variable of block data that can be referenced throughout your FBJS.

❑   `object.setTextValue(string)` — This method accepts a single parameter, the string that the element's text is to be set to.

❑   `object.setInnerFBML(token)` — This method accepts a single token representing the `fb:js-string` FBML entity block that the object's data will be set to.

Consider the following example:

```
<div id="contentroot" style="margin: 5px;">
  <p><span id="greeting"></span> <span id="myname"></span>.</p>
</div>
<fb:js-string var="loggedinname">
  <fb:name uid="loggedinuser" useyou="false" />
</fb:js-string>
<script>
<!--
function update_content() {
  document.getElementById('greeting').setTextValue('Hello');
  document.getElementById('myname').setInnerFBML(loggedinname);
}
update_content();
//-->
</script>
```

In this example, several things take place that change the content of the greeting and myname span elements. Immediately above the script block, you create an fb:js-string FBML entity, setting the variable loggedinname to the value of the fb:name FBML entity for the currently logged-in user.

In FBJS, you must create the update_content function that references both span elements and sets the content appropriately. The first calls the setTextValue method to set the content of the greeting element to the plaintext value "greetings." The second calls the setInnerFBML method with the loggedinname variable as set by the fb:js-string FBML entity.

> *Note that using the setInnerFBML method without a fb:js-string FBML entity will fail silently. The FBML rendering engine does not validate your FBJS or check for the existence of used variables.*

JavaScript and CSS Includes

The Facebook Platform allows developers to have Include files containing relevant Cascading Style Sheet (CSS) and JavaScript in application Canvas pages. These Includes are treated like traditional Includes and are capable of being cached locally by your browser.

When referencing included JavaScript, the src attribute is applied to a script HTML entity as usual. The FBML rendering treats this external resource much like it treats images. It caches the resource locally, and the URL displayed on the application Canvas page is the local Facebook URL.

```
<script src="http://example.com/js/include.js"></script>
```

Following are some rules and caveats that developers should be aware of when using this feature:

- ❑ There is a hard limit of 1,000 Include file references.
- ❑ Facebook will remove cached Include files as it sees fit.
- ❑ The cache policy on included files is such that they are set to never expire. Developers should take the necessary steps to ensure that when releasing new versions of included files, the intended files are referenced. This can easily be done by including a version query string parameter in the FBML referencing the included files, as shown here:

```
<script src="http://example.com/js/include.js?build=123332"></script>
```

- ❑ Facebook recommends limiting the total number of include references per page to 10 or less.

FBML Blocks with fb:js-string

As mentioned above, the fb:js-string FBML entity can be used to render FBML content within a JavaScript variable for later use in your FBJS. This has numerous benefits, and, in some ways, is vital to developing some of the more advanced features found in existing Facebook applications.

Following is the required parameter:

- ❑ var — The name of the JavaScript variable that the content of the FBML entity is set to.

In its most simple form, simple FBML is rendered into a string for later use.

```
<fb:js-string var="myname">
<fb:name uid="loggedinuser" useyou="false" />
</fb:js-string>
<script>
obj.setInnerFBML(myname);
</script>
```

It is also possible to populate array elements with this FBML entity. When setting the name, each key must begin with a letter. This means that `people` and `people.uid123` are valid key names, although `people.123` is invalid.

```
<fb:js-string var="people.uid123" ><fb:name uid="123" /><fb:js-string>
<fb:js-string var="people.uid234" ><fb:name uid="234" /><fb:js-string>
<fb:js-string var="people.uid345" ><fb:name uid="345" /><fb:js-string>
<script>
obj1.setInnerFBML(people['uid1239']);
obj2.setInnerFBML(people['uid2349']);
obj3.setInnerFBML(people['uid3459']);
</script>
```

Element and ID Renaming

The FBML rendering engine has special rules for processing variable and function names within a given block of FBML. In most cases, developers don't have to worry about the processed variable and function names. But, in some cases, it may be useful to understand what happens under the hood.

As the FBML rendering engine encounters a variable or function, it prepends the string "a", the application ID, and an underscore ("_"). This moves the majority of your application's code into a sandbox, preventing it from interfering with the FBJS of any other applications, as shown here:

```
<script>
  var myname = "Nick Gerakines";
  function describe_username(name) {
    return name + " is awesome";
  }
  describe_username(myname);
</script>
```

Given this example, if your application ID is 44556677, the preceding code is processed and rendered as follows:

```
<script>
  var a44556677_myname = "Nick Gerakines";
  function a44556677_describe_username(name) {
    return a44556677_name + " is awesome";
  }
 a44556677_describe_username(a44556677_myname);
</script>
```

These rules also affect how element IDs are rendered, as well as the CSS and styles that apply to those elements. When renaming HTML and CSS element IDs, they are prepended with the string "app," the Facebook application ID, and an underscore ("_"), as shown here:

```
<style>
#bodycontent {
  margin: 0px 20px 20px 20px;
}
.header {
  font-size: 150%;
  font-weight: bold;
}
li {
  color: blue;
}
</style>
<div id="bodycontent">
  <p class="header">Activities</p>
  <p>I play in the rain.</p>
  <p class="header">Favorite Authors</p>
  <ul>
    <li>Neil Stevenson</li>
    <li>William Gibson</li>
    <li>Leslie M. Orchard</li>
    <li>Mercedes Lackey</li>
  </ul>
</div>
```

The markup in this example is transformed into the following:

```
<style type="text/css">
.app_content_44556677 #app44556677_bodycontent { margin: 0px 20px 20px; }
.app_content_44556677 .header { font-size: 150%; font-weight: bold; }
.app_content_44556677 li { color: blue; }
</style>
<div id="app44556677_bodycontent" fbcontext="bdbu3ad3dsa">
  <p class="header">Activities</p>
  <p>I play in the rain.</p>
  <p class="header">Favorite Authors</p>
  <ul>
    <li>Neil Stevenson</li>
    <li>William Gibson</li>
    <li>Leslie M. Orchard</li>
    <li>Mercedes Lackey</li>
  </ul>
</div>
```

You'll also note that when the `style` HTML element is processed, all of the CSS rules are prepended with the class `.app_content _44556677`, which corresponds with the root element of the rendered FBML for the given application Canvas page. This allows Facebook to force all styles defined by the application to be processed only within the context and scope of the FBML given.

> When including medium-sized code blocks of CSS, the `fb:ref` FBML entity can come in quite handy. With it, your application can set a block of FBML that can be cached and referenced as the need arises. This can dramatically clean up your FBML and ease the development process.

FBML Canvas Rules and Caveats

Facebook imposes several rules and conditions to protect the privacy of its users, as well as to enhance the overall security of the web site.

- ❑ Public Canvas pages (such as user profiles) impose some rules about what is displayed:

    - ❑ The `fb:name` FBML entity will only display the user's first name to limit the exposure to users who would not normally see that user.

    - ❑ The `fb:profile-pic` FBML entity is allowed, but only if users have set themselves as publicly searchable. If the users have limited the visibility of their profile pictures, a blank image with a question mark is displayed for consistency.

- ❑ When using the `fb:swf`, `fb:flv`, `fb:mp3`, or `fb:silverlight` FBML entities, they must be "activated" in order to start or work. This is done by clicking on the entity in question.

- ❑ When using JavaScript, FBJS events, or FBML events (such as the visibility attributes) on a User Profile page, the actions defined will not start on their own. They must be activated in a similar fashion as media objects. This includes all mouseover and click events.

FBJS DOM Objects

The majority of the differences between FBJS and traditional JavaScript come from the way that the document object model (DOM) is read and manipulated. Within FBJS, there are a number of methods designed to over-ride and extend the functionality provided in traditional JavaScript. Many of these changes are because of the way element identifiers are renamed and handled; others are because of security concerns.

The primary way to directly read and find an object is through the `document.getElementByID` method. Creating new elements is done through the `document.createElement` method. At any point, developers can use `this` to reference the current object.

When placing objects, the `appendChild`, `insertBefore`, `removeChild`, and `cloneNode` methods work as expected. Many of the methods that manipulate or read object properties have been replaced with getter and setter methods.

Table 4-1 shows the JavaScript methods and functions that have been replaced.

Table 4-1: Replaced JavaScript Methods and Functions

Method or Function	Getter	Description	Setter	Description
parentNode	getParentNode()	Returns the object's parent node	N/A	
nextSibling	getNextSibling()	Returns the object's next sibling node	N/A	
previousSibling	getPreviousSibling()	Returns the object's previous sibling node	N/A	
firstChild	getFirstChild()	Returns the first child node of the object	N/A	
lastChild	getLastChild()	Returns the last child node of the object	N/A	
childNodes	getChildNodes()	Returns a list of the child nodes of the object	N/A	
innerHTML	N/A		setInnerFBML(name)	Used with the fb:js-string FBML entity to set the content of the object to the named fb:js-string FBML entity's content
innerText and textContent	N/A		setTextValue(text)	Sets the text node of the object to the passed text. If the object has any children, they will be removed. Only plaintext may be passed (no HTML or FBML).
action	getAction()	Returns the value of the action attribute on the object	setAction(name)	Sets the action attribute of the object
value	getValue()	Returns the value of the value attribute on the object	setValue(var)	Sets the value attribute on the object
href	getHref	Returns the value of the href attribute on the object	setHref(var)	Sets the value of the href attribute
target	getTarget()	Returns the value of the target attribute on the object	setTarget(var)	Sets the value of the target attribute
src	getSrc()	Returns the value of the src attribute on the object	setSrc(var)	Sets the value of the src attribute

Method or Function	Getter	Description	Setter	Description
className	getClassName()	Returns the value of the class attribute	setClassName(var)	Sets the value of the class attribute
tagName	getTagName()	Returns the tag name of the object	N/A	
id	getId()	Returns the ID of the object	setId(var)	Sets the ID of the object
dir	getDir()	Returns the reading direction of the document/object	setDir(var)	Sets the reading direction of the document/object
checked	getChecked()	Returns the current state of the checkbox	setChecked()	Sets the checked state of the checkbox
clientWidth	getClientWidth()		N/A	
clientHeight	getClientHeight()		N/A	
offsetWidth	getOffsetWidth()		N/A	
offsetHeight	getOffsetHeight()		N/A	
scrollTop	getScrollTop()		setScrollTop()	
scrollLeft	getScrollLeft()		setScrollLeft()	
scrollHeight	getScrollHeight()		N/A	
scrollWidth	getScrollWidth()		N/A	
tabIndex	getTabIndex()	Returns the tab order of an object	setTabIndex(var)	Sets the tab order of an object
title	getTitle()	Returns the value of the title attribute	setTitle(var)	Sets the value of the title attribute
name	getName()	Returns the value of the name attribute	setName(var)	Sets the value of the name attribute
cols	getCols()	Returns the number of columns of an object	setCols(var)	Sets the number of columns of an object
rows	getRows()	Returns the number of rows an object has	setRows(var)	Sets the number of rows an object has
accessKey	getAccessKey()	Returns the access key of an object	setAccessKey(var)	Sets the access key of an object
disabled	getDisabled()	Returns the disabled state of an object	setDisabled(var)	Sets the disabled state of an object
readOnly	getReadOnly()	Returns whether an object is read-only or not	setReadOnly(var)	Sets an object's read-only state

Table continued on following page

Method or Function	Getter	Description	Setter	Description
type	getType()	Returns the value of an object's type attribute	setType(var)	Sets the value of an object's type attribute
selectedIndex	getSelectedIndex()	Returns the index of the selected child of an object	setSelected-Index(var)	Sets the selected child of an object
selected	getSelected()	Returns whether or not an object is selected	setSelected(var)	Sets an object as selected or not
location	N/A		setLocation()	Sets the location of the browser. Used for client-side browser redirection.

In addition to the methods shown in Table 4-1, the following new methods have been introduced:

- ❏ getAbsoluteTop() — Returns the element's absolute position relative to the top of the page. This is provided because of the lack of the offsetParent property.

- ❏ getAbsoluteLeft() — Returns the element's absolute position relative to the left of the page

- ❏ getRootElement() — Returns the root element of the Canvas area

```
document.getRootElement().getFirstChild().setStyle('margin', '10px');
```

- ❏ removeClassName() — Clears the class value of an object

- ❏ toggleClassName(var) — Clears the class value of an object if it exists; otherwise, sets the class

- ❏ hasClassName(var) — Returns whether or not the object has the given class

CSS and Styling

The style attribute was intentionally removed, and instead the setStyle method has been provided. The setStyle method accepts two parameters. The first is the name of the style to apply to the object, and the second is the value to apply to the key.

```
myobj.setStyle('color', 'red');
```

Multiple attributes can also be set using a JavaScript Object Notation (JSON) encoded string.

```
myobj.setStyle({ color: 'red', background: '#0064009 });
```

> When setting any sort of numeric value indicating a size or measurement, you must
> include the character suffix indicating the type.

```
myobj.setStyle('margin', '20'); // bad
myobj.setStyle('margin', '20px'); // good
```

Event Handling

FBJS events operate much like traditional JavaScript events. Events are set using the
`object.addEventListener(...)` method. The exception is that the third parameter indicating
that the user wants to initiate the capture is not supported.

```
<div id="contentroot">
  <p><a id="drinkmeobj" href="#">Drink Me</a></p>
  <p><a id="eatmeobj" href="#">Eat Me</a></p>
  <p id="alice">What a curious feeling!</p>
</div>
<script type="text/javascript">
function shrinkText() {
  document.getElementById("alice").setStyle('fontSize', '50%');
}
function growText() {
  document.getElementById("alice").setStyle('fontSize', '200%');
}
function load() {
  document.getElementById("drinkmeobj").addEventListener("click", shrinkText);
  document.getElementById("eatmeobj").addEventListener("click", growText);
}
load();
</script>
```

This example handles the `click` event on two different objects using the `addEventListener` method as
defined in the `load()` function. The `drinkmeobj` and `eatmeobj` are bound to the `shrinkText()` and
`growText()` and manipulate the alive object appropriately.

In addition to the standard methods and functions provided, two additional FBJS methods are provided:

❑ `object.listEventListeners(eventname)` — This method returns a JavaScript array of all
of the event listeners associated with the named event for the given object. Events that have
been added through FBML using the `on*` attributes are also included in the returned list.

❑ `object.purgeEventListeners(eventname)` — This method removes all event listeners on
the object for the given event name. This will also remove all of the event listeners assigned
through FBML.

When an event listener fires, the event handler is called with an object containing information about the event. When event handlers are added as attributes, the passed object is accessible through the `event()` method. The event makes available the following properties:

❏   `target` — The object that is the target of the event

❏   `type` — The named type of event that fired

❏   `pageX` — The horizontal position of the event

❏   `pageY` — The vertical position of the event

❏   `ctrlKey` — The control key used to fire the event (if any)

❏   `keyCode` — The key pressed used to fire the event (if any)

❏   `metaKey` — The meta key pressed used to fire the event (if any)

❏   `shiftKey` — The shift key pressed to fire the event (if any)

The following methods are also available:

❏   `stopPropagation` — This method prevents the event from propagating to any other elements that may exist further up in the DOM tree.

❏   `preventDefault` — This method removes the default behavior of the event without stopping the propagation of other events.

Ajax

One of the most useful objects provided through FBJS is the `Ajax` object. Through it, developers can implement and create true Ajax interfaces to enhance their applications and improve the already present features.

Developers should be aware that all `Ajax` requests are actually made through a proxy where a post-processing filter scrubs the response data. This includes JSON-encoded data and also allows the use of FBML replacement in Ajax response data.

Creating a new `Ajax` object is simple:

```
var ajaxobj = new Ajax
```

The `Ajax` object supports several properties used to interact, manipulate, and submit the request:

❏   `requireLogin` — This property sets a Boolean flag used to indicate that the `Ajax` call can only be made by a user who has logged into the application. If this condition is met, the `Ajax` call is made with the standard `fb_sig_*` parameters containing the user's information. If the condition is not met and the user does not log in, the `Ajax` call will fail.

❏   `responseType` — This property sets the response type of the `Ajax` object.

❏   `Ajax.RAW` — This response type indicates that the response is made in its original form. No processing or parsing has been made.

❏ `Ajax.JSON` — This response type indicates that the response has been parsed as a valid JSON object and has been processed accordingly. The returned response to the callback function will be in the form of an object. The properties of the JSON object that are prefixed with `fbml_` are parsed as individual FBML strings and returned as FBML blocks. These blocks can be used on a DOM object with the `setInnerFBML` method. Each variable and its value in the response is limited to a combined length of 5,000 characters.

❏ `Ajax.FBML` — This response type indicates that the response has been parsed as an FBML block, and the data returned to the callback function are a reference to that FBML block. This response type can be used with the `document.setInnerFBML` FBJS function.

The `post` and `abort` methods are used to submit or abort the `Ajax` request.

❏ `post(url, query)` — This method submits the `Ajax` request. The `url` parameter must be an absolute URL pointing to a remote address. The `query` parameter must be a string or an object that can be converted to a string.

❏ `abort()` — This method aborts the `Ajax` request.

The `Ajax` object can also respond to several internal events.

❏ `ondone(data)` — This event fires when the `Ajax` request object returns a response. The type of variable sent to the function handling the event directly corresponds to the response type indicated by the `responseType()` `Ajax` object method.

❏ `onerror` — This event fires when an error occurs within the `Ajax` object.

To demonstrate the functionality of the `Ajax` object and its functionality, let's create a simple example application. The ajaxidigg example application is available for download on this book's web site.

Creating this application through the Developers application is very much like the setup of the "Hello World" example project in Chapter 2.

❏ Using the Facebook Developers Application, create a new application with a unique name and URL. For this project, use your initials and *ajaxidigg*. When developing this application for this book, *ngajaxidigg* was used as the name and URL.

❏ Upload the included project files to a publicly accessible web space, and point the callback URL in the configuration options to the htdocs/index.php file.

This project consists of two files and the Facebook PHP Client Library. The first file is the `AppConfig` class found at `lib/AppConfig.class.php`. This class contains the Facebook application URL, the API key, and the secret key for the application.

```
class AppConfig {
  public static $app_name = 'Ajax-i-Digg';
  public static $app_url = 'http://apps.facebook.com/ngajaxidigg/';
  public static $app_callback = 'http://fbapps.socklabs.com/ngajaxidigg/';
  public static $app_id = '75818452919;
  public static $api_key = '09972efed5f03eefefbada8cfd2527af';
  public static $secret  = '5f75adc9751e712751156f6dc38cd71d';
}
```

The `AppConfig` class is not used directly. Therefore, it is excluded from public access, putting it outside of the htdocs directory.

The htdocs/index.php file is the main Canvas page for this application. This is the page requested by the callback URL and returns the content to render on the Canvas for the user. This is the only publicly accessible page for the application's users.

This example application doesn't have some of the stricter application requirements as previous applications. Because of this, you can exclude the Facebook PHP Client Library altogether.

The first block of PHP code includes the `AppConfig` class and also sets the URL that the `Ajax` object will be calling.

```php
<?php
  include_once 'lib/AppConfig.class.php';
  $ajax_url = AppConfig::$app_callback . 'update.php';
?>
```

The FBML that builds the page is broken into two parts. The first part is the simple markup that outlines and encloses the content that you will display through the `Ajax` calls. The second is a `script` HTML entity that contains the majority of the FBJS code.

```
<fb:dashboard></fb:dashboard>
<div id="bodyroot" style="margin: 0 20px 20px 20px">
  <div id="ajaxstatus"></div>
  <div id="ajaxcontent"></div>
</div>
<fb:js-string var="pleasewait">
<fb:success>
  <fb:message>Please wait while the feed updates.</fb:message>
</fb:success>
</fb:js-string>
<fb:js-string var="errorgeneral">
<fb:error>
  <fb:message>There was an error updating the feed.</fb:message>
</fb:error>
</fb:js-string>
<script>
  var statuselem = document.getElementById('ajaxstatus');
  var contentelem = document.getElementById('ajaxcontent');

  function loadDiggContent() {
    var ajax = new Ajax();
    ajax.responseType = Ajax.FBML;
    ajax.onerror = function() {
      contentelem.setStyle('display', 'none');
      statuselem.setInnerFBML(errorgeneral);
      statuselem.setStyle('display', '');
    }
    ajax.ondone = function(data) {
      contentelem.setInnerFBML(data);
      statuselem.setStyle('display', 'none');
      contentelem.setStyle('display', '');
    }
```

```
      ajax.requireLogin = 0;
      ajax.post('<?= $ajax_url ?>', '');
  }

  function reloadData() {
    loadDiggContent();
    setTimeout(function() { reloadData() }, 1000 * 50); // 3 minutes
  }

  statuselem.setInnerFBML(pleasewait);
  reloadData();
</script>
```

In the first portion of the FBML markup, you create the `bodyroot` element with two empty `div` elements, `ajaxstatus` and `ajaxcontent`. You also create two `fb:js-string` FBML entities that store the different status messages used by the application.

In the FBJS block, you define two functions, `loadDiggContent` and `reloadData`. You also create two variables, `statuselem` and `contentelem`, that reference the `ajaxstatus` and `ajaxcontent` elements in the markup. Immediately after the function definitions, you make a reference to the `setInnerFBML` method on the `statuselem` object, setting the content of that element to the message defined by the `fb:js-string` FBML entity keyed `pleasewait`.

The process is kicked off by calling the `reloadData()` method. That method immediately calls the `loadDiggContent()` method and then sets a timer that calls the `reloadData()` method again after three minutes.

In the `loadDiggContent()` method, you construct an `Ajax` object and submit the request. This example uses the `Ajax.FBML` request type because you know that the requested data will be able to be cleanly inserted directly into the markup without needing to create any additional elements within the FBJS.

The `onerror` and `ondone` events are captured to set status messages and toggle the visibility of the `ajaxstatus` and `ajaxcontent` elements accordingly. Note that the requirement for the viewing user to be logged in to submit the `Ajax` request is turned off.

The htdocs/update.php file is the destination of the `Ajax` request and parses the Digg data into an FBML block that can be displayed.

```php
<?php

function fetch_diggs() {
  $ch = curl_init();
  curl_setopt($ch, CURLOPT_URL, 'http://services.digg.com/stories/
?type=json&count=10&appkey=http%3A%2F%2Fwrox.com');
  curl_setopt($ch, CURLOPT_RETURNTRANSFER, 1);
  curl_setopt($ch, CURLOPT_USERAGENT, 'ExampleFacebookApp/0.1');
  $body = curl_exec($ch);
  if (curl_errno($ch)) {
    return array();
  } else {
```

(continued)

(continued)

```
      curl_close($ch);
      $data = json_decode($body);
      return $data;
   }
}

$data = fetch_diggs();

?>
<p>Displaying <?= $data->count ?> articles.</p>
<ul>
<?php foreach ($data->stories as $story) { ?>
<li><a href="<?= $story->href ?>"><?= $story->title ?></a></li>
<?php } ?>
</ul>
```

This page consists of the function `fetch_diggs()` that creates a curl request to fetch the 10 most recent Digg articles. Internally, it uses the PHP `json_decode(...)` function to parse the JSON-encoded response. Immediately after the PHP code block, you simply iterate through the JSON object to create a simple list of articles and relative links to those articles.

Dialogs

Another of the FBJS-provided objects is the `Dialog` object, which enables developers to construct the Dialog windows used throughout Facebook. Using Dialog widgets wisely can reduce site bandwidth, as well as save developers and designers a good amount of time designing and developing pages that could simply be handled through Dialog widgets and API end points.

Constructing a `Dialog` object is similar to any other object. It requires a parameter indicating the type of dialog to create.

❑   `Dialog.DIALOG_POP` — A Dialog widget style shown when removing a Wall post

❑   `Dialog.DIALOG_CONTEXTUAL` — A Dialog widget style shown when removing a Mini-Feed story

```
dialogobj = new Dialog(Dialog.DIALOG_POP);
```

The `Dialog` object provides several properties and methods that interact and manipulate the Dialog widget.

❑   `setStyle` — This method is used to set the style of the parent Dialog widget.

❑   `showMessage(title, content, button_confirm)` — This method displays a Dialog widget. The only visible component when displayed is a Confirmation button. The `title` and `content` parameters can be strings or references to FBML blocks set by the `fb:js-string` FBML entity. The `button_confirm` parameter is used to set the text of the button displayed. It is optional, defaulting to the text `Okay` if not set.

❑   `showChoice(title, content, button_confirm, button_cancel)` — This method displays a Dialog widget containing both of the Confirm and Cancel buttons. The `title` and `content` can be set as strings or as references to FBML blocks set by the `fb:js-string` FBML entity. The `button_confirm` and `button_cancel` parameters are used to set the text on the Confirm and Cancel buttons, respectively. If not set, they default to "Okay" and "Cancel."

❏ `setContext` — This method only applies to Dialog widgets created with the `Dialog.DIALOG_CONTEXTUAL` parameter. This method sets the context of the Dialog widget. The context is a reference to the element that the Dialog widget should be focused on.

❏ `hide` — This method sets the visibility of the Dialog widget as Hidden.

In addition to the properties and methods listed, the following two events can be captured:

❏ `onconfirm` — This event is fired when the Confirm button is selected.

❏ `oncancel` — This event is fired when the Cancel button is selected.

To demonstrate the functionality of the `Dialog` object, let's create a simple example application. The ngdialogs example application is available for download on this book's web site.

Creating this application through the Developers application is very much like the setup of the "Hello World" example project in Chapter 2.

❏ Using the Facebook Developers Application, create a new application with a unique name and URL. For this project, use your initials and **yapa**. When developing this application for this book, *ngpaya* was used as the name and URL.

❏ Upload the included project files to a publicly accessible web space, and point the callback URL in the configuration options to the htdocs/index.php file.

❏ This project is small enough to not warrant a need for an `AppConfig` class, so one is not included.

The htdocs/index.php file is the main Canvas page for this application. This is the page requested by the callback URL and returns the content to render on the Canvas for the user. This page is the only page publicly accessible by the application's users.

This example application doesn't have some of the stricter application requirements for previous applications. Because of this, you can exclude the Facebook PHP Client Library altogether. All of the code on this page is on the client's side. Therefore, no PHP code exists.

The FBML that builds the page is broken into two parts. The first part includes the `fb:js-string` FBML entities defining some of the messages displayed, as well as the `script` HTML entity that houses all of the FBJS.

```
<fb:js-string var="pinchconfirmstr">
<fb:success>
  <fb:message>You pinched them!</fb:message>
</fb:success>
</fb:js-string>
<fb:js-string var="pinchcancelstr">
<fb:error>
  <fb:message>Chicken ... *brrgock*</fb:message>
</fb:error>
```

(continued)

(continued)

```
    </fb:js-string>
    <script>
      var statuelem = document.getElementById('actionstatus');

      function HugThemConfirm(username) {
        diaobj = new Dialog(Dialog.DIALOG_POP);
        var msg = 'You just gave ' + username + ' a big hug!';
        diaobj.showMessage('Show the love', msg);
      }

      function PokeThemConfirm(context, username) {
        diaobj = new Dialog(Dialog.DIALOG_CONTEXTUAL);
        diaobj.setContext(context);
        var msg = 'Do you really want to poke ' + username + '?';
        diaobj.showChoice(
          'Please Confirm',
          msg,
          'Poke',
          'Nevermind'
        );
      }

      function PinchThemConfirm(context, username) {
        diaobj = new Dialog(Dialog.DIALOG_CONTEXTUAL);
        diaobj.setContext(context);
    diaobj.onconfirm = function() {
          statuelem.setInnerFBML(pinchconfirmstr);
          statuelem.setStyle('display', '');
          setTimeout(function() { statuelem.setStyle('display', 'none') }, 1000 * 10);
        };
    diaobj.oncancel = function() {
          statuelem.setInnerFBML(pinchcancelstr);
          statuelem.setStyle('display', '');
          setTimeout(function() { statuelem.setStyle('display', 'none') }, 1000 * 10);
        };
        diaobj.showChoice(
          'Please Confirm',
          'Do you really want to pinch ' + username + '?',
          'Pinch',
          'Nevermind'
        );
      }
    </script>
    <div id="bodyroot" style="margin: 0 20px 20px 20px">
      <h3>YAPA (Yet Another Poke App)</h3>
      <p>Your friends are listed below. Do stuff to them.</p>
      <ul>
        <li>Nick -
          <a href="#" onclick="PokeThemConfirm(this, 'Nick'); return false;">Poke</a>,
          <a href="#" onclick="HugThemConfirm('Nick'); return false;">Hug</a>,
          <a href="#" onclick="PinchThemConfirm(this, 'Nick'); return false;">Pinch</a>.
      </ul>
      <div id="actionstatus"></div>
    </div>
```

In the first portion of the page, you define two `fb:js-string` FBML entities, `pinchconfirmstr` and `pinchcancelstr`. Next, you have the script HTML entity, where you define one variable and three functions. The variable defined is a reference to the `actionstatus` element used to display messages when events fire. The functions you define are `HugThemConfirm`, `PokeThemConfirm`, and `PinchThemConfirm`. Figure 4-1 shows the Dialog widget displayed by the `Hug` action.

Figure 4-1: The Dialog widget displayed by the Hug action.

The `HugThemConfirm` function creates the most basic form of the Dialog widget. It accepts the `username` parameter, corresponding to the user who is the target of the hug. The type defined during object construction is `Dialog.DIALOG_POP`, and the purpose is to display a simple message to the user indicating that the action was processed. Figure 4-2 shows the Dialog displayed by the `Poke` action.

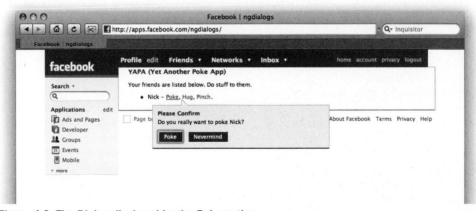

Figure 4-2: The Dialog displayed by the Poke action.

This type of Dialog widget is extremely simple to use and implement. At the lowest level, it can be deployed to give users confirmation that whatever action they recently took has happened. This type of feedback builds user confidence that your application is doing what it is supposed to.

The next function defined is `PokeThemConfirm`. It accepts the `context` and `username` parameters referencing the parent object that the Dialog references and the name of the user who was the target of the poke. The `Dialog` object created here is given the `Dialog.DIALOG_CONTEXTUAL` type, indicating that the Dialog widget displayed should be relative to one of the rendered objects on the FBML Canvas. This is useful when relating an action to a specific element on a page where normally a user could be confused as to what the Dialog is referencing. When displaying the Dialog widget, you call the `showChoice` method, which presents the user with two options when the Dialog is displayed.

The last function defined is `PinchThemConfirm`. Like the `PokeThemConfirm` function, it accepts the `context` and `username` parameters. This function demonstrates the capability to capture `Dialog` object events and act on them. In this case, when the user selects the Confirmation button, the anonymous function defined sets the `actionstatus` element's content to the FBML defined in the `pinchconfirmstr` `fb:js-string` FBML entity. When the user selects the Cancel button, the anonymous function defined sets the `actionstatus` element's content to the FBML defined in the `pinchcancelstr` `fb:js-string` FBML entity. In both cases, you also set a timer to hide the `actionstatus` element after 10 seconds.

The FBML rendered on the page is relatively simple. In this example application, you display a simple list of users with poke, hug, and pinch links with `onclick` attributes to the appropriate FBJS functions.

Summary

By now, you should be able to take any of the mock-Ajax and visibility FBML attributes and replace them with your own FBJS. While, in most cases, what is provided fits nicely, you now have the option to extend the features and functionality of your Facebook applications with true Ajax calls.

Chapter 5 continues the trend of taking a focused look at specific Facebook Platform components and moves on to the Facebook API.

Using the Facebook API

The Facebook API consists of a wide range of API methods available to developers to interact on a deeper level with the Facebook Platform. With these methods, you can enable your applications to retrieve user data, create and interact with photos and albums, update user profile content, and more.

Chapters 3 and 4 unearthed the complex world of FBML and user-interface development. The FBML entities covered can be used to create the rich and unique interfaces that your users expect. This chapter takes you deeper into the Facebook Platform, enabling you to bring more functionality to your applications.

This chapter explores the Facebook API, including the formats and structures of the requests and responses of the API methods, as well as error handling and some of the special cases you may encounter while developing your applications. Web applications and Desktop applications both benefit from information in this chapter equally. Desktop application developers will find this chapter most useful, as it is the gateway to the Facebook Platform.

Each API method reviewed contains several standard elements. These include a description and overview of the API method, the required and optional request parameters, the structure of the default successful response, and the error codes that can be returned.

The Method Request

The method request is a combination of the method parameters and request destination. In brief, an API request is a specially crafted HTTP POST request to http://api.facebook.com/ restserver.php. A set of default parameters is included in every request, and some API methods do have special cases, but the process is very straightforward. An API client can be as simple as a wrapper around a web request library such as curl, lowering the requirements to interact with the Facebook Platform.

The following HTTP request is an example of a `facebook.users.isAppAdded` API method call. The request is crafted as a HTTP 1.1 `POST` request to the `api.facebook.com` server URI `/restserver.php`. The request is submitted under the content type `application/x-www-form-urlencoded`.

```
POST /restserver.php HTTP/1.1
Host: api.facebook.com
Connection: close
User-Agent: ErlyFBClient/1.2 (Macintosh; U; Intel Mac OS X; en-us)
Accept: text/xml, application/xml
Accept-Language: en-us
Content-type: application/x-www-form-urlencoded
Content-length: 203

sig=955588f356e2aa1c8a8a0b11a0c14cd5&api_key=cde8787f00c09c05e8a6d562aa4f129a&call_
id=1200781421044311&method=facebook.users.isAppAdded&session_key=d74543fc74d0aa3117
df74ac-31232124&uid=500025891&v=1.0
```

There isn't any trickery or anything special going on under the hood. The server's response is also very plain, as shown here:

```
HTTP/1.1 200 OK
Date: Sat, 12 Jan 2008 22:22:22 GMT
Server: Apache/1.3.37.fb1
Expires: Mon, 26 Jul 1997 05:00:00 GMT
Cache-Control: private, no-store, no-cache, must-revalidate, post-check=0, pre-
check=0
Pragma: no-cache
Keep-Alive: timeout=60, max=875
Connection: Keep-Alive
Transfer-Encoding: chunked
Content-Type: text/xml;charset=utf-8

<?xml version=\"1.0\" encoding=\"UTF-8\"?>
<users_isAppAdded_response xmlns=\"http://api.facebook.com/1.0/\"
xmlns:xsi=\"http://www.w3.org/2001/XMLSchema-instance\"
xsi:schemaLocation=\"http://api.facebook.com/1.0/
http://api.facebook.com/1.0/facebook.xsd\">1</users_isAppAdded_response>
```

Common Request Parameters

All of the API methods available to developers have a default set of method parameters that must be included with every request. These method parameters are used to direct the request internally and verify the authenticity of the request.

Following are several request parameters that are standard across all API methods:

❑ `method` — This is the method name. Without this parameter, the Facebook API cannot direct your request. An example value is `facebook.fql.query`.

❑ `v` — This is the version of the API. The only supported version available to developers is "1.0."

❑ `api_key` — This parameter is the `api_key` of the requesting application.

❑   `sig` — This parameter is the API method request signature. This signature is generated by hashing the sorted key/value pairs of the request, and follows the same structure as the signatures generated by the `POST` requests through Facebook to your application.

There are several optional arguments as well:

❑   `format` — This parameter represents the desired response format of the request. The two response formats available are JSON and XML. The default value is XML.

❑   `call_id` — This parameter represents a unique incrementing request ID set by the client. With every request, the value of this parameter must be greater than the value sent in the previous request. Common practice by developers and API client libraries is to use the current UNIX time stamp or a microtime value.

❑   `callback` — This parameter is used to specify a callback function used to wrap JSON responses. If the `format` parameter is not set to JSON, this parameter is ignored.

Responses

The Facebook API may return an error or a successful structure for any given API method request. Successful responses vary from request to request in the payload and structure of the body.

Error Handling

A standard structure for API errors and failures for each response type is available. The base structure will always include the `error_code`, `error_msg`, and `request_args` keys. The `request_args` element is a list of the key/value pairs sent in the initial request to the API method.

The `error_code` element is a unique numeric error code associated with an error condition. There are several error codes that may be used across all of the API methods. Some error codes are method-specific, but will still be unique. The `error_msg` is a human-readable error message explaining the error or failure.

Listing 5-1 shows a JSON-serialized `facebook.fql.query` error, and Listing 5-2 shows an XML `facebook.fql.query` error.

Listing 5-1: A JSON-serialized `facebook.fql.query` error.

```
{
"error_code":602,
"error_msg":"xyz is not a member of the user table.",
"request_args":[
  {"key":"query","value":"SELECT name FROM user\nWHERE uid = xyz"},
  {"key":"callback","value":""},
  {"key":"app_id","value":"2227470867"},
  {"key":"session_key","value":"cd617c16ca615e3ee73aa02e-500025891"},
  {"key":"v","value":"1.0"},
  {"key":"format","value":"json"},
  {"key":"method","value":"facebook.fql.query"},
  {"key":"api_key","value":"0289b21f46b2ee642d5c42145df5489f"},
  {"key":"call_id","value":"1189742501.7153"},
  {"key":"sig","value":"d750527eac855a6195da6f73fb1e1358"}
]
}
```

Listing 5-2: An XML `facebook.fql.query` error.

```xml
<error_response xmlns="http://api.facebook.com/1.0/"
xmlns:xsi="http://www.w3.org/2001/XMLSchema-instance">
  <error_code>602</error_code>
  <error_msg>xyz is not a member of the user table.</error_msg>
  <request_args list="true">
    <arg>
      <key>query</key>
      <value>SELECT name FROM user WHERE uid = xyz</value>
    </arg>
    <arg>
      <key>callback</key>
      <value/>
    </arg>
    <arg>
      <key>app_id</key>
      <value>2227470867</value>
    </arg>
    <arg>
      <key>session_key</key>
      <value>cd617c16ca615e3ee73aa02e-500025891</value>
    </arg>
    <arg>
      <key>v</key>
      <value>1.0</value>
    </arg>
    <arg>
      <key>method</key>
      <value>facebook.fql.query</value>
    </arg>
    <arg>
      <key>api_key</key>
      <value>0289b21f46b2ee642d5c42145df5489f</value>
    </arg>
    <arg>
      <key>call_id</key>
      <value>1189743089.6994</value>
    </arg>
    <arg>
      <key>sig</key>
      <value>5729d584dc95a032d9a357a8d119c7e3</value>
    </arg>
  </request_args>
</error_response>
```

There are few differences between the XML- and JSON-serialized errors. The notable exception here is that when parsing an XML response, you can easily determine that the response resulted in an error by looking at the root `error_response` element. When parsing the JSON-formatted response, the developer must do a little more to verify the success of a response.

XML

XML-serialized responses have a standard format for the root response element. The root element's name will be the method group name, method name, and word response joined by an underscore. In other words, when making an API request to `facebook.fql.query`, the root response node will be `fql_query_response`. In the case of an error, the root element name is `error_response`, as seen in Listing 5-1.

XML-serialized responses also include several XMLNS declarations in the root element. The default XML namespace is defined and set to `http://api.facebook.com/1.0/`. The `xsi` XML namespace is also defined, and the `xsi:schemalocation` attribute is defined and set to

```
http://api.facebook.com/1.0/
http://api.facebook.com/1.0/facebook.xsd.
```

JSON

JSON-serialized responses have a more fluid structure, depending on the API method called.

Method Definitions

The next few subsections of this chapter provide definitions of the available Facebook API methods, and example responses will be given. The methods are grouped by general functionality.

Authentication

The `auth.*` methods are used to verify and assert the validity of application and user authentication information. These include `facebook.auth.createToken` and `facebook.auth.getSession`.

facebook.auth.createToken

The `facebook.auth.createToken` method creates a single-use token unique to the application and user that is used to create a `session_key` for a user and application. This application is primarily used by Desktop applications to kick off the authentication process.

There are no optional method parameters available for this API method.

A successful response contains a freshly created `auth` token:

```
<auth_createToken_response ... >
3e4a22bb2f5ed75114b0fc9995ea85f1
</auth_createToken_response>
```

Error codes include the following:

❑　1 — An unknown error has occurred.

❑　2 — Service temporarily unavailable

❑　4 — Application request limit reached

❑   5 — Unauthorized source IP address

❑   101 — The API key submitted is not associated with any known applications.

❑   104 — Incorrect signature

facebook.auth.getSession

The `facebook.auth.getSession` API method returns a `session_key` bound to a user and application based on a valid `auth` token. This method should be called immediately after a user logs in and the `auth_token` is returned.

Following is a required parameter:

❑   `auth_token` — This parameter is a valid authentication token.

A successful response is a structure containing the `session_key`, `uid`, and `expires` elements. The `expires` element is the date and time (in UNIX time-stamp format) when the `session_key` expires. If the `expires` element is 0, then the session will not expire unless the user explicitly logs out.

```
<auth_getSession_response ... >
    <session_key>5f34e11bfb97c762e439e6a5-8055</session_key>
    <uid>8055</uid>
    <expires>1173309298</expires>
</auth_getSession_response>
```

Error codes include the following:

❑   1 — An unknown error has occurred.

❑   2 — Service temporarily unavailable

❑   4 — Application request limit reached

❑   5 — Unauthorized source IP address

❑   100 — Invalid parameter

❑   101 — The API key submitted is not associated with any known applications.

❑   104 — Incorrect signature

News Feed and Mini-Feed

The `feed.*` API methods are used to post content to the News Feed or Mini-Feed of a user. These include `facebook.feed.publishStoryToUser`, `facebook.feed.publishActionOfUser`, and `facebook.feed.publishTemplatizedAction`.

facebook.feed.publishStoryToUser

The `facebook.feed.publishStoryToUser` API method publishes a story to the News Feed of a user associated with the `session_key` parameter. A feed item consists of a title, optional body, and up to four images that are displayed in the feed.

Following are required parameters:

❑   `title` — The markup rendered in the title of the feed item

❑   `session_key` — The session token for a user and application

Following are optional parameters:

❑   `body` — The markup rendered in the body of the feed item

❑   `image_1` — The URL of an image to be displayed in the feed item

❑   `image_1_link` — The URL destination after a click on the image referenced by `image_1`

❑   `image_2` — The URL of an image to be displayed in the feed item

❑   `image_2_link` — The URL destination after a click on the image referenced by `image_2`

❑   `image_3` — The URL of an image to be displayed in the feed item

❑   `image_3_link` — The URL destination after a click on the image referenced by `image_3`

❑   `image_4` — The URL of an image to be displayed in the feed item

❑   `image_4_link` — The URL destination after a click on the image referenced by `image_4`

This method has several restrictions and caveats:

❑   The `title` parameter is limited to 60 displayable characters. This does not include HTML or FBML entities.

❑   The title may contain zero or one `<a>` HTML element. No other FBML or HTML may be used.

❑   The body is optional and is limited to 200 displayable characters. It can include `<a>`, `<b>`, and `<i>` HTML elements.

❑   Each image must be a fully qualified URL or the photo ID of a photo within Facebook. The images will be resized by Facebook to 75 by 75 pixels and cached.

❑   Each image must have a link associated with it.

❑   Applications are limited to calling this API method once every 12 hours for each user.

Not all posts to the News Feed will show up in the News Feed of the user's friends. Facebook allows users to heavily customize the content displayed in the user's News Feed, and there is no guarantee that your item in the feed will be displayed.

Developers can submit an unlimited number of `facebook.feed.publishStoryToUser` *requests to encourage testing and display tweaks. This only works when submitting requests to their own account.*

A successful response body includes a simple true value (`1`). If the response body is a false value (`0`), this indicates that there was a permission error when submitting the request. All other failures are represented by the standard error structure.

```
<feed_publishStoryToUser_response ... >
1
</feed_publishStoryToUser_response>
```

Error codes include the following:

- ❏ 1 — An unknown error has occurred.

- ❏ 2 — Service temporarily unavailable

- ❏ 4 — Application request limit reached

- ❏ 5 — Unauthorized source IP address

- ❏ 100 — Invalid parameter

- ❏ 101 — The API key submitted is not associated with any known applications.

- ❏ 102 — The session key was improperly submitted, or has reached its time-out. Direct the user to the login page to obtain a fresh session key.

- ❏ 103 — The submitted `call_id` was not greater than the previously submitted `call_id` for this session.

- ❏ 104 — Incorrect signature

facebook.feed.publishActionOfUser

The `facebook.feed.publishActionOfUser` API method is used to publish an action to the user's News Feed. This method is very similar to the `facebook.feed.publishStoryToUser` API method. The notable difference centers on its lax rules for the `title` and `body` parameters regarding the HTML and FBML entities available.

Following are required parameters:

- ❏ `title` — The markup rendered in the title of the feed item

- ❏ `session_key` — The session key associated with a user whose feed the item will be published to

Following are optional parameters:

- ❏ `body` — The markup rendered in the body of the feed item
- ❏ `image_1` — The URL of an image to be displayed in the feed item
- ❏ `image_1_link` — The URL destination after a click on the image referenced by `image_1`
- ❏ `image_2` — The URL of an image to be displayed in the feed item
- ❏ `image_2_link` — The URL destination after a click on the image referenced by `image_2`
- ❏ `image_3` — The URL of an image to be displayed in the feed item
- ❏ `image_3_link` — The URL destination after a click on the image referenced by `image_3`
- ❏ `image_4` — The URL of an image to be displayed in the feed item
- ❏ `image_4_link` — The URL destination after a click on the image referenced by `image_4`

There are also several restrictions to the `title` and `body` parameters:

❑ The `title` parameter is limited to 60 displayable characters. This does not include HTML or FBML entities.

❑ One `fb:userlink` FBML entity is allowed, and the `uid` must be the user ID (UID) of the user associated with the session key. If the entity is not included, the `fb:userlink` FBML entity will automatically be prefixed to the `title`. Submitting, "**Josh fights spam**" as the `title` will result in "`Josn (No Network) Josh fights spam`".

❑ The `fb:name` FBML entity is allowed and can be used multiple times.

❑ The `body` parameter is optional and may include any number of `fb:userlink`, `fb:name`, a, b, and i FBML and HTML elements.

❑ Each image must be a fully qualified URL or the photo ID of a photo within Facebook. The images will be resized by Facebook to 75 by 75 pixels and cached.

❑ Each image must have a link associated with it.

❑ Applications are limited to calling this API method 10 times for each user in a rolling 48-hour window.

Much like the `facebook.feed.publishStoryToUser` API method, not all posts to the News Feed will show up in the News Feed of the user's friends. Facebook allows users to heavily customize the content displayed in the user's News Feed, and there is no guarantee that your item in the feed will be displayed.

> *This method affects all of the friends of the user. This method is subject to the limits, regardless if the developer is the subject or not. This is different from the behavior of the* `facebook.feed` `.publisStoryToUser` *method.*

A successful response is indicated by a true (1) value in the body. If the body is a false (0) value, this indicates that there was a permission error when submitting the request. All other response failures are represented by error codes.

```
<feed_publishActionOfUser_response ... >
1
</feed_publishActionOfUser_response>
```

Error codes include the following:

❑ 1 — An unknown error has occurred.

❑ 2 — Service temporarily unavailable

❑ 4 — Application request limit reached

❑ 5 — Unauthorized source IP address

❑ 100 — Invalid parameter

❑ 101 — The API key submitted is not associated with any known applications.

❑ 102 — The session key was improperly submitted, or has reached its time-out. Direct the user to the login page to obtain a fresh session key.

❑ 103 — The submitted `call_id` was not greater than the previously submitted `call_id` for this session.

❑ 104 — Incorrect signature

Action versus Story

The `feed.publishActionOfUser` and `feed.publishStoryToUser` methods are very similar but have dramatically different effects that may cause confusion among developers. Table 5-1 compares the two methods.

Table 5-1: Comparison of `publishActionOfUser` and `publishStoryToUser`

	PublishActionOfUser	PublishStoryToUser
Limits on usage	Limited always	Unlimited for developers
Send restrictions	10 times per user in a rolling 48-hour period	Once per user every 12 hours
Tags allowed in title	`1x fb:userlink, 1xa, fb:name`	`a`
Tags allowed in body	`fb:name, a`	`a, b, i`

facebook.feed.publishTemplatizedAction

The `facebook.feed.publishTemplatizedAction` is used to publish a story to a user or page Mini-Feed. When publishing to a Facebook user, the story will also be published to the News Feed of the user's friends.

Following are required parameters:

❑ `actor_id` — The user or page ID performing the action. The user or page represented by this ID must have the application added for this call to succeed.

❑ `title_template` — The markup template used to render the story title

Following are optional parameters:

❑ `title_data` — A JSON-encoded associative array of the key/value pairs used to represent variables in the title template

❑ `body_template` — The markup template used to render the story title

❑ `body_data` — A JSON-encoded associative array of the key/value pairs used to represent variables in the body template

❑ `body_general` — Free-form markup that is specific to a given story. When more than one story is aggregated, only one of the `body_general` values is included in the displayed story.

❑ `image_1` — The URL of an image to be displayed in the feed item

- ❏ `image_1_link` — The URL destination after a click on the image referenced by `image_1`
- ❏ `image_2` — The URL of an image to be displayed in the feed item
- ❏ `image_2_link` — The URL destination after a click on the image referenced by `image_2`
- ❏ `image_3` — The URL of an image to be displayed in the feed item
- ❏ `image_3_link` — The URL destination after a click on the image referenced by `image_3`
- ❏ `image_4` — The URL of an image to be displayed in the feed item
- ❏ `image_4_link` — The URL destination after a click on the image referenced by `image_4`
- ❏ `target_ids` — A comma-separated list of Facebook user ID tokens used when the `{target}` variable is used within a template to reference Facebook users that were targeted by the story action

When using this method, it is important to fully understand all of the rules that apply to the content and distribution of the story.

- ❏ The `title_template` parameter is limited to 60 characters, not including tags.
  - ❏ The "`{actor}`" variable must be included in the markup and represents the Facebook user or page that performed the action.
  - ❏ The "`{target}`" variable may be included in the markup and is used to hint to the Facebook Platform the structure of the story. If this variable is used, the `target_ids` parameter must be included.
  - ❏ Variable substitutions are made by enclosing variables in curly brackets and including them within the `title_data` parameter.
  - ❏ The `fb:name`, `fb:pronoun`, `fb:if-multiple-actors` and a FBML and HTML entities are allowed in the title. No other FBML entities are processed.
- ❏ The `body_template` is combined with the `body_general` parameter and together is limited to 200 characters.
  - ❏ The "`{actor}`" and "`{target}`" variables may be included in the markup.
  - ❏ The `fb:userlink`, `fb:name`, `fb:pronoun`, `fb:if-multiple-actors`, a, b, and i FBML and HTML entities are allowed in the body. No other FBML entities are processed.
- ❏ Two or more News Feed stories published by the `facebook.feed .publishTemplatizedAction` method may be aggregated.
  - ❏ Stories with identical `title_template` and `body_template` values are aggregated when possible. Additionally, the `target_ids` and associative arrays for the key/value pairs representing the `title_data` and `body_data` parameters must also be identical.
  - ❏ If two or more stories are aggregated, the "`{actor}`" variable is replaced with the names of all of the users or Facebook pages whose actions are being aggregated.
- ❏ The `body_general` markup is intended to be related to the story, but not necessary to its understanding.
- ❏ With story aggregates, the `body_general` variable and images (if available) will come from the same story source.

- ❏ A maximum of four images will be displayed for any given story or story aggregate. Images will be resized to fit a 75 by 75 square, cached, and reformatted by the Facebook Platform.

- ❏ The Facebook Platform imposes a limit of 10 method calls for each user or page in a rolling 48-hour window.

- ❏ When a new template is registered, it is possible to enable the option to display published stories to users who do not have the application installed.

A successful response is indicated by a true (1) value in the body. If the body is a false (0) value, this indicates that there was a permission error when submitting the request. All other response failures are represented by error codes.

```
<feed_publishTemplatizedAction_response ...>
1
</feed_publishTemplatizedAction_response>
```

Error codes include the following:

- ❏ 1 — An unknown error has occurred.

- ❏ 2 — Service temporarily unavailable

- ❏ 4 — Application request limit reached

- ❏ 5 — Unauthorized source IP address

- ❏ 100 — Invalid parameter

- ❏ 101 — The API key submitted is not associated with any known applications.

- ❏ 102 — The session key was improperly submitted, or has reached its time-out. Direct the user to the login page to obtain a fresh session key.

- ❏ 103 — The submitted `call_id` was not greater than the previously submitted `call_id` for this session.

- ❏ 104 — Incorrect signature

- ❏ 330 — The markup was invalid.

- ❏ 360 — Feed story `title_data` argument was not a valid JSON-encoded array.

- ❏ 361 — Feed story title template either missing required parameters or did not have all parameters defined in the `title_data` array.

- ❏ 362 — Feed story `body_data` argument was not a valid JSON-encoded array.

- ❏ 363 — Feed story body template either missing required parameters or did not have all parameters defined in the `body_data` array.

- ❏ 364 — Feed story photos could not be retrieved, or bad image links were provided.

- ❏ 366 — One or more of the target IDs for this story are invalid. They must all be IDs of friends of the acting user.

FQL

The Facebook Query Language (FQL) is a powerful and flexible query language that allows developers to mine data from the Facebook Platform. The `fql.*` methods are the interface.

facebook.fql.query

The `facebook.fql.query` API method evaluates an FQL query and returns the requested information, if available.

Following are required parameters:

❏ `session_key` — The session key of the requesting user

❏ `query` — The FQL query to evaluate

Queries range from the simple to the complex. Chapter 6 examines FQL in more detail, as well as its uses and caveats.

A successful response includes the complex element structure based on the fields requested. The following response is from the FQL query "`SELECT name FROM user WHERE uid = 500025891`":

```
<fql_query_response ... >
  <user>
    <name>Nick Gerakines</name>
  </user>
</fql_query_response>
```

Error codes include the following:

❏ 1 — An unknown error has occurred.

❏ 2 — Service temporarily unavailable

❏ 4 — Application request limit reached

❏ 5 — Unauthorized source IP address

❏ 100 — Invalid parameter

❏ 101 — The API key submitted is not associated with any known applications.

❏ 102 — The session key was improperly submitted or has reached its time-out. Direct the user to the login page to obtain a fresh session key.

❏ 103 — The submitted `call_id` was not greater than the previously submitted `call_id` for this session.

❏ 601 — Error while parsing FQL statement

❏ 602 — The field you requested does not exist.

❏ 603 — The table you requested does not exist.

- ❑ 604 — Your statement is not indexable.

- ❑ 605 — The function you called does not exist.

- ❑ 606 — Wrong number of arguments passed into the function.

Friends

The `friends.*` API methods are used to build and explore the social graph of user relationships that Facebook maintains. These include `facebook.friends.areFriends`, `facebook.friends.get`, and `facebook.friends.getAppUsers`.

facebook.friends.areFriends

The `facebook.friends.areFriends` API methods return the relationship between two or more people.

This API method is very similar to evaluating a specially crafted FQL query:

```
SELECT uid1, uid2 FROM friend WHERE uid1 = <x> AND uid2 = <y>
```

Following are required parameters:

- ❑ `uids1` — The comma-separated list of UIDs compared to `uids2`

- ❑ `uids2` — The comma-separated list of UIDs compared to `uids1`

The `uids1` and `uids2` parameters are comma-separated lists of UIDs. Keep in mind that both lists must contain an equal number of UIDs to compare, because the lists are compared row by row. In other words, the first users in `uids1` and `uids2` are compared, then the second `uids1` and `uids2` users, and so on.

A successful response includes a list of `friend_info` elements. These elements define the relationship between two users using `uid1`, `uid2`, and `are_friends` child elements. The `uid1` and `uid2` elements contain the two UIDs that were compared. The `are_friends` element is a true (1) or false (0) value, indicating that the two users are or are not friends. All other response failures are represented by error codes.

```
<friends_areFriends_response ... >
  <friend_info>
    <uid1>500025891</uid1>
    <uid2>1559580004</uid2>
    <are_friends>1</are_friends>
  </friend_info>
</friends_areFriends_response>
```

> When requesting the relationship status for users and one or more of the users are not visible to the Facebook Platform (as determined by the user's privacy settings), the following `friend_info` block will contain an `are_friends` element with an `xsi:nill` attribute set to `"true"`:

```
<friend_info>
  <uid1>500025891</uid1>
  <uid2>1559580004</uid2>
  <are_friends xsi:nill="true" />
</friend_info>
```

Error codes include the following:

- ❏ 1 — An unknown error has occurred.

- ❏ 2 — Service temporarily unavailable

- ❏ 4 — Application request limit reached

- ❏ 5 — Unauthorized source IP address

- ❏ 100 — Invalid parameter

- ❏ 101 — The API key submitted is not associated with any known applications.

- ❏ 102 — The session key was improperly submitted or has reached its time-out. Direct the user to the login page to obtain a fresh session key.

- ❏ 103 — The submitted `call_id` was not greater than the previously submitted `call_id` for this session.

- ❏ 104 — Incorrect signature

facebook.friends.get

The `facebook.friends.get` API method returns the available and visible friends for a user associated with a session key. This method can be replaced by the following FQL query:

```
SELECT uid2 from FRIEND WHERE uid1 = loggedInUid
```

Following is a required parameter:

- ❏ `session_key` — A session key

A successful response includes a list of `uid` elements containing the friends of the user of the `session_key`.

```
<friends_get_response ... >
    <uid>1233</uid>
    <uid>1234</uid>
</friends_get_response>
```

This method will only return UIDs that are visible to the Facebook Platform. This list may not include all available content.

Error codes include the following:

- ❏ 1 — An unknown error has occurred.

- ❏ 2 — Service temporarily unavailable

❑   4 — Application request limit reached

❑   5 — Unauthorized source IP address

❑   101 — The API key submitted is not associated with any known applications.

❑   102 — The session key was improperly submitted or has reached its time-out. Direct the user to the login page to obtain a fresh session key.

❑   103 — The submitted `call_id` was not greater than the previously submitted `call_id` for this session.

❑   104 — Incorrect signature

facebook.friends.getAppUsers

The `facebook.friends.getAppUsers` API method returns a list of users who have added the application and are considered friends of the user associated with the `session_key`. This method can be replaced by the following FQL query:

```
SELECT uid
FROM user
WHERE uid IN (
    SELECT uid2 FROM friend WHERE uid1 = loggedInUser
) AND is_app_user
```

Following is a required parameter:

❑   `session_key` — The session key of the requesting user

A successful response includes zero or more `uid` elements representing the users.

```
<friends_getappusers_response ... >
    <uid>1233</uid>
    <uid>1234</uid>
</friends_getappusers_response>
```

This method will only return UIDs that are visible to the Facebook Platform. This list may not include all available content.

Error codes include the following:

❑   1 — An unknown error has occurred.

❑   2 — Service temporarily unavailable

❑   4 — Application request limit reached

❑   5 — Unauthorized source IP address

❑   101 — The API key submitted is not associated with any known applications.

❑   102 — The session key was improperly submitted or has reached its time-out. Direct the user to the login page to obtain a fresh session key.

❑ 103 — The submitted `call_id` was not greater than the previously submitted `call_id` for this session.

❑ 104 — Incorrect signature

Notifications

The `notifications.*` methods are used to send and receive notifications and requests in Facebook. Notifications are one of the staples of communication between users and applications. These include `facebook.notifications.get`, `facebook.notifications.send`, `facebook.notifications.sendrequest`, and `facebook.notifications.sendEmail`.

facebook.notifications.get

The `facebook.notifications.get` API method returns the notifications for the user associated with the `session_key`.

Following is a required parameter:

❑ `session_key` — The session key of the target user of the request

A successful response contains the `messages`, `pokes`, `shares`, `friend_requests`, `group_invites`, and `event_invites` elements. Those elements will include the `unread` and `most_recent` child elements. The `unread` element defines the number of unread notifications of the parent element type. The `most_recent` element contains a comma-separated list of IDs that are considered "recent" of the parent element type. The exception is the `friend_requests` element, which contains a list of `uid` elements representing the users who have made friend requests to this user.

```
<notifications_get_response ... >
<messages>
  <unread>1</unread>
  <most_recent>1170644932</most_recent>
</messages>
<pokes>
  <unread>0</unread>
  <most_recent>0</most_recent>
</pokes>
<shares>
  <unread>1</unread>
  <most_recent>1170657686</most_recent>
</shares>
<friend_requests list="true">
  <uid>2231342839</uid>
  <uid>2231511925</uid>
  <uid>2239284527</uid>
</friend_requests>
</ notifications_get_response>
```

In cases where the `unread` element for a notification type is 0, the `most_recent` element will be empty.

> When displaying a user's notifications on your application, Facebook encourages you to use the following logic.
>
> ```
> if (unread > 0 && most_recent > old_most_recent) {
>   // display notifications
> }
> old_most_recent = most_recent
> ```
>
> This method will only return IDs that are visible to the platform. This list may not include all available content.

Error codes include the following:

- ❑ 1 — An unknown error has occurred.
- ❑ 2 — Service temporarily unavailable
- ❑ 4 — Application request limit reached
- ❑ 5 — Unauthorized source IP address
- ❑ 101 — The API key submitted is not associated with any known applications.
- ❑ 102 — The session key was improperly submitted or has reached its time-out. Direct the user to the login page to obtain a fresh session key.
- ❑ 103 — The submitted `call_id` was not greater than the previously submitted `call_id` for this session.
- ❑ 104 — Incorrect signature

facebook.notifications.send

The `facebook.notifications.send` API method can be called to send notifications to one or more users on behalf of the application.

Following are required parameters:

- ❑ `session_key` — The session key of the sending user
- ❑ `to_ids` — The comma-separated list of UIDs to send notifications to
- ❑ `notification` — The FBML rendered on the notification page

Following is an optional parameter:

- ❑ `email` — The FBML rendered in the e-mail sent. If this parameter is not passed, no e-mail will be sent.

This API method has several restrictions and caveats that developers should be aware of:

❑   When sending notifications to users who have not added the application, the response body will include a URL that the user must follow. The user will be presented with the notification that he or she must acknowledge and explicitly submit. If all of the users that the notification is being sent to have added the application, this step is not required.

❑   An application can send at most 40 notifications on behalf of a single user per day. In addition to this restriction, only 10 of those notifications may include e-mail content.

❑   The sender's name is automatically prefixed to the e-mail body.

❑   There can be at most 10 notifications sent at once.

❑   The FBML allowed in the notification body and e-mail body are stripped heavily, and result in plaintext and links. The exception to this rules is when setting the email parameter, the fb:notif-subject FBML entity can be used to set the e-mail subject.

A successful response includes the notification confirmation URL.

```
<notifications_send_response ... >
http://www.facebook.com/send_email.php?from=1&id=5551234
</notifications_send_response>
```

Error codes include the following:

❑   1 — An unknown error has occurred.

❑   2 — Service temporarily unavailable

❑   4 — Application request limit reached

❑   5 — Unauthorized source IP address

❑   101 — The API key submitted is not associated with any known applications.

❑   102 — The session key was improperly submitted or has reached its time-out. Direct the user to the login page to obtain a fresh session key.

❑   103 — The submitted call_id was not greater than the previously submitted call_id for this session.

❑   104 — Incorrect signature

facebook.notifications.sendrequest

The facebook.notifications.sendRequest method has been deprecated and is no longer supported.

facebook.notifications.sendEmail

The facebook.notifications.sendEmail API method is used to send e-mail notifications to users who have added the application specified by the API key.

Following are required parameters:

- ❑ `session_key` — The session key of the sending user
- ❑ `recipients` — A comma-separated list of Facebook user IDs. These users must have already added the application, and up to 100 can be specified at a time.
- ❑ `subject` — The e-mail subject

Following are optional parameters:

- ❑ `text` — The plaintext body of the message. This must be included if the `fbml` parameter is not given.
- ❑ `fbml` — The body of the message to be rendered by the FBML rendering engine. This parameter must be included if the `text` parameter is not given.

Developers should be aware that when setting the `fbml` parameter, the only tags allowed are those that result in plaintext, links, and line breaks. These include the `p`, `a`, and `br` HTML entities.

A successful response is composed of a comma-separated list of the Facebook user IDs to whom the e-mail was sent. This does not indicate that the users have read or received the message.

```
<notifications_sendEmail_response ...>
123,234,345
</notifications_sendEmail_response>
```

Error codes include the following:

- ❑ 1 — An unknown error has occurred.
- ❑ 2 — Service temporarily unavailable
- ❑ 4 — Application request limit reached
- ❑ 5 — Unauthorized source IP address
- ❑ 101 — The API key submitted is not associated with any known applications.
- ❑ 102 — The session key was improperly submitted or has reached its time-out. Direct the user to the login page to obtain a fresh session key.
- ❑ 103 — The submitted `call_id` was not greater than the previously submitted `call_id` for this session.
- ❑ 104 — Incorrect signature

Profile

The `profile.*` methods are used to read and manipulate the user profile. These include `facebook .profile.getFBML` and `facebook.profile.setFBML`.

facebook.profile.getFBML

The `facebook.profile.getFBML` API method returns the FBML set to the application profile box for an application user.

Following are required parameters:

- ❏ `uid` — The UID of the target user
- ❏ `session_key` — The session key of the requesting user

A successful response contains the profile FBML in the response body.

```
<profile_getFBML_response ... >
Virtus Junxit Mors Non Separabit
</profile_getFBML_response>
```

Error codes include the following:

- ❏ 1 — An unknown error has occurred.
- ❏ 2 — Service temporarily unavailable
- ❏ 4 — Application request limit reached
- ❏ 5 — Unauthorized source IP address
- ❏ 100 — Invalid or missing parameter
- ❏ 101 — The API key submitted is not associated with any known applications.
- ❏ 102 — The session key was improperly submitted or has reached its time-out. Direct the user to the login page to obtain a fresh session key.
- ❏ 103 — The submitted `call_id` was not greater than the previously submitted `call_id` for this session.
- ❏ 104 — Incorrect signature

facebook.profile.setFBML

The `facebook.profile.setFBML` API method is called to set the profile content of a user. This content includes the application profile box FBML, as well as the profile action links. Once this method is called for a user, the profile content will not change unless this method is called again.

Following are required parameters:

- ❏ `session_key` — The session key of the requesting user
- ❏ `markup` — The FBML rendered in the application profile box

Following is an optional parameter:

- ❏ `uid` — The UID of the target user. If this parameter is not set, then the user associated with the `session_key` is used.

Developers should account for a 64-kB (after GZIP compression) content size restriction when setting profile FBML content. Another caveat to be aware of is that desktop applications are only allowed to update the profile of the user associated with the session key.

A successful response is indicated by the FBML content used to set the application profile box.

```
<profile_setFBML_response>
Artephii Liber Secretus
</profile_setFBML_response>
```

Error codes include the following:

- ❑ 1 — An unknown error has occurred.

- ❑ 2 — Service temporarily unavailable

- ❑ 4 — Application request limit reached

- ❑ 5 — Unauthorized source IP address

- ❑ 100 — Invalid or missing parameter

- ❑ 101 — The API key submitted is not associated with any known applications.

- ❑ 102 — The session key was improperly submitted or has reached its time-out. Direct the user to the login page to obtain a fresh session key.

- ❑ 103 — The submitted `call_id` was not greater than the previously submitted `call_id` for this session.

- ❑ 104 — Incorrect signature

- ❑ 240 — The UID cannot be specified from a Desktop application.

- ❑ 330 — The markup was invalid.

User

The `users.*` methods are used to retrieve user information and metadata associated with Facebook users. These include `facebook.users.isAppAdded`, `facebook.users.getInfo`, `facebook.users.getLoggedInUser`, `facebook.users.hasAppPermission`, `facebook.users.hasAppAdded`, and `facebook.users.setStatus`.

facebook.users.isAppAdded

The `facebook.users.isAppAdded` API method can be called to determine whether the user of a session key has added the application.

Following is a required parameter:

- ❑ `session_key` — The session key of the user in question

A successful response includes either a true (1) or false (0) value indicating that the user has or has not added the application.

```
<users_isAppAdded_response ... >
1
</users_isAppAdded_response>
```

Error codes include the following:

- ❏ 1 — An unknown error has occurred.
- ❏ 2 — Service temporarily unavailable
- ❏ 4 — Application request limit reached
- ❏ 5 — Unauthorized source IP address
- ❏ 101 — The API key submitted is not associated with any known applications.
- ❏ 102 — The session key was improperly submitted or has reached its time-out. Direct the user to the login page to obtain a fresh session key.
- ❏ 103 — The submitted `call_id` was not greater than the previously submitted `call_id` for this session.
- ❏ 104 — Incorrect signature

facebook.users.getInfo

The `facebook.users.getInfo` API method returns information about one or more users.

Following are required parameters:

- ❏ `session_key` — The session key of the requesting user. This field is used to verify the fields available to the requesting user.
- ❏ `uids` — The comma-separated list of UIDs to retrieve information on
- ❏ `fields` — The comma-separated list of fields requested

This API method is very similar to evaluating a specially crafted FQL query such as the following:

```
SELECT uid, fields FROM user WHERE uid IN (uids)
```

A successful response includes one of the many available complex data structures based on the `fields` parameter passed when the API method was called. These data structures are wrapped in `user` elements to separate multiple UID requests.

```
<users_getInfo_response ... >
<user>
  <uid>12345</uid>
  <name>Nick Gerakines</name>
  <field2 />
</user>
</users_getInfo_response>
```

Each user element will always contain the `uid` child element as the first element in each `user` element. All other data structures are specified through the `fields parameter`.

The `about_me` field returns the user-defined content corresponding to the "About Me" section of the user profile page. The `activities` field returns the user-defined content corresponding to the Activities section of the user profile page.

The `affiliations` field is used return a complex data structure representing the network affiliations the user has. Each `affiliation` element contained in the `affiliations` parent element contains the `nid`, `name`, `type`, `year`, and `status` child elements. The user's primary network affiliation will always be listed first. The `nid` element is the unique identifier of the network. The four values for the `type` element are `high school`, `college`, `work`, and `region`. The value of the `status` element has a value if the `affiliation` type is `college` and represents the graduation status of that user.

Listing 5-3 shows an example of the `affiliations` data structure.

Listing 5-3: Example of the `affiliations` data structure.

```
<user>
  <uid>500025891</uid>
  <affiliations list="true">
    <affiliation>
      <nid>3160</nid>
      <name>F&amp;AM</name>
      <type>organization</type>
      <status/>
      <year>0</year>
    </affiliation>
  </affiliations>
</user>
```

The `birthday` and `books` fields are available to return the user-defined content pertaining to the Birthday and Favorite Books profile sections.

The `current_location` and `hometown_location` fields represent the user-defined Current Location profile and Hometown sections, respectively. These two data structures are composed of the `city`, `state`, `country`, and `zip` child elements. Listing 5-4 shows an example of the `current_location` and `hometown_location` data structures.

Listing 5-4: Example of the `current_location` and `hometown_location` data structures.

```
<user>
  <uid>500025891</uid>
  <current_location>
    <city>Mountain View</city>
    <state>CA</state>
    <country>United States</country>
    <zip>94041</zip>
  </current_location>
  <hometown_location>
```

```
      <city>New Orleans</city>
      <state>LA</state>
      <country>United States</country>
      <zip/>
   </hometown_location>
  </user>
```

The education_history field returns the educational history for a user. Requesting these data will only result in the college information at this time. Each education_info element returned contains the name, year, and concentrations child elements. Each child element of the concentrations element is a user-defined school focus or concentration. Listing 5-5 shows an example of the education_history data structure.

Listing 5-5: Example of the education_history data structure.

```
<user>
  <uid>14000941</uid>
  <education_history list="true">
    <education_info>
      <name>Union</name>
      <year>2007</year>
      <concentrations list="true">
        <concentration>Hating Cold Weather</concentration>
      </concentrations>
    </education_info>
    <education_info>
      <name>City College of San Francisco</name>
      <year>0</year>
      <concentrations list="true">
        <concentration>General Requirements</concentration>
      </concentrations>
    </education_info>
  </education_history>
</user>
```

The has_added_app and is_app_user fields are used to return user metadata associated with the requesting application as defined by the api_key in the request. The has_added_app field returns a true (1) or false (0) value indicating that the user has added the application to his or her Facebook account. The is_app_user field returns a true (1) or false (0) value indicating whether the user has ever added or used the application.

The first_name, last_name, and name elements return values derived from the Name profile section. Listing 5-6 shows an example of the first_name, last_name, and name data structures.

Listing 5-6: Example of the first_name, last_name, and name data structures.

```
<user>
   <uid>500025891</uid>
   <first_name>Nick</first_name>
   <last_name>Gerakines</last_name>
   <name>Nick Gerakines</name>
  </user>
```

The `hs_info` field returns a user's high school information. This data structure consists of the `hs1_name`, `hs2_name`, `grad_year`, `hs1_id`, and `hs2_id` elements. Listing 5-7 shows an example of the `hs_info` data structure.

Listing 5-7: Example of the `hs_info` data structure.

```
<user>
   <uid>500025891</uid>
   <hs_info>
     <hs1_name>Mandeville High School</hs1_name>
     <hs2_name/>
     <grad_year>2002</grad_year>
     <hs1_id>8570</hs1_id>
     <hs2_id>0</hs2_id>
   </hs_info>
</user>
```

The `interests`, `music`, and `movies` fields return the user-defined content map to the Interests, Favorite Music, and Favorite Movies profile sections, respectively.

The `meeting_for` and `meeting_sex` fields can be called to return the types of relationships and opposite sex(es) the user is interested in. The values returned correspond to the "Looking For" and "Interested In" profile sections. Both of these fields are visible only if the user has added the application. Listing 5-8 shows an example of the `meeting_for` and `meeting_sex` data structures.

Listing 5-8: The `meeting_for` and `meeting_sex` data structures.

```
<user>
   <uid>500033387</uid>
   <meeting_for list="true">
     <seeking>Friendship</seeking>
   </meeting_for>
   <meeting_sex list="true">
     <sex>female</sex>
   </meeting_sex>
</user>
```

The `notes_count` field returns the total number of notes written or imported by the user.

The `pic`, `pic_big`, `pic_small`, and `pic_square` fields contain the profile picture of the user in different sizes, as shown in Table 5-2.

Table 5-2: Sizes of `pic`, `pic_small`, `pic_big`, and `pic_square` Fields

	Height	Width
Pic	100 pixels	300 pixels
pic_big	200 pixels	600 pixels
pic_small	50 pixels	150 pixels
pic_square	50 pixels	50 pixels

The `political` field returns the user-defined value associated with the "Political View" profile field.

The `profile_update_time` field returns the time (in seconds) since Epoch that the user's profile was last updated. If the user's profile has never been updated, the value is `0`.

The `quotes` field is the user-defined content displayed in the "Favorite Quotes" profile section.

The `relationship_status` and `significant_other_id` fields can be requested to define the relationship status of a user. The `relationship_status` field represents one of the relationship types available when editing your Facebook profile. If the value of the `relationship_status` field is not `Single`, the user can select another Facebook user as the other member of the relationship. The UID of that user is represented in the `significant_other_id` field. The `significant_other_id` field will return a value only if both users have added the application making the request. Listing 5-9 shows the `relationship_status` and `significant_other_id` data structures.

Listing 5-9: The `relationship_status` and `significant_other_id` data structures.

```
<user>
   <uid>500033387</uid>
   <relationship_status>Married</relationship_status>
   <significant_other_id xsi:nil="true" />
</user>
```

The `religion` field returns the user-defined value associated with the "Religious Views" profile field. This field is only visible for users who have added the application.

The `sex` field is the user-defined sex that the user associates with. The available values are `Male`, `Female`, and `None`.

The `status` field returns the user-defined status message. This structure includes the `message` element that contains the user-defined message and the `time` element that represents the time (in seconds) since Epoch that the user set the status. Listing 5-10 shows an example of the `status` data structure.

Listing 5-10: Example of the `status` data structure.

```
<user>
   <uid>500025891</uid>
   <status>
     <message>at the DMV.</message>
     <time>1189793740</time>
   </status>
</user>
```

The `timezone` field is the user-set time zone of the user.

The `tv` field is the user-defined content associated with the "Favorite TV Shows" profile section.

The `wall_count` field returns the total number of Wall posts that have been written to the user's Wall.

The `work_history` field can be used to retrieve the work history for a user. Each `work_info` element contains the `location`, `company_name`, `position`, `description`, `start_date`, and `end_date` elements. The `location` element is composed of a `city`, `state`, and `country`. If the `end_date` element is empty, it is understood that the user is still with the company. Listing 5-11 shows an example of the `work_history` data structure.

Listing 5-11: Example of the `work_history` data structure.

```
<user>
   <uid>500025891</uid>
   <work_history list="true">
     <work_info>
       <location>
         <city>Sunnyvale</city>
         <state>CA</state>
         <country>United States</country>
       </location>
       <company_name>Yahoo</company_name>
       <position>Software Engineer, Delicious</position>
       <description/>
       <start_date>2006-11</start_date>
       <end_date/>
     </work_info>
   </work_history>
</user>
```

Fields that are not visible to the Facebook Platform, requesting user, or application will be returned as empty with the `xsi:null` attribute set to `"true"`.

```
<significant_other_id xsi:nil="true"/>
```

Error codes include the following:

- ❑ 1 — An unknown error has occurred.

- ❑ 2 — Service temporarily unavailable

- ❑ 4 — Application request limit reached

- ❑ 5 — Unauthorized source IP address

- ❑ 100 — One of the parameters was not specified or invalid.

- ❑ 101 — The API key submitted is not associated with any known applications.

- ❑ 102 — The session key was improperly submitted or has reached its time-out. Direct the user to the login page to obtain a fresh session key.

- ❑ 103 — The submitted `call_id` was not greater than the previously submitted `call_id` for this session.

- ❑ 104 — Incorrect signature

facebook.users.getLoggedInUser

The `facebook.users.getLoggedInUser` API method returns the UID associated with a given `session_key`. The UID returned should be cached or stored locally to avoid calling this method too much.

Following is a required parameter:

❑   `session_key` — The session key

A successful response contains the UID associated with the `session_key`.

```
<users_getLoggedInUser_respons ... >
1240077
</users_getLoggedInUser_response>
```

Error codes include the following:

❑   1 — An unknown error has occurred.

❑   2 — Service temporarily unavailable

❑   4 — Application request limit reached

❑   5 — Unauthorized source IP address

❑   101 — The API key submitted is not associated with any known applications.

❑   102 — The session key was improperly submitted or has reached its time-out. Direct the user to the login page to obtain a fresh session key.

❑   103 — The submitted `call_id` was not greater than the previously submitted `call_id` for this session.

❑   104 — Incorrect signature

facebook.users.hasAppPermission

The `facebook.users.hasAppPermission` API method is used to determine whether or not the given user has opted into one of the extended application permissions.

Following are required parameters:

❑   `session_key` — The session key for the user in question

❑   `ext_perm` — The permission in question. Must be one of `status_update`, `create_listing`, or `photo_upload`.

A successful response contains a true (1) value indicating that the user's status has been updated. A false (0) value indicates that the status was not updated. All other errors are indicated by error codes.

```
<users_hasAppPermission_response ... >
1
</users_hasAppPermission_response>
```

Error codes include the following:

- ❏ 1 — An unknown error has occurred.
- ❏ 2 — Service temporarily unavailable
- ❏ 4 — Application request limit reached
- ❏ 5 — Unauthorized source IP address
- ❏ 101 — The API key submitted is not associated with any known applications.
- ❏ 102 — The session key was improperly submitted or has reached its time-out. Direct the user to the login page to obtain a fresh session key.
- ❏ 103 — The submitted `call_id` was not greater than the previously submitted `call_id` for this session.
- ❏ 104 — Incorrect signature

facebook.users.hasAppAdded

The `facebook.users.hasAppAdded` API method is used to determine whether or not the given user has added the application to the user's Facebook account.

Following is a required parameter:

- ❏ `session_key` — The session key for the user in question

A successful response contains true (1) or false (0). All other errors are indicated by error codes.

```
<users_hasAppAdded_response ... >
1
</users_hasAppAdded_response>
```

Error codes include the following:

- ❏ 1 — An unknown error has occurred.
- ❏ 2 — Service temporarily unavailable
- ❏ 4 — Application request limit reached
- ❏ 5 — Unauthorized source IP address
- ❏ 101 — The API key submitted is not associated with any known applications.
- ❏ 102 — The session key was improperly submitted or has reached its time-out. Direct the user to the login page to obtain a fresh session key.
- ❏ 103 — The submitted `call_id` was not greater than the previously submitted `call_id` for this session.
- ❏ 104 — Incorrect signature

facebook.users.setStatus

The `facebook.users.setStatus` API method is used to set the status message for a user. This method requires the `status_update` extended application permission. The presence of that permission can be verified with the `facebook.users.hasAppPermission` API method.

Following is a required parameter:

❑   `session_key` — The session key for the user in question

Following are optional parameters:

❑   `status` — A string representing the status message to set

❑   `clear` — A Boolean value indicating that the user's status is to be cleared, as opposed to set to a message

❑   `status_includes_verb` — A Boolean value indicating that the `status` parameter includes a verb and the string `is` should not be prepended to the status when set

A successful response contains a true (`1`) or false (`0`) indicating that the request action has or has not been performed. All other errors are indicated by error codes.

```
<users_setStatus_response ... >
1
</users_setStatus_response>
```

Error codes include the following:

❑   1 — An unknown error has occurred.

❑   2 — Service temporarily unavailable

❑   4 — Application request limit reached

❑   5 — Unauthorized source IP address

❑   101 — The API key submitted is not associated with any known applications.

❑   102 — The session key was improperly submitted or has reached its time-out. Direct the user to the login page to obtain a fresh session key.

❑   103 — The submitted `call_id` was not greater than the previously submitted `call_id` for this session.

❑   104 — Incorrect signature

Events

The `events.*` methods are used to retrieve general information and the membership of Facebook events. These include `facebook.events.get` and `facebook.events.getMembers`. Currently, there is no way to create events through the Facebook API.

facebook.events.get

The `facebook.events.get` API method is used to retrieve information on one or more user-created events. The events returned can be filtered by users who are members of the event and/or by specific event IDs.

Following is a required parameter:

❏   `session_key` — The session key for the requesting user

Following are optional parameters:

❏   `uid` — A Facebook UID to filter the events by. When set, all of the events available will be filtered to those that this user is a member of.

❏   `eids` — This comma-separated list of event IDs limits the events returned to these event IDs.

❏   `start_time` — When this parameter is included and is not zero, it provides the lower bound to included events. This is an integer representing a time in UNIX time-stamp format.

❏   `end_time` — When this parameter is included and is not zero, it provides an upper bound to the included events. This is an integer representing a time in UNIX time-stamp format.

❏   `rsvp_status` — This parameter filters the events returned by RSVP status.

If the `uid` and `eids` parameters are not set, then the events returned will be those that the user associated with the `session_key` has membership in.

The results returned by this method can be retrieved using an FQL query.

```
SELECT eid, name, tagline, nid, pic, pic_big, pic_small, host, description,
       event_type, event_subtype, start_time, end_time, creator, update_time,
       location, venue
FROM event
WHERE
  eid IN (
    SELECT eid FROM event_member WHERE uid=uid AND rsvp_status=rsvp_status
  ) AND eid IN (eids)
  AND end_time >= start_time
  AND start_time < end_time
```

A successful response includes zero or more event structures. An event structure contains the `eid`, `name`, `tagline`, `nid`, `pic`, `pic_big`, `pic_small`, `host`, `description`, `event_type`, `event_subtype`, `start_time`, `end_time`, `creator`, `update_time`, `location`, and `venue` child elements.

```
<events_get_response ... >
<event>
  <eid>5316827308</eid>
  <name>An evening in Azeroth</name>
  <tagline>Because who doesn't want to PVP after launch week?</tagline>
  <nid>0</nid>
  <pic/>
  <pic_big/>
  <pic_small/>
  <host>Medivh</host>
```

```
        <description>Log in, Slay some Horde and Hang out</description>
        <event_type>Party</event_type>
        <event_subtype>LAN Party</event_subtype>
        <start_time>1189832400</start_time>
        <end_time>1189843200</end_time>
        <creator>500025891</creator>
        <update_time>1189723648</update_time>
        <location>Iron Forge</location>
        <venue>
          <street/>
          <city/>
          <state/>
          <country/>
        </venue>
      </event>
    </events_get_response>
```

The eid element is the unique event ID set on event creation. The start_time, end_time, and update_time elements are date/time values represented in seconds since Epoch. The venue element is a complex data structure composed of the street, city, state, and country child elements. The events returned by this API method are considered public; secret events cannot be returned. The nid element is set to 0 on global events.

The pic_* elements follow the following size rules:

❑   pic — 100 pixels (width) by 300 pixels (height)

❑   pic_big — 200 pixels by 600 pixels.

❑   pic_small — 50 pixels by 150 pixels.

If the user who created the event is not visible to the Facebook Platform, the application, or requesting user associated with the session_key parameter, the creator element is empty and will contain the xsi:null attribute set to "true".

```
    <creator xsi:nil="true"/>
```

Error codes include the following:

❑   1 — An unknown error has occurred.

❑   2 — Service temporarily unavailable

❑   4 — Application request limit reached

❑   5 — Unauthorized source IP address

❑   101 — The API key submitted is not associated with any known applications.

❑   102 — The session key was improperly submitted or has reached its time-out. Direct the user to the login page to obtain a fresh session key.

❑   103 — The submitted call_id was not greater than the previously submitted call_id for this session.

❑   104 — Incorrect signature

facebook.events.getMembers

The `facebook.events.getMembers` API method returns several lists of users who are considered members of an event.

Following are required parameters:

❑   `session_key` — The session key for the requesting user

❑   `eid` — The event ID to obtain the membership of

The results returned by this method can be retrieved using an FQL query.

```
SELECT uid, eid, rsvp_status FROM event_member WHERE eid=eid
```

A successful response includes several lists of `uid` elements grouped by membership type. These groups are represented through the `attending`, `unsure`, `declined`, and `not_replied` child elements.

```
<events_getMembers_response ... >
  <attending list="true">
    <uid>500025891</uid>
  </attending>
  <unsure list="true"/>
  <declined list="true"/>
  <not_replied list="true">
    <uid>4810273</uid>
    <uid>6851120</uid>
    <uid>12450363</uid>
    <uid>22702059</uid>
    <uid>509160944</uid>
    <uid>516463201</uid>
    <uid>1559580004</uid>
  </not_replied>
</events_getMembers_response>
```

This API method will not return the UIDs of users who have not added the application.

Error codes include the following:

❑   1 — An unknown error has occurred.

❑   2 — Service temporarily unavailable

❑   4 — Application request limit reached

❑   5 — Unauthorized source IP address

❑   101 — The API key submitted is not associated with any known applications.

❑   102 — The session key was improperly submitted or has reached its time-out. Direct the user to the login page to obtain a fresh session key.

❑   103 — The submitted `call_id` was not greater than the previously submitted `call_id` for this session.

❑   104 — Incorrect signature

Groups

The groups.* methods are used to retrieve general and membership information of Facebook groups. These include facebook.groups.get and facebook.groups.getMembers. These methods have many elements in common with the Events method group.

facebook.groups.get

The facebook.groups.get API method can be called to retrieve information about the user-created groups within Facebook.

Following is a required parameter:

❑   session_key — The session key for the requesting user

Following are optional parameters:

❑   uid — A UID used to filter the groups returned. When this parameter is set, the groups returned must have this user as a member.

❑   gids — A comma-separated list of group IDs to filter the results by

If no uid or gids parameters are set, the API method will return groups as though the uid parameter is set to the user associated with the session_key.

The results returned by this method can be retrieved using an FQL query.

```
SELECT gid, name, nid, description, group_type, group_subtype, recent_news,
       pic, pic_big, pic_small, creator, update_time, office, website, venue
FROM group
WHERE
   gid IN (SELECT gid FROM group_member WHERE uid=uid)
   AND gid IN (gids)
```

A successful response includes zero or more group data structures. The group data structure is defined by the gid, name, nid, description, group_type, group_subtype, recent_news, pic, pic_big, pic_small, creator, update_time, office, website, and venue elements. The venue is composed of the street, city, state, and country child elements.

```
<groups_get_response ... >
  <group>
    <gid>17831253704</gid>
    <name>Wrox : Programmer to Programmer</name>
    <nid>0</nid>
    <description>Wrox Press, established in 1992 ... </description>
    <group_type>Internet &amp; Technology</group_type>
    <group_subtype>Languages &amp; Formats</group_subtype>
    <recent_news>Wrox is now providing news ... </recent_news>
    <pic>http://prof...359/22/s17831253704_7117.jpg</pic>
    <pic_big>http://prof...359/22/n17831253704_7117.jpg</pic_big>
    <pic_small>http://prof...359/22/t17831253704_7117.jpg</pic_small>
```

(continued)

(continued)

```
      <creator>677101506</creator>
      <update_time>1189643054</update_time>
      <office/>
      <website>http://www.wrox.com/</website>
      <venue>
        <street>10475 Crosspoint Blvd</street>
        <city>Indianapolis</city>
        <state>IN</state>
        <country>United States</country>
      </venue>
    </group>
  </groups_get_response>
```

All of the groups returned by this API method should be considered public and not set as secret by the creator.

The `pic_*` elements follow the following size rules:

❑ `pic` — 100 pixels (width) by 300 pixels (height)

❑ `pic_big` — 200 pixels by 600 pixels

❑ `pic_small` — 50 pixels by 150 pixels

If the user that created the group is not visible to the Facebook Platform, the application, or requesting user associated with the `session_key` parameter, the `creator` element is empty and will contain the `xsi:null` attribute set to `"true"`.

```
  <creator xsi:nil="true"/>
```

Error codes include the following:

❑ 1 — An unknown error has occurred.

❑ 2 — Service temporarily unavailable

❑ 4 — Application request limit reached

❑ 5 — Unauthorized source IP address

❑ 101 — The API key submitted is not associated with any known applications.

❑ 102 — The session key was improperly submitted or has reached its time-out. Direct the user to the login page to obtain a fresh session key.

❑ 103 — The submitted `call_id` was not greater than the previously submitted `call_id` for this session.

❑ 104 — Incorrect signature

facebook.groups.getMembers

The `facebook.groups.getMembers` API method returns several lists of users who are considered members of a group.

Following are required parameters:

❑ `session_key` — The session key of the requesting user

❑ `gid` — The group ID to obtain the membership of

The results returned by this method can be retrieved using an FQL query.

```
SELECT uid, gid, positions FROM group_member WHERE gid=gid
```

A successful response will include zero or more `uid` elements grouped by their membership type. The membership types are represented by the `members`, `admins`, `officers`, and `not_replied` elements.

```
<groups_getMembers_response ... >
  <members list="true">
    <uid>5117310</uid>
    <uid>24301449</uid>
    <uid>64800210</uid>
    <!-- ... -->
  </members>
  <admins list="true">
    <uid>660558037</uid>
    <uid>677101506</uid>
    <uid>680415718</uid>
  </admins>
  <officers list="true">
    <uid>660558037</uid>
    <uid>677101506</uid>
    <uid>680415718</uid>
  </officers>
  <not_replied list="true"/>
</groups_getMembers_response>
```

This API method will not return the UIDs of users who have not added the application.

Error codes include the following:

❑ 1 — An unknown error has occurred.

❑ 2 — Service temporarily unavailable

❑ 4 — Application request limit reached

❑ 5 — Unauthorized source IP address

❑ 101 — The API key submitted is not associated with any known applications.

❑ 102 — The session key was improperly submitted or has reached its time-out. Direct the user to the login page to obtain a fresh session key.

❏ 103 — The submitted `call_id` was not greater than the previously submitted `call_id` for this session.

❏ 104 — Incorrect signature

Photos

The `photos.*` methods are used to create, manipulate, and retrieve photos within Facebook. These include `facebook.photos.upload`, `facebook.photos.createAlbum`, `facebook.photos.get`, `facebook.photos.getAlbums`, `facebook.photos.addtag`, and `facebook.photos.getTags`.

facebook.photos.upload

The `facebook.photos.upload` API method is used by applications to upload photos to a photo album on behalf of a user. The uploaded photo is held for approval, wherein the user must explicitly approve a photo before it can be seen by other users throughout Facebook. Photos that are uploaded through this API method belong to the user.

Following are required parameters:

❏ `session_key` — The session key of the requesting user

❏ `data` — The raw image data

Following are optional parameters:

❏ `aid` — The album ID of the destination album. If this value is not specified, the photo will be added to a default album for the application. If the default album does not exist, it will be created.

❏ `caption` — An optional caption

Regular albums have a size limit of 60 photos. Application albums have a size limit of 1,000 photos.

This API method has special requirements when submitting the request. The request *must* be sent as a MIME multipart message through an HTTP POST request. Each method parameter must be specified as a separate chunk of form data.

A successful response includes the `pid`, `aid`, `owner`, `src`, `src_big`, `src_small`, `link`, and `caption` elements. The `pid` element is the unique internal ID of the uploaded photo. This should not be confused with the `pid` query string parameter when viewing photos in the web browser.

```
<photos_upload_response ... >
    <pid>940915697041656</pid>
    <aid>940915667462717</aid>
    <owner>219074</owner>
    <src>http://ip002.face...74/s219074_31637752_5455.jpg</src>
    <src_big>http://ip002.face...74/n219074_31637752_5455.jpg</src_big>
    <src_small>http://ip002.face...74/t219074_31637752_5455.jpg</src_small>
    <link>http://www.facebook.com/photo.php?pid=31637752&id=219074</link>
    <caption>Under the sunset</caption>
</photos_upload_response>
```

Error codes include the following:

- ❑ 1 — An unknown error has occurred.
- ❑ 2 — Service temporarily unavailable
- ❑ 4 — Application request limit reached
- ❑ 5 — Unauthorized source IP address
- ❑ 101 — The API key submitted is not associated with any known applications.
- ❑ 102 — The session key was improperly submitted or has reached its time-out. Direct the user to the login page to obtain a fresh session key.
- ❑ 103 — The submitted `call_id` was not greater than the previously submitted `call_id` for this session.
- ❑ 104 — Incorrect signature
- ❑ 120 — Invalid album ID
- ❑ 321 — Album is full.
- ❑ 324 — Missing or invalid image file
- ❑ 325 — Too many unapproved photos pending

facebook.photos.createAlbum

The `facebook.photos.createAlbum` API method creates a named album for a user on behalf of that user by the application.

Following are required parameters:

- ❑ `session_key` — The session key of the requesting user
- ❑ `name` — The album name

Following are optional parameters:

- ❑ `location` — The location associated with this album
- ❑ `description` — The user-defined description of the album

A successful response includes the `aid`, `cover_pid`, `owner`, `name`, `created`, `modified`, `description`, `location`, `link`, and `size` elements that define the album. The `owner` element should always be the user associated with the `session_key` parameter. The `cover_pid` will always be set to `0` upon album creation.

Developers should note that the `aid` element returned is the internal album ID used to identify the album within the Facebook Platform. This is not the same `aid` parameter that appears in the query string used to view the album in the browser.

```
<photos_createAlbum_response ...>
    <aid>34595963571485</aid>
    <cover_pid>0</cover_pid>
    <owner>8055</owner>
    <name>Films you will never see</name>
    <created>1132553109</created>
    <modified>1132553363</modified>
    <description>No I will not make out with you</description>
    <location>York, PA</location>
    <link>http://www.facebook.com/album.php?aid=2002205&id=8055</link>
    <size>0</size>
</photos_createAlbum_response>
```

Error codes include the following:

- ❑ 1 — An unknown error has occurred.

- ❑ 2 — Service temporarily unavailable

- ❑ 4 — Application request limit reached

- ❑ 5 — Unauthorized source IP address

- ❑ 101 — The API key submitted is not associated with any known applications.

- ❑ 102 — The session key was improperly submitted or has reached its time-out. Direct the user to the login page to obtain a fresh session key.

- ❑ 103 — The submitted call_id was not greater than the previously submitted call_id for this session.

- ❑ 104 — Incorrect signature

facebook.photos.get

The facebook.photos.get API method is used to return all of the visible photos as defined by the filters set in the method parameters.

Following is a required parameter:

- ❑ session_key — The session key of the requesting user

At least one of the following parameters must be supplied:

- ❑ subj_id — Limits the photos returned to those who have this user in them.

- ❑ aid — Limits photos to those in this album.

- ❑ pid — Limits photos to this photo ID.

The results returned by this method can be retrieved using an FQL query.

```
SELECT pid, aid, owner, src, src_big, src_small, link, caption, created
FROM photo
WHERE
  pid IN (SELECT pid FROM photo_tag WHERE subject=subj_id)
  AND aid=aid
  AND pid IN (pids)
```

A successful response includes zero or more photo data structures containing the information on the photos available. A photo data structure contains the pid, aid, owner, src, src_big, src_small, link, caption, and created elements.

```
<photos_get_response ... >
  <photo>
    <pid>2147594848998313850</pid>
    <aid>2147594848998262913</aid>
    <owner>500025891</owner>
    <src>http://photos.../s500025891_53114_350.jpg</src>
    <src_big>http://photos.../n500025891_53114_350.jpg</src_big>
    <src_small>http://photos.../t500025891_53114_350.jpg</src_small>
    <link>http://www.facebook.com/photo.php?pid=53114&amp;id=500025891</link>
    <caption>Christmas 2006</caption>
    <created>1177514360</created>
  </photo>
  <!-- ... -->
</photos_get_response>
```

If the user who created the photo is not visible to the Facebook Platform, the application, or requesting user associated with the session_key parameter, the owner element is empty and will contain the xsi:null attribute set to "true".

```
<owner xsi:nil="true"/>
```

Error codes include the following:

- ❑ 1 — An unknown error has occurred.

- ❑ 2 — Service temporarily unavailable

- ❑ 4 — Application request limit reached

- ❑ 5 — Unauthorized source IP address

- ❑ 101 — The API key submitted is not associated with any known applications.

- ❑ 102 — The session key was improperly submitted or has reached its time-out. Direct the user to the login page to obtain a fresh session key.

- ❑ 103 — The submitted call_id was not greater than the previously submitted call_id for this session.

- ❑ 104 — Incorrect signature

facebook.photos.getAlbums

The `facebook.photos.getAlbums` method returns all of the photo albums that are included in the requesting user's filters.

Following is a required parameter:

❏   `session_key` — The session key of the requesting user

At least one of the following parameters must be supplied.

❏   `uid` — Limit the albums returned to those created by this user.

❏   `pid` — Limit albums to those that are containers to the photos in this comma-separated list of photo IDs.

The results returned by this method can be retrieved using an FQL query.

```
SELECT aid, cover_pid, owner, name, created, modified, description, location
FROM album
WHERE
  owner = uid
  AND aid IN (aids)
```

A successful response contains zero or more album data structures composed of the `aid`, `cover_pid`, `owner`, `name`, `created`, `modified`, `description`, `location`, `link`, and `size` child elements.

```
<photos_getAlbums_response ... >
  <album>
    <aid>2147594848998260741</aid>
    <cover_pid>2147594848998260805</cover_pid>
    <owner>500025891</owner>
    <name>Santa Cruz</name>
    <created>1151815857</created>
    <modified>1151816736</modified>
    <description/>
    <location>Santa Cruz, CA</location>
    <link>http://www.facebook.com/album.php?aid=5&amp;id=500025891</link>
    <size>14</size>
  </album>
</photos_getAlbums_response>
```

Error codes include the following:

❏   1 — An unknown error has occurred.

❏   2 — Service temporarily unavailable

❏   4 — Application request limit reached

❏   5 — Unauthorized source IP address

❏   101 — The API key submitted is not associated with any known applications.

❏ 102 — The session key was improperly submitted or has reached its time-out. Direct the user to the login page to obtain a fresh session key.

❏ 103 — The submitted `call_id` was not greater than the previously submitted `call_id` for this session.

❏ 104 — Incorrect signature

facebook.photos.addtag

The `facebook.photos.addTag` API method is called to "tag" one or more users in a photo on behalf of a user. Photo tags on Facebook are not the traditional tags used by other web sites or services. Facebook considers a tag as a reference to a user.

Following are required parameters:

❏ `session_key` — The session key of the requesting user setting the tag

❏ `pid` — The ID of the photo to tag

❏ `x` — The horizontal position of the tag as a percentage from 0 to 100 from the left

❏ `y` — The vertical position of the tag as a percentage from 0 to 100 from the top

One of the following parameters must be included:

❏ `tag_uid` — The UID of the Facebook user in the photo

❏ `tag_text` — Free-form text describing the person being identified in the photo. This parameter is ignored if the `tag_uid` parameter is set.

Following is an optional parameter:

❏ `tags` — A JSON-serialized list of tags to be added to the photo

A successful response is composed of a true (0) value indicating that the tag(s) was applied to the photo.

```
<photos_addTag_response ... >
1
</photos_addTag_response>
```

Error codes include the following:

❏ 1 — An unknown error has occurred.

❏ 2 — Service temporarily unavailable

❏ 4 — Application request limit reached

❏ 5 — Unauthorized source IP address

❏ 101 — The API key submitted is not associated with any known applications.

❏ 102 — The session key was improperly submitted or has reached its time-out. Direct the user to the login page to obtain a fresh session key.

❑ 103 — The submitted `call_id` was not greater than the previously submitted `call_id` for this session.

❑ 104 — Incorrect signature

facebook.photos.getTags

The `facebook.photos.getTags` API method returns the tags associated with a photo. This method will only return the tags that directly reference a Facebook user. Free-text tags are not returned.

Following are required parameters:

❑ `session_key` — The session key of the requesting user

❑ `pid` — The photo to fetch the tags of

The results returned by this method can be retrieved using an FQL query.

```
SELECT pid, subject, xcoord, ycoord FROM photo_tag WHERE pid IN (pids)
```

A successful response includes zero or more `photo_tag` data structures. A `photo_tag` is composed of the `pid`, `subject`, `xcoord`, and `ycoord` elements.

```
<photos_getTags_response ... >
    <photo_tag>
      <pid>34995991612795</pid>
      <subject>1240078</subject>
      <xcoord>51.4901</xcoord>
      <ycoord>23.6203</ycoord>
    </photo_tag>
</photos_getTags_response>
```

This method will not return any `photo_tag` data structures where the creator of the tag has made the tag hidden from the Facebook Platform.

Error codes include the following:

❑ 1 — An unknown error has occurred.

❑ 2 — Service temporarily unavailable

❑ 4 — Application request limit reached

❑ 5 — Unauthorized source IP address

❑ 101 — The API key submitted is not associated with any known applications.

❑ 102 — The session key was improperly submitted or has reached its time-out. Direct the user to the login page to obtain a fresh session key.

❑ 103 — The submitted `call_id` was not greater than the previously submitted `call_id` for this session.

❑ 104 — Incorrect signature

FBML

These methods are used to assist the FBML rendering engine by notifying Facebook that content needs to be refreshed. These include `facebook.fbml.refreshimgsrc`, `facebook.fbml.refreshRefUrl`, and `facebook.fbml.setrefhandle`.

facebook.fbml.refreshimgsrc

The `facebook.fbml.refreshImgSrc` API method is used to notify the Facebook Platform that an image should be invalidated and fetched again. This API method applies to images used on non-Canvas pages (the News Feed, a notification, the user profile, etc.).

Following are required parameters:

❑   `session_key` — The session key of the requesting user

❑   `url` — The absolute URL of the image to cache

A successful response includes a true (1) value indicating that the Facebook Platform has acknowledged the request.

```
<fbml_refreshImgSrc_response ... >
1
</fbml_refreshImgSrc_response>
```

Error codes include the following:

❑   1 — An unknown error has occurred.

❑   2 — Service temporarily unavailable

❑   4 — Application request limit reached

❑   5 — Unauthorized source IP address

❑   101 — The API key submitted is not associated with any known applications.

❑   102 — The session key was improperly submitted or has reached its time-out. Direct the user to the login page to obtain a fresh session key.

❑   103 — The submitted `call_id` was not greater than the previously submitted `call_id` for this session.

❑   104 — Incorrect signature

facebook.fbml.refreshRefUrl

The `facebook.fbml.refreshRefUrl` API method is used to notify the Facebook Platform that the content of a URL used in an `fb:ref` FBML entity has changed.

Following are required parameters:

❑   `session_key` — The session key of the requesting user

❑   `url` — The absolute URL of the image to cache

A successful response includes a true (1) value indicating that the Facebook Platform has acknowledged the request.

```
<fbml_refreshRefUrl_response ... >
1
</fbml_refreshRefUrl_response>
```

Error codes include the following:

- ❑ 1 — An unknown error has occurred.

- ❑ 2 — Service temporarily unavailable

- ❑ 4 — Application request limit reached

- ❑ 5 — Unauthorized source IP address

- ❑ 101 — The API key submitted is not associated with any known applications.

- ❑ 102 — The session key was improperly submitted or has reached its time-out. Direct the user to the login page to obtain a fresh session key.

- ❑ 103 — The submitted `call_id` was not greater than the previously submitted `call_id` for this session.

- ❑ 104 — Incorrect signature

facebook.fbml.setrefhandle

The `facebook.fbml.setRefHandle` API method is used to set the FBML content for a given key used by the `fb:ref` FBML entity that is associated with the requesting application.

Facebook encourages developers to use the `fb:ref` FBML entity when showing the same content for many different users. This practice reduces the overall load generated by the application through making `facebook.profile.setFBML` API method requests.

Following are required parameters:

- ❑ `session_key` — The session key of the requesting user

- ❑ `handle` — The handle key known to Facebook

- ❑ `fbml` — The FBML rendered by the `fb:ref` FBML entity when using the given handle

A successful response includes a true (1) value indicating that the Facebook Platform has acknowledged the request.

```
<fbml_setRefHandle_response ... >
1
</fbml_setRefHandle_response>
```

Error codes include the following:

- ❏ 1 — An unknown error has occurred.
- ❏ 2 — Service temporarily unavailable
- ❏ 4 — Application request limit reached
- ❏ 5 — Unauthorized source IP address
- ❏ 101 — The API key submitted is not associated with any known applications.
- ❏ 102 — The session key was improperly submitted or has reached its time-out. Direct the user to the login page to obtain a fresh session key.
- ❏ 103 — The submitted `call_id` was not greater than the previously submitted `call_id` for this session.
- ❏ 104 — Incorrect signature

Marketplace

These methods allow developers to interact and manipulate the Facebook Marketplace, allowing deep integration into Facebook. These include `facebook.marketplace.createListing`, `facebook.marketplace.getCategories`, `facebook.marketplace.getSubCategories`, `facebook.marketplace.getListings`, `facebook.marketplace.removeListing`, and `facebook.marketplace.search`.

facebook.marketplace.createListing

The `facebook.marketplace.createListing` API method is used to create and update Facebook Marketplace listings on behalf of a user. Additionally, listings can only be created for users who have set the `create_listing` extended application permission.

Following is a required parameter:

- ❏ `session_key` — The session key of the requesting user. This method can only create or update listings for the user associated with this session key.

Following are optional parameters:

- ❏ `listing_id` — The ID of the listing being modified. If this parameter is not included with the request, a new listing is created.
- ❏ `show_on_profile` — This Boolean parameter directs the Facebook Platform to display the listing on the user's profile.
- ❏ `listing_attrs` — A JSON-serialized string of attributes that define the listing.

The following Marketplace Listing attributes should be included with every request:

- ❏ `category`
- ❏ `subcategory`
- ❏ `title`
- ❏ `description`

In addition to these attributes, there are additional attributes that should be included with each request based on the category and subcategory. The following is a list of categories that require special attributes.

> This is not the definitive list of categories and subcategories available when using the Facebook Marketplace API methods. That list can be acquired from the `facebook.marketplace.getCategories` and `facebook.marketplace` `.getSubCategories` API methods.

- ❏ FORSALE
    - ❏ GENERAL — `price`
    - ❏ BOOKS — `price, isbn, condition`
    - ❏ TICKETS — `price`
    - ❏ ELECTROICS — `price, condition`
    - ❏ FURNITURE — `price, condition`
    - ❏ AUTOS — `price, condition`
- ❏ HOUSING
    - ❏ GENERAL — `num_beds, num_baths, dogs, cats, smoking, square_footage, street, crossstreet, postal`
    - ❏ RENTALS — `num_beds, num_baths, dogs, cats, smoking, square_footage, street, crossstreet, postal, rent`
    - ❏ SUBLETS — `num_beds, num_baths, dogs, cats, smoking, square_footage, street, crossstreet, postal, rent`
    - ❏ REALESTATE — `num_beds, num_baths, dogs, cats, smoking, square_footage, street, crossstreet, postal, price`
- ❏ JOBS — `pay, full, intern, summer, nonprofit, pay_type`
- ❏ FORSALE_WANTED
    - ❏ BOOKS_WANTED — `condition, isbn`
    - ❏ FURNITURE_WANTED — `condition`
    - ❏ AUTOS_WANTED — `condition`

- ❏ ELECTRONICS_WANTED — `condition`

- ❏ GENERAL_WANTED — `num_beds`, `num_baths`, `dogs`, `cats`, `smoking`, `square_footage`, `street`, `crossstreet`, `postal`

- ❏ SUBLETS_WANTED — `num_beds`, `num_baths`, `dogs`, `cats`, `smoking`, `square_footage`, `street`, `crossstreet`, `postal`

- ❏ REALESTATE_WANTED — `num_beds`, `num_baths`, `dogs`, `cats`, `smoking`, `square_footage`, `street`, `crossstreet`, `postal`

When including the `condition` attribute, its value can only be ANY, NEW, or USED.

A successful response includes the ID of the listing that was created or modified. If the `listing_id` parameter was included in the API request, the return value should match.

```
<marketplace_createListing_response ... >
7444312
</marketplace_createListing_response>
```

Error codes include the following:

- ❏ 1 — An unknown error occurred. Please resubmit the request.

- ❏ 2 — The service is not available at this time.

- ❏ 4 — The application has reached the maximum number of requests allowed. More requests are allowed once the time window has completed.

- ❏ 5 — The request came from a remote address not allowed by this application.

- ❏ 100 — One of the parameters specified was missing or invalid.

- ❏ 101 — The API key submitted is not associated with any known application.

- ❏ 102 — The session key was improperly submitted or has reached its time-out. Direct the user to log in again to obtain another key.

- ❏ 103 — The submitted `call_id` was not greater than the previous `call_id` for this session.

- ❏ 104 — Incorrect signature

- ❏ 140 — Invalid category

- ❏ 141 — Invalid subcategory

- ❏ 142 — Invalid title

- ❏ 143 — Invalid description

- ❏ 280 — The extended permission `create_listing` has not been granted to this application.

facebook.marketplace.getCategories

The `facebook.marketplace.getCategories` API method can be used to return all of the available Facebook Marketplace categories.

Following is a required parameter:

❑   `session_key` — The session key of the requesting user

A successful response includes an XML structure of the available categories.

```
<marketplace_getCategories_response ... list="true">
  <marketplace_category>FORSALE</marketplace_category>
  <marketplace_category>HOUSING</marketplace_category>
  <marketplace_category>JOBS</marketplace_category>
  ...
</marketplace_getCategories_response>
```

Error codes include the following:

❑   1 — An unknown error has occurred.

❑   2 — Service temporarily unavailable

❑   4 — Application request limit reached

❑   5 — Unauthorized source IP address

❑   100 — One of the parameters was missing or invalid.

❑   101 — The API key submitted is not associated with any known applications.

❑   102 — The session key was improperly submitted or has reached its time-out. Direct the user to the login page to obtain a fresh session key.

❑   103 — The submitted `call_id` was not greater than the previously submitted `call_id` for this session.

❑   104 — Incorrect signature

facebook.marketplace.getSubCategories

The `facebook.marketplace.getCategories` API method can be used to return all of the available Facebook Marketplace categories.

Following are required parameters:

❑   `session_key` — The session key of the requesting user

❑   `category` — The name of the category to retrieve the subcategories of

A successful response includes an XML structure of the available categories.

```
<marketplace_getSubCategories_response ... list="true">
  <marketplace_category>AUTOS</marketplace_category>
  <marketplace_category>BOOKS</marketplace_category>
  <marketplace_category>FURNITURE</marketplace_category>
  ...
</marketplace_getSubCategories_response>
```

Error codes include the following:

❏ 1 — An unknown error has occurred.

❏ 2 — Service temporarily unavailable

❏ 4 — Application request limit reached

❏ 5 — Unauthorized source IP address

❏ 100 — One of the parameters was missing or invalid.

❏ 101 — The API key submitted is not associated with any known applications.

❏ 102 — The session key was improperly submitted or has reached its time-out. Direct the user to the login page to obtain a fresh session key.

❏ 103 — The submitted `call_id` was not greater than the previously submitted `call_id` for this session.

❏ 104 — Incorrect signature

facebook.marketplace.getListings

The `facebook.marketplace.getListings` API method is used to retrieve one or more Facebook Marketplace listings filtered by user or specific listing IDs.

Following is a required parameter:

❏ `session_key` — The session key of the requesting user

At least one of the following parameters must be included:

❏ `listing_ids` — A comma-separated list of Facebook Marketplace listing IDs

❏ `uids` — A comma-separated list of Facebook user IDs corresponding to the creators of those listings

A successful response includes an XML structure of matching Facebook Marketplace listings.

```
<marketplace_getListings_response ... list="true">
  <listing>
    <listing_id>31603160</listing_id>

<url>http://www.facebook.com/marketplace/listing.php?classified_id=31603160</url>
    <title>Brotherly Love, Relief, and Truth</title>
```

(continued)

(continued)

```
    <description>What more could you want?</description>
    <poster>500025891</poster>
    <update_time>1200727571</update_time>
    <category>FREE</category>
    <subcategory>GENERAL</subcategory>
    <image_urls list="true"/>
  </listing>
</marketplace_getListings_response>
```

This API method is very similar to evaluating a specially crafted FQL query:

```
SELECT listing_id, url , title, description, price, poster, update_time, category,
subcategory, image_urls, condition, isbn,num_beds,num_baths,dogs,cats, smoking,
square_footage, street, crossstreet, postal, rent, pay, full,intern, summer,
nonprofit, pay_type
FROM listings
WHERE poster in (uids) AND listing_id in (listing_ids)SELECT uid1, uid2 FROM friend
WHERE uid1 = <x> AND uid2 = <y>
```

Error codes include the following:

- ❑ 1 — An unknown error has occurred.

- ❑ 2 — Service temporarily unavailable

- ❑ 4 — Application request limit reached

- ❑ 5 — Unauthorized source IP address

- ❑ 100 — One of the parameters was missing or invalid.

- ❑ 101 — The API key submitted is not associated with any known applications.

- ❑ 102 — The session key was improperly submitted or has reached its time-out. Direct the user to the login page to obtain a fresh session key.

- ❑ 103 — The submitted `call_id` was not greater than the previously submitted `call_id` for this session.

- ❑ 104 — Incorrect signature

facebook.marketplace.removeListing

The `facebook.marketplace.removeListing` API method is used to delete a Facebook Marketplace listing. Additionally, listings can only be deleted for users who have set the `create_listing` extended application permission.

Following is a required parameter:

- ❑ `session_key` — The session key of the requesting user. This method can only remove listings for the user associated with this session key.

Following is an optional parameter:

❑   `status` — A string indicating the reason why the listing was removed. Possible values are `SUCCESS`, 'DEFAULT, and `NOT_SUCCESS`.

A successful response is indicated by a true (1) value. All other responses are expressed as an error.

```
<marketplace_removeListing_response ...>
1
</marketplace_removeListing_response>
```

Error codes include the following:

❑   1 — An unknown error has occurred.

❑   2 — Service temporarily unavailable

❑   4 — Application request limit reached

❑   5 — Unauthorized source IP address

❑   100 — One of the parameters was missing or invalid.

❑   101 — The API key submitted is not associated with any known applications.

❑   102 — The session key was improperly submitted or has reached its time-out. Direct the user to the login page to obtain a fresh session key.

❑   103 — The submitted `call_id` was not greater than the previously submitted `call_id` for this session.

❑   104 — Incorrect signature

❑   210 — The logged-in user does not have permission to edit the specified listing.

❑   280 — The application does not have the extended permission `create_listing`.

facebook.marketplace.search

The `facebook.marketplace.search` API method allows Facebook applications to find listings in the Facebook Marketplace by category, subcategory, or search term.

Following is a required parameter:

❑   `session_key` — The session key of the requesting user

At least one of the following parameters must be included:

❑   `category` — A Facebook Marketplace listing category to filter listings by

❑   `subcategory` — A Facebook Marketplace listing subcategory to filter listings by. The `category` parameter must be included in the API request when including this parameter.

❑   `query` — A query string processed by the Facebook Platform to retrieve Facebook Marketplace listings.

A successful response is indicated by zero or more listings matching the search criteria. Developers should note that an empty result set is not an error. The listings returned may span more than one category, resulting in cases in which different listings will have different XML structures, depending on any additional listing attributes associated with the category of those listings.

```
<marketplace_removeListing_response ...>
  <listing />
  <listing />
  ...
</marketplace_removeListing_response>
```

Error codes include the following:

- 1 — An unknown error has occurred.
- 2 — Service temporarily unavailable
- 4 — Application request limit reached
- 5 — Unauthorized source IP address
- 100 — One of the parameters was missing or invalid.
- 101 — The API key submitted is not associated with any known applications.
- 102 — The session key was improperly submitted or has reached its time-out. Direct the user to the login page to obtain a fresh session key.
- 103 — The submitted `call_id` was not greater than the previously submitted `call_id` for this session.
- 104 — Incorrect signature

Summary

The Facebook API has proven to be useful to web developers as well as Desktop Application developers. Through the Facebook API, developers can build high-value features quickly and easily. The plain and candid responses to the API methods available are indicative of the philosophy that APIs should always be useful first, and extensive second.

If you step back, you will notice that the majority of the API methods have little to no effect on actual user data. The closest any API method comes is the capability to create photos and photo albums for users, but in that case, the user still maintains full control over the privacy of those photos. Facebook has made it very clear that the applications developed and used through the Facebook Platform should be self-contained. As an application developer, you have access to a vast amount of user data, but you have a limited effect on the users themselves.

Throughout this chapter, there have been small examples of the usefulness of FQL, and you have seen how, in many ways, it can replace several of the Facebook API methods completely. Chapter 6 explores the FQL in more detail.

6

Data Mining with FQL

The Facebook Query Language (FQL) is a generic SQL-like query language used to retrieve data from the Facebook Platform. In many ways, FQL is one of the core components that other components (such as the Facebook API) build on top of. As seen in Chapter 5, there are several methods that can be made obsolete by crafting FQL queries.

The emphasis of Chapter 5 was on the Facebook API and its role in the Facebook Platform. The API methods available were grouped by functionality with the method parameters, and the discussion described the data structures returned.

This chapter continues where Chapter 5 left off with the FQL. This chapter discusses the tables and fields that are available, as well as the common data structures returned by those fields. Additionally, there are several advanced features provided in the FQL processor that allow developers to interact with the data guarded by the Facebook Platform. This chapter also discusses complex data structures within FQL responses, anonymous fields, and complex subqueries.

FQL Requests

An FQL query is exercised through the `facebook.fql.query` API method. Although this method was discussed in Chapter 5, the following provides a brief recap:

❑ FQL queries are executed by sending an HTTP POST request to the Facebook Platform via the `facebook.fql.query` API method. The two parameters involved are `session_key` and `query`. The `session_key` parameter represents the requesting user and is used to control the user's access to data. The `query` parameter is the FQL query that you want to execute.

❑ The response will contain either a root `error_response` or `fql_query_response` element indicating the success or failure of the query.

> It is important to remember that the `fql_query_response` element can be empty
> without the request failing. This indicates that the query was executed, but no
> results are available under the query conditions.

FQL Responses

Once a query is crafted and sent to the Facebook Platform, the query response must be parsed and
understood by the client making the request. As defined in Chapter 5, the `facebook.fql.query` request
returns a root `fql_query_response` element containing zero or more data structures.

XML

Extensible Markup Language (XML) is recognized as the most commonly used response format. In an
FQL query, the response format is defined by the table and fields request. Within the root `fql_query_`
`response` element, there will be zero or more table elements with child elements of the fields requested.

Anonymous fields are the special case here. All anonymous field values are contained in `anon` elements.
Developers should make careful note that the fields returned will be in the same order that they were
requested in. Consider the following example:

```
SELECT "hello", "world" FROM user where uid = 500025891
```

This will return the following XML:

```
<fql_query_response ... >
  <user>
    <anon>hello</anon>
    <anon>world</anon>
  </user>
</fql_query_response>
```

When requesting data from the `user` table, fields are enclosed in a `user` element. The following query
returns the names of a user's friends that are in a specified group:

```
SELECT name FROM user WHERE uid IN (
  SELECT uid FROM group_member WHERE gid = 2204910717)
AND uid IN (
  SELECT uid2 FROM friend WHERE uid1 = 500025891
)
```

JSON

Developers using JavaScript Object Notation (JSON) as the response type for FQL queries benefit from a
very slim and compact response body. In many ways, JSON is ideal for high-bandwidth Facebook
applications. JSON parsing has become very fast, and in many languages, breaks down to very simple
structures that can be handled easily.

> **More information on JSON and the parsers available can be found at**
> www.json.org/.

The Facebook Platform returns JSON structures as simple lists and hashes. The response is composed of a list that can contain zero or more hashes representing the key/value pairs of the fields requested. Consider the following FQL statement:

```
SELECT name FROM group WHERE gid = 17831253704
```

Following is the JSON response for that statement:

```
[{"name":"Wrox : Programmer to Programmer"}]
```

Complex data structures such as the affiliations field of the user table are also represented in the list and hash format. Consider the following FQL query:

```
SELECT name, current_location FROM user WHERE uid = 500025891
```

Following is the response:

```
[
{"current_location":
  {"city":"Mountain View",
    "state":"CA",
    "country":"United States",
    "zip":"94041"}
  , "name":"Nick Gerakines"}
]
```

It is important to note that the order of the key/value pairs in the response is not the same order that the fields were requested in.

The big caveat with JSON requests centers on anonymous fields and how they are represented. Because of the simple key/value pair structure returned for each item in the response, only one anonymous field is returned. Consider the following FQL statement:

```
SELECT name, "hello", "world", uid FROM user where uid = 500025891
```

As shown here, the response will contain the last anonymous field requested:

```
[{"name":"Nick Gerakines","uid":500025891,"anon":"world"}]
```

For some applications, this is a showstopper; but for developers who seldom use anonymous fields, this is an acceptable flaw.

FQL Syntax

An FQL query is broken into three components that answer the following questions:

- ❏ What is requested?
- ❏ Where are the requested data located?
- ❏ What conditions are there on the results?

This translates directly into the SELECT, FROM, and WHERE clauses of a SQL statement, respectively.

```
SELECT
  field
  [, field .. ]
  [, expression ... ]
FROM
  table
WHERE
  [ condition ... ]
```

The SELECT component answers the question, "What is requested?" by providing a place to define what data are being requested by the FQL query. The fields or expressions here correspond to the available fields and functions provided by the Facebook Platform.

The FROM component answers the question, "Where are the requested data located?" by defining the tables in which the listed fields in the SELECT component exist.

The WHERE component answers the question, "What conditions are there on the results?" by providing a place to add filters and conditions that apply to the results of the FQL query.

These three components translate into a very SQL-like query structure that can easily be parsed by the Facebook Platform. While it does share many of the qualities of SQL, there are heavy restrictions in place, and some more advanced SQL components are unavailable.

Three of these caveats will require developers to rethink how they query data from the Facebook Platform:

- ❏ **Developers Cannot Specify the Sort Order of a Query** — The Facebook Platform sorts the results of a query, and that sort order may change without notice. Developers should not rely on that sort order to be consistent if it matters to their applications.

- ❏ **There Is No Way to Set a Limit or Offset When Selecting Data** — The LIMIT and OFFSET SQL components are not available to developers when creating FQL requests. This prevents pagination.

- ❏ **When Building FQL Statements, the Facebook Platform Does Not Allow Unbounded Queries** — There is no way to request all possible rows of a given table. There must always be an indexed field set in the WHERE component of an FQL query.

Even with those restrictions on queries, FQL doesn't lose its usefulness.

Available Fields and Tables

The nine tables that can be queried include the following:

- ❏ user
- ❏ friend
- ❏ group
- ❏ group_members
- ❏ event
- ❏ event_member
- ❏ album
- ❏ photo
- ❏ photo_tag

The user Table

The user table contains much of the information pertaining to the standard Facebook User Account. This table is notably the largest and most complex of the tables available. It has a high number of unique data structures associated with its fields.

The fields on this table include the following:

about_me	last_name	profile_update_time
activities	meeting_for	quotes
affiliations	meeting_sex	relationship_status
birthday	movies	religion
books	music	sex
current_location	name	significant_other_id
education_history	notes_count	status
first_name	pic	timezone
has_added_app	pic_big	tv
hometown_location	pic_small	uid
hs_info	pic_square	wall_count
interests	political	work_history
is_app_user		

The fields available all correspond to the fields outlined in the Chapter 5 section, "`Facebook.users`
`.getinfo`," which discusses the API method. Refer to that section for more information regarding the
data structures that these fields represent, as well as examples of those data structures.

The two fields that are indexed on this table are `uid` and `name`. Following is an example query using the
`user` table:

```
SELECT concat(name, " is ", relationship_status) FROM user WHERE uid = 500025891
```

Following is the JSON response for the previous query:

```
[{"anon":"Nick Gerakines is Married"}]
```

The friend Table

The `friend` table stores the user-to-user relationship mapping that makes the social graph that Facebook
maintains. The only information returned is the presence of a relationship between two users. The
absence of information means that the two users are not friends.

The two available fields are `uid1` and `uid2`. The `uid1` field is always indexable, and the `uid2` field is
indexable when the field `uid1` is included in the query condition.

Following is an example query using the `friend` table:

```
SELECT uid1, uid2 from friend where uid1 = 500025891 and uid2 = 516463201
```

Following is the JSON response for the previous query:

```
[{"uid1":"500025891","uid2":"516463201"}]
```

Queries against the `friend` table are often subqueries for queries against other tables. In the following
example, the inner query selects all of the users that are friends with the user defined by `uid1`. The outer
query then looks up the names of all of the users returned by the inner query.

```
select name from user where uid in (select uid2 from friend where uid1 = 500025891)
```

Following is the JSON response for the previous query:

```
[{"name":"Corey Jackson"},{"name":"Leonard Lin"},{"name":"Dave McClure"}, ...]
```

Developers should be aware the fields specified in subqueries are not listed in the output of parent
queries. In the previous example, it is important to note that the `uid2` field is not directly displayed in
the FQL response.

The group Table

The `group` table is the repository of information about the Facebook groups.

The fields available include the following:

```
gid          pic            creator

name         description    update_time

nid          group_type     office

pic_small    group_subtype  website

pic_big      recent_news    venue
```

The gid field is the only indexed field for this table. The fields returned map directly to the fields returned in the facebook.groups.get API method. Refer to the section, "Facebook.groups.get," in Chapter 5 for more information.

Following is an example query using the group table:

```
select name from group where gid = 17831253704
```

Following is the JSON response for the previous query:

```
[{"name":"Wrox : Programmer to Programmer"}]
```

The group_members Table

The group_members table stores the users that are members of one or more groups. This table also stores the position field that tracks the rank of the group member, providing a hint at the permissions the user has with the group.

The fields in this table include uid, gid, and position. The indexed fields are uid and gid. Following is an example query using the group_members table.

```
SELECT uid, gid, positions FROM group_member WHERE uid = 500025891
```

Queries against the group_members table are often subqueries used to retrieved data from tables.

Consider the following example and the nested queries. The innermost query retrieves the friends of the user as per the WHERE component "uid1 = 500025891." The result of that query is then fed into a query that returns all of the group IDs based on group memberships for those users. The result of that query is then fed into the outermost query that retrieves the names of those groups.

```
SELECT name FROM group WHERE gid IN (
  SELECT gid FROM group_member WHERE uid IN (
    SELECT uid2 FROM friend WHERE uid1 = 500025891
  )
)
```

Following is the JSON response for the previous query:

```
[{"name":"Lunch 2.0"},{"name":"Facebook Developers"},{"name":"OpenID"}, ...]
```

The event Table

The `event` table stores all of the user-created events within Facebook.

The fields available include the following:

eid	pic, host	end_time
name	description	creator
tagline	event_type	update_time
nid	event_subtype	location
pic_small	start_time	venue
pic_big		

The `eid` field is the only field that is indexed. The fields returned map directly to the fields returned in the `facebook.events.get` API method. Refer to the section, "Facebook.events.get," in Chapter 5 for more information.

Following is an example query using the `event` table:

```
SELECT name FROM event WHERE eid = 5316827308
```

Following is the JSON response for the previous query:

```
[{"name":"An evening in Azeroth"}]
```

The event_member Table

The `event_member` table maps all of the members of an event to an event, as well as the RSVP information specified by the user.

The fields for the table include `uid`, `eid`, and `rsvp_status`. Both the `uid` and `eid` fields are indexed. Following is an example query using the `event_member` table:

```
SELECT eid from event_member where uid = 500025891
```

Following is the JSON response for the previous query:

```
[{"eid":"8442662657"},{"eid":"8846751954"},{"eid":"14310280583"}, ...]
```

Queries against the `event_member` table are often subqueries for queries against other tables. The following example query returns the names of future events to which a user has accepted the RSVP:

```
SELECT name FROM event WHERE eid IN (
  SELECT eid FROM event_member WHERE uid = 500025891 AND rsvp_status = 'attending'
) AND start_time > now()
```

Following is the JSON response for the previous query:

```
[{"name":"Superbowl Party"}]
```

The album Table

The `album` table contains information about user-created photo albums.

This table has the `aid`, `cover_pid`, `owner`, `name`, `created`, `modified`, `description`, `location`, and `size` fields. The `aid`, `cover_pid`, and `owner` fields are indexed, thus allowing developers to search album owners and find albums that use a photo as the album cover photo.

Following is an example query using the `album` table:

```
SELECT name FROM album WHERE owner = 500025891
```

Following is the JSON response for the previous query:

```
[{"name":"Friends and Places"},{"name":"Life at home"}, ... ]
```

The photo Table

The `photo` table contains the metadata about a user-uploaded photo on Facebook. This table does not store the actual photo data.

The `pid`, `aid`, `owner`, `src_small`, `src_big`, `link`, `caption`, and `created` fields are available to query. This table is indexed by the `pid` and `aid` fields. Following is an example query using the `photo` table:

```
SELECT src_small FROM photo WHERE aid IN (
  SELECT aid FROM album WHERE owner = 500025891
)
```

The photo_tag Table

The `photo_tag` table stores all of the photo-to-tag relationships that are created by Facebook users. In Facebook, when a user tags another user in a photo, that user literally marks the coordinates where the user appears in the photo. This location is available for developers to process when reading photo tag data. Photos play a more user-centric role in Facebook through creating connections between other Facebook users and events or places.

The `pid`, `subject`, `text`, `xcoord`, `ycoord`, and `created` fields are available. Both the `pid` and `subject` fields are indexed on this table. Following is an example query using the `photo_tag` table:

```
SELECT subject FROM photo_tag WHERE pid IN (
  SELECT pid FROM photo WHERE aid IN (
    SELECT aid FROM album WHERE owner = 500025891
  )
) AND subject != ''
```

Following is the JSON response for the previous query:

```
[{"subject":"500025891"},{"subject":"1559580004"}, ...]
```

A `photo_tag` record can also have free-form text that is used to identify a user or object not in Facebook. The general rule is that with every `photo_tag` record, the `text` field will have content. If the `photo_tag` record is referencing a Facebook user, then the `subject` field will contain the Facebook user ID of that user.

Additional Query Components

In addition to the field and table components of a query, there are anonymous fields, conditional statements, and functions. *Anonymous fields* are fields created by a function, simple string, or a mathematical operation. Following is an example of an anonymous field:

```
SELECT (2 + (1/1)) FROM user WHERE uid = 500025891
```

Following is the JSON response for the previous query:

```
[{"anon":3}]
```

Following is the XML response for the previous query:

```
<fql_query_response ... list="true">
  <user>
    <anon>3</anon>
  </user>
</fql_query_response>
```

The caveat to anonymous fields is that when selecting one or more anonymous fields in an FQL query, you must still provide a table and indexed field to validate the query.

The conditions of a query are set to filter the results pertaining to the field and table requested. When constructing FQL, you should be aware of the following rules:

1. All queries must reference at least one indexed field for that table.

2. More than one index can be referenced.

3. Once an indexed field is referenced, you can apply additional conditions on non-indexed fields.

4. Boolean comparison operators such as =, >, <=, and so on, can be used in query conditions. Parentheses and nested Boolean comparisons can be used as well. Arithmetic operators such as +, −, *, and /, as well as query functions, can also be referenced at any point in a query. With functions and some operators, anonymous fields can be returned.

Functions are useful for complex comparisons and data manipulation. Facebook provides a limited number of functions to developers, including the following:

❑ `concat(string [, string ...])` — Concatenates several strings.

❑ `lower(string)` — Returns the lowercase value of a `string`.

❑ `now` — Returns the current time.

❑ `strlen(string)` — Returns the length of a `string`.

❑   strpos(string1, string2) — Returns the position of string2 in string1. If string2 isn't found, then this function returns -1.

❑   substr(string, start, length) — Returns a string that is length long starting at position start of string.

❑   upper — Returns the uppercase value of a string.

Following is an example of a query that uses functions and operators:

```
SELECT concat("You tagged ", text, " in photo ", pid) FROM photo_tag WHERE pid IN (
    SELECT pid FROM photo WHERE aid IN (
      SELECT aid FROM album WHERE owner = 500025891
    )
  ) AND subject != ''
```

Following is the JSON response for the previous query:

```
[{"anon":"You tagged Nick Gerakines in photo 2147594848998313850"}, ... ]
```

Fields with Complex Data Structures

There are several fields (especially in the user table) that represent complex data structures. FQL allows you to specify named components of those complex data structures when building your FQL queries.

Consider the following example, where you want to retrieve the affiliations for a user:

```
SELECT affiliations FROM user where uid = 500025891
```

Following is the JSON response for the previous query:

```
[{"affiliations":[
   {"nid":67108896,"name":"Silicon Valley,
CA","type":"region","status":"","year":0},
   {"nid":50432537,"name":"Yahoo!","type":"work","status":"","year":0}]
}]
```

If you only want to retrieve the names of those affiliations, you can easily set the name attribute of the affiliations field when building your query.

Consider the following example, where you want to retrieve the affiliations for a user:

```
SELECT affiliations.name FROM user where uid = 500025891
```

Following is the JSON response for the previous query:

```
[{"affiliations":[{"name":"Silicon Valley, CA"},{"name":"Yahoo!"}]}]
```

Using This in Your Applications

FQL can play an important role in your applications, but its use tends to be specific to the functionality that your application provides.

Method Replacement

As seen in Chapter 5, FQL can be used directly to replace the functionality of many of the API methods available to developers. The most common use case is selecting only the fields you want out of a table where an API method would otherwise return many fields that you don't need or want.

The `facebook.friends.areFriends` method can be replaced by creating an FQL query to verify that a user-to-user relationship exists in the `friend` table between one or more users. The following example shows how to craft an FQL query to validate the relationship of one user to several other users:

```php
<?php
$pfriends = array(680415718, 660558037, 677101506);
$myid = 500025891;
$fql = 'SELECT uid2 FROM friend WHERE uid1 = ' . $myid . ';
$fql .= ' AND uid2 IN ( ' . implode(', ', $pfriends) . ')';
$rlist = $facebook->api_client->fql_query($fql);
$rfriends = array();
foreach($rlist as $ritem) {
  array_push($rfriends, $ritem['uid2']);
}
foreach($pfriends as $user) {
  if (in_array($user, $rfriends)) {
    print "You are friends with $user.\n";
  } else {
    print "You are not friends with $user.\n";
  }
}
?>
```

Storing Data

The Facebook Platform Terms of Service state that only a few key pieces of data can be stored by Facebook applications indefinitely. It also states that user data can be stored up to 24 hours from the time that they are fetched to improve application performance, as well as to limit the number of requests made against the Facebook Platform.

The following list represents the fields that can be stored indefinitely by Facebook Application Developers. All of the fields, with the exception of the `notes_count` and `profile_update_time` fields, are stored as 64-bit integers. The `notes_count` and `profile_update_time` can be stored as regular integers.

❑ uid — Facebook user ID

❑ nid — Primary network ID

❑ eid — Event ID

174

- ❏   `gid` — Group ID
- ❏   `pid` — Photo ID
- ❏   `aid` — Photo album ID
- ❏   `notes_count` — The number of notes written or posted by a user
- ❏   `profile_update_time` — The last time that a user's profile was updated

Summary

FQL is a powerful data-mining tool to retrieve the vast amount of user-generated data and metadata associated with users, their relationships with other users, groups, and photos. Chapter 5 discussed and gave examples of the construction and deconstruction of an FQL query, and also the components that make an FQL query.

Chapter 7 discusses authentication and its role in the Facebook Platform. Much like FQL, authentication is a key piece of the Facebook Platform that all applications take advantage of in one way or another.

7

Authentication

Authentication is one of the key pieces to the Facebook Platform, as well as application development. It is used by every other component of the Facebook Platform in some form or fashion. Chapter 5 described the `facebook.auth` methods, and throughout the book, there are clear examples of signature creation and validation, which are all part of authentication.

While Chapter 6 examined FQL, this chapter delves deep into authentication and examines how its components are spread throughout the Facebook Platform.

Authentication is really a combination of pieces and parts that individually may belong to another piece of the Facebook Platform, but as a whole, play a part in the complex authentication and validation process.

So many different pieces have come into existence because of the different types of authentication available. Internal, external, and desktop applications all have unique forms of authentication with a wide degree of variance between them. This chapter explains the different types of authentication and provides you with example projects to demonstrate how authentication really works.

Authentication Components

From a developer's point of view, the authentication process includes the following key components:

❑ **Authentication Tokens** — The *API key, secret key,* and *session key* fall under the realm of *authentication tokens*. These are generally handled internally by the application. These components are used to validate and verify requests and responses throughout the authentication process.

❑ **User Login Credentials** — The *user login credentials* include the obvious user login and user password, but also application access control and permissions. Within Facebook, users can specify different permissions given to applications. There is also a distinct difference between a user who has granted an application access and a user who has added the application to his or her account, as well as the different types of information and control that a user might give an application to his or her account. These options are available to users when they first add the application or give it access to their accounts. They can also be found on the "My Privacy" page located at the following URL: www.facebook.com/privacy.php.

❏ **Signatures** — A *signature* is its own class of token. Signatures are used throughout the Facebook Platform to validate requests and responses.

❏ **Application Configuration Options and Combinations** — Different *application configuration options and combinations* also affect how the Facebook Platform regards and references your application.

❏ **URL and URL Query String Parameters** — There are also several *URL and URL query string parameters* that affect the authentication flow and process.

❏ **Authentication API Methods** — The *authentication API methods* play a more supportive role in the authentication process by creating auth tokens for external and desktop authentication. But they also provide a means of retrieving session and user information during the authentication process.

Identifying an Application

Within the Facebook Platform, there are three things that define an application and make it unique:

1. API key
2. Secret
3. Application ID

When an application is created, those three fields are generated by the Facebook Platform and made available to the application owner and developers through the official Developer Application.

An *API key* is an application-unique string that is used to create and validate requests, as well as to identify an application throughout the Facebook Platform. The API is the public portion of a public/ private key model.

The *secret* is a token that is also used to create and validate requests. The secret represents the private key in a public/private key model. Whereas an API key is a visible parameter for an API method or application Canvas page request, the secret is not directly visible and is used in the request signature.

> It is called a *secret* for a reason! Do not give out the secret or leave it available in a public place. Anyone having the API key and secret of an application can masquerade as the application and thus have total control over its users and data.

The generated *application ID* (usually represented by a large number) isn't necessary for general development. Several locations within Facebook can use the application ID to reference an individual application, including an application About page, Settings page, and the Application Statistics page.

Sessions

A *session* (generally referred to as a *session key*) is an object that represents a user's access to an application for a period of time. Within the Facebook Platform, a session key is represented by a globally unique string. Each session generated is completely unique, and no other applications or users will have the same session key.

Session keys come in two formats:

- ❏ A session that expires: 6749c477929db0ac9bf14fc8
- ❏ A session that does not expire: 6749c477929db0ac9bf14fc8-500025891

Note that both formats include an alphanumeric string, while the second format includes a dash and Facebook user ID appended to the alphanumeric string.

There are several ways to create a session. Most developers will rely on a session being created in the background and passed to an application through Application Canvas requests. In those cases, Facebook creates the session because it is already aware of the state of the user accessing the application.

Sessions can also be created using the Facebook API method `facebook.auth.getsession`. The parameters and response of this API method were outlined in Chapter 5.

Given that a session is the combination of a user and its privileges with an application for a period of time, that period of time can be infinite. Infinite session keys are crucial to having services that interact with Facebook on behalf of a user without the user initiating the action directly. An example of this is having a Schedule Task add an item to the News Feed of a user as an event is triggered on an external web site.

There are two ways to create an infinite session:

1. When the user is directed to a login page as part of an authentication process, the user willingly selects the "Remember My Information" checkbox. This box is unchecked by default and can be hidden with a named query string parameter.

2. An application can direct users to a special URL that will generate an `auth` token that an application can use as the `auth_token` input to the `facebook.auth.getSession` API method.

   ```
   http://www.facebook.com/code_gen.php?v=1.0&api_key=[API_KEY]
   ```

When a session is created or requested, the `auth` token of the request plays an important part. An `auth` token is a temporary token used to associate a user with an application. In this case, to create a session, an application must create an `auth` token that is then, in turn, associated with a user to create a session.

Signatures

A *signature* is a token used to validate and secure requests both to and from the Facebook Platform. Signatures are used in every incoming and outgoing request to verify the arguments of the request. Therefore, they have very wide coverage throughout the Facebook Platform.

To create a signature, you join a list of parameters in conjunction with the application secret key and hash the joined list, as shown here:

```
arguments = alphabetically_sort arguments
tmpstr = secret
for each arg in arguments
  tmpstr .= arg_name + '=' + arg_value
end
signature = md5(tmpstr)
```

While signatures can verify the validity of a request, they cannot verify where the request is coming from, or who made it.

As seen in the Facebook PHP Client Library, creating a signature is a quick and painless process, as shown in the following `generate_sig` function:

```
public static function generate_sig($params_array, $secret) {
  $str = '';
  ksort($params_array);
  foreach ($params_array as $k => $v) {
    $str .= "$k=$v";
  }
  $str .= $secret;
  return md5($str);
}
```

Application Authentication

Authentication has many use cases, including the following:

- ❏ A Facebook application wants to verify that incoming requests are valid with a passing signature.

- ❏ A Facebook application wants to force all incoming requests to be from users who have granted the application access to their accounts.

- ❏ An external application wants to associate a local user with a Facebook user.

- ❏ A desktop application wants to create a session and make API requests.

Validating Requests

Validating application requests is a very common task for Facebook applications. This involves reading the request arguments and comparing the signature of the request to a generated signature. Included with this chapter is the `auth_signature` example application.

Creating this application through the Developers Application is very much like the setup of the "Hello World" example project in Chapter 2.

1. Using the Facebook Developers Application, create a new application with a unique name and URL. For this project, use your initials and signature. When developing this application for this book, I used *ngsignature* as the name and URL.

2. Upload the included project files to a publicly accessible web space and point the callback URL in the configuration options to the htdocs/index.php file.

This project consists of two files and the Facebook PHP Client Library. The first is AppConfig class found at lib/AppConfig.class.php. As shown in Listing 7-1, this class contains the Facebook application URL, the API key, and secret key for the application.

Listing 7-1: The lib/AppConfig.class.php PHP class.

```php
class AppConfig {
  public static $app_name = 'Signature';
  public static $app_url  = 'http://apps.facebook.com/ngsignature/';
  public static $app_id   = '6321806094';
  public static $api_key  = '153a6a42e42bc27a0f1a0e7985b4496d';
  public static $secret   = '2bad2d025de71b5162142e1fbd87d088';
}
```

The AppConfig class is not used directly; therefore, you exclude it from a public access, putting it outside of the htdocs directory.

The htdocs/index.php file is the main Canvas page for this application. This is the page requested by the callback URL, and returns the content to render on the Canvas for the user. This page is used to demonstrate how generated signatures are verified.

The first few lines of code of this Canvas page build a Facebook class object and do some initial validation. The api_key and secret variables are set in the AppConfig class as inputs to the Facebook class constructor. Then, the following requirements for the page are set:

1. The incoming request must be made through a valid Facebook frame.

2. The requesting user must be logged in and the application must have been granted access to that user.

3. The requesting user is required to add the application and set permission levels.

As shown in Listing 7-2, the default index page demonstrates how to parse incoming Facebook requests and validate them against a signature.

Listing 7-2: The htdocs/index.php Canvas page.

```php
<?php

include_once '../lib/client/facebook.php';
include_once '../lib/AppConfig.class.php';

// Create a new Facebook client object
```

(continued)

Listing 7-2 *(continued)*

```php
$facebook = new Facebook(AppConfig::$api_key, AppConfig::$secret);

// Prevent this page from being viewed outside the context of
// http://app.facebook.com/appname/
$facebook->require_frame();

// Prevent this page from being viewed without a valid logged in user
// -- NOTE: This does not mean that the logged in user has added the application
$user = $facebook->require_login();

// Require the viewing user to have added the application.
$facebook->require_add();

// Use the get_valid_fb_params to return an array of the fb_sig_* parameters
$app_params = $facebook->get_valid_fb_params($_POST, 48*3600, 'fb_sig');

// Use the generate_sig method to create a signature from the application
// parameters and the secret
$request_sig = $facebook::generate_sig($app_params, AppConfig::$secret);

$sig_match = $facebook->verify_signature($app_params, $request_sig);

?>
<div style="padding: 10px;">
  <h2>Hello <fb:name firstnameonly="true" uid="<?= $user ?>" useyou="false"/>!</h2>
<?php if ($sig_match) { ?>
  <p>The signature "<?= $request_sig ?>" does match the request parameters.</p>
<?php } else { ?>
  <p>The signature "<?= $request_sig ?>" does not match the request parameters.</p>
<?php } ?>
  <p>When we add foo => bar we get a mismatch.</p>
<?php
$app_params['foo_sig_foo'] = "bar";
$new_sig = $facebook::generate_sig($app_params, AppConfig::$secret);
?>
  <p>The signature "<?= $new_sig ?>" does not match the request parameters.</p>
  <hr />
  <p>When we add fb_sig_foo => bar we get a mismatch.</p>
<?php
$app_params["fb_sig_foo"] = "bar";
$new_sig = $facebook::generate_sig($app_params, AppConfig::$secret);
$sig_match = $facebook::verify_signature($app_params, $new_sig);
?>
<?php if ($sig_match) { ?>
  <p>The signature "<?= $request_sig ?>" does match the request parameters.</p>
<?php } else { ?>
  <p>The signature "<?= $request_sig ?>" does not match the request parameters.</p>
<?php } ?>
</div>
```

The block of PHP prepares the rest of the logic by including the required libraries and configuration files used. Immediately, you then build a valid Facebook object as per the Facebook PHP Client Library and pass in the API key and secret key stored in the configuration class, lib/AppConfig.class.php.

You then call the `require_frame`, `require_login`, and `require_add` methods as per the Facebook object to verify and force all requests to be made through the Facebook application Canvas and by a valid, logged-in user who has added the application to his or her Facebook account.

The following block of PHP code brings some of the signature validation out from behind the scenes. The `get_valid_fb_params` class method is first called to return all of the `fb_sig_*` request parameters. Next, the `generate_sig` function creates a signature from the parameters and the application secret key. Lastly, the `verify_signature` method compares the signature found in the request with the one that you compared.

The first set of FBML returned displays different messages based on whether or not the signature created from the parameters matches the one found in the request signature.

Now that you have proven success, you can try different combinations of request parameters prove failure. You can do this by adding a new parameter to the list of application parameters to the list returned by the `get_valid_fb_params` class method. Because the parameter is not part of the original request, it would not have been included in the signature generated by the Facebook Platform.

Now that you have been through the code and components of this Facebook application, you can point your browser to the application Canvas page (Figure 7-1). In this case, it is `http://apps.facebook .com/ngsignature`. The rendered content on the page will show the current signature, and then give two examples of parameter adjustments that create signatures that do not match.

Figure 7-1: The application Canvas page for the ngSignature application.

Forcing Views

In the previous section (as well as the example project used in Chapter 2), several steps taken ensure that the incoming request is made by a valid user, is executed through the Facebook application Canvas, and that the user has added the application. All of the real work behind these rules is done in the background by the Client Library, but understanding how these rules are enforced is important.

When a request is made to your application, the Facebook Platform includes several POST parameters. Those parameters can be used to determine where the request came from, by whom, and what are the conditions of the request.

❑   `fb_sig_in_canvas` — When this parameter has a value of 1, the request was made through the Facebook application Canvas. To force a user through the Facebook application Canvas, when this parameter is set to 0, redirect the user to the Facebook application URL.

```
http://apps.facebook.com/[application]
```

❑   `fb_sig_user` — This parameter is the user ID of the user who made the request. The absence of this parameter indicates that the user who made the request has not granted access to your application. When this request parameter is absent or unset, you can force the viewing users to log in by redirecting them to the appropriate login page.

```
http://www.facebook.com /login.php?v=1.0&api_key=[API KEY]
```

❑   `fb_sig_added` — When this parameter has a value of 1, the requesting user has added the application, not just granted the application access to the user's account. When this parameter is not set to 1, you can require that users viewing the application have the application added by redirecting them to the appropriate Application Add page.

```
http://www.facebook.com/add.php?api_key=[API KEY]
```

External Application Authentication

External application authentication is the trickiest and least-documented of the authentication processes. Because the Facebook Platform does not make requests to the application through the application Canvas, external applications must rely on the user and the `facebook.auth.getSession` API method to create a valid session key for its users.

External application users usually start or engage the process outside the context of the Facebook Platform. They visit a web site that has a pseudo-service that interacts with Facebook, but to do so, the external web site must have its user associate with Facebook users.

From the user's point of view, the process of adding an external application is as simple as following a link, logging into Facebook (if required), adding the Facebook application, and being taken back to the external web site. From the developer's point of view, the external web site must take several steps to verify the identity of the user on the external web site, both through Facebook and the Facebook Platform.

A perfect candidate for an external application would be a wiki that would like to allow its editors and contributors to display their pages and content to their friends on Facebook. Creating an external application through the Developers Application, the wiki owner sets a callback URL that performs the actual work of associating its wiki users with Facebook users.

As logged-in wiki users view the user pages, they are presented with a link to a Facebook login page associated with the wiki's Facebook application by appending the `api_key` in the query string, as shown here:

```
https://login.facebook.com/login.php?v=1.0&api_key=XYZ1ABC
```

The users are taken to Facebook, where they must do two things: log in and grant access to the application. If the user isn't logged in, the user is presented with the standard login form. If the user has never granted access to the application, the user is presented with a form to do so. The notable feature of the form is a checkbox where the user can allow the application to remember his or her information. The selection of this checkbox is vital to the creation of an infinite session key for the user and application.

Once the user is logged in and the appropriate permissions are granted, the user is redirected to the callback URL set by the application in the application configuration.

As another example, let's say that a wiki wants to allow its contributors to display their edits and pages on their Facebook profiles. When users are logged onto the wiki, they are presented with a link that takes them to a Facebook login page.

External applications are the topic of Chapter 10 and will be examined much more closely there. For now, take note of the `auth_external` example application. In addition, the query string contains a fresh `auth_token` that was created by the Facebook Platform and associated with the application and user. This token is the subject of a `facebook.auth.getsession` API method request to retrieve a session for the user. Once the session is retrieved, the application has everything it needs to make subsequent API method requests, query the Facebook Platform using FQL, and interact with the Platform in general.

Creating this application through the Developers Application is very much like the setup of the "Hello World" example project in Chapter 2:

- ❑ Using the Facebook Developers Application, create a new application with a unique name and URL. For this project, use your initials and **external**. When developing this application for this book, I used *ngexternal* as the name and URL.

- ❑ Upload the include project files to a publicly accessible web space and point the callback URL in the application configuration options to the htdocs/callback.php file.

- ❑ This application uses a database to store a local user and associate them with Facebook user account information. In this database, you store the session key, session expiration time, and Facebook user ID retrieved through the `facebook.auth.getsession` API method (Listing 7-2).

The `auth_external` example application (Listing 7-3) contains four files, as well as the Facebook PHP Client Library files.

Listing 7-3: The database schema used by the auth_external project.

```
CREATE TABLE facebook_accounts (
    user_id INT(11) NOT NULL,
    fb_user_id INT(11) NOT NULL,
    session_key VARCHAR(44) NOT NULL,
    session_expires INT(11) NOT NULL,
    row_created INT(11) NOT NULL
);
```

The first (shown in Listing 7-4) is the `AppConfig` class found at lib/AppConfig.class.php. This class contains the Facebook application URL, the API key, and the secret key for the application. The database connection information is also contained in this class to be referenced by the application class.

Listing 7-4: The lib/AppConfig.class.php PHP class.

```php
<?php
class AppConfig {
  public static $app_name = 'SuperStore';
  public static $app_url = 'http://apps.facebook.com/ngexternal/';
  public static $app_id = '6321806094';
  public static $api_key = '153a6a42e42bc27a0f1a0e7985b4496d';
  public static $secret  = '2bad2d025de71b5162142e1fbd87d088';
  public static $db_ip = '127.0.0.1';
  public static $db_user = 'user';
  public static $db_pass = 'password';
  public static $db_name = 'ngexternal';
}
```

The `AppConfig` class is not used directly; therefore, it has been excluded from a public access, putting it outside of the htdocs directory.

The lib/SuperStore.class.php class (shown in Listing 7-5) defines and contains all of the business logic used by the Facebook application. It also handles any database class or Facebook API method requests that are made. The `SuperStore` class opens with several internal variables set to reference the Facebook class object used, and the account used by the external web site.

Listing 7-5: The lib/SuperStore.class.php PHP class.

```php
<?php
class SuperStore {

  public $fbclient;
  public $account;

  //! Create a new SuperStore object
  /*! \param fbclient The facebook client object
   */
  public function __construct($fbclient) {
    // On creation, set the facebook client
    $this->fbclient = $fbclient;
  }

  // Return a user id representing some made-up Super Store 2000 user.
  function get_user_id() {
    return 3;
  }

  function has_account($user_id = null) {
    if (! $user_id) { $user_id = $this->get_user_id(); }
    if ($this->account['fb_user_id']) { return true; }
    $udata = $this->get_user($user_id);
    if (! $udata) { return false; }
    $this->account = $udata;
    return true;
  }

  function get_user($id) {
```

```
    $conn = $this->get_db_conn();
    // nkg: id should be escaped ... raw vars in sql = quick but bad
    $sql = "SELECT user_id, fb_user_id, session_key, session_expires, row_created
FROM facebook_accounts WHERE user_id = $id LIMIT 1";
    $res = mysql_query($sql, $conn);
    // nkg: error checking? ... nah
    $data = array();
    while ($row = mysql_fetch_assoc($res)) {
        $data = $row;
    }
    return $data;
}

function account_id() {
    $has_account = $this->has_account();
    if (! $has_account) { return 0; }
    return $this->account['fb_user_id'];
}

function account_expires() {
    $has_account = $this->has_account();
    if (! $has_account) { return false; }
    return $this->account['session_expires'];
}

function account_has_expired() {
    $has_account = $this->has_account();
    if (! $has_account) { return true; } // nkg: makes sense to me
    $now = time;
    $expires = $this->account_expires();
    if ($expires > $now) { return true; }
    return false;
}

function tie_account() {
    $auth_token = $_GET['auth_token'];
    if (! $auth_token) { return false; }
    $session_response = $this->fbclient->api_client->auth_getSession($auth_token);
    $skey = $session_response['session_key'];
    $sexp = $session_response['expires'];
    $fbuid = $session_response['uid'];
    $uid = $this->get_user_id();
    $this->account = array('user_id' => $uid, 'fb_user_id' => $fbuid, 'session_key'
=> $skey, 'session_expires' => $sexp);
    try {
        $conn = $this->get_db_conn();
        $sql = "INSERT INTO facebook_accounts SET user_id = $uid, fb_user_id =
$fbuid, session_key = \"$skey\", session_expires = $sexp, row_created =
UNIX_TIMESTAMP(NOW())";
        mysql_query($sql, $conn);
    } catch (Exception $e) {
        return false;
    }
```

(continued)

Listing 7-5 (continued)

```
      return true;
    }

    //! Return a database connection
    function get_db_conn() {
      $conn = mysql_connect(
        AppConfig::$db_ip,
        AppConfig::$db_user,
        AppConfig::$db_pass
      );
      //! \exception Exception Error connecting to database
      if (! $conn) {
        throw new Exception('Error connecting to database: ' . mysql_error());
      }
      $success = mysql_select_db(AppConfig::$db_name, $conn);
      //! \exception Exception Error connecting to database
      if (! $success) {
        throw new Exception('Error connecting to database: ' . mysql_error());
      }
      return $conn;
    }
  }
```

The SuperStore class starts by defining two variables used internally, $fbclient and $account. The constructor for the class accepts one parameter, a Facebook object (as per the Facebook PHP Client Library) that is used internally.

The get_user_id class method abstracts a user ID that would be the logged-in user of the web site. The has_account method is used to perform an internal lookup of a user to see if that user has associated his or her account with a Facebook account. If the user has, the data are stored in the account class variable.

The get_user class method performs the actual lookup of the potential user association data stored locally by the external application.

The account_id, account_expires, and account_has_expired class methods are simple accessor methods to the data stored in the account class variable. These are used instead of direct access to the variable for error checking and validation. If the account variable hasn't been populated or the data don't exist, they will return "0" or false.

When a user has gone through the required steps of associating with a Facebook account, you then want to store the session information locally for later use. The tie_account method takes the necessary steps to do so. The method first fetches the auth_token query string parameter that is passed from the Facebook Platform once a user has initiated the external application authentication process. You then immediately make a facebook.auth.getsession API method request to retrieve the session information.

Once you have the session information, you stuff the account class variable with the appropriate data and write the session information to the database for later use.

Next is the htdocs/index.php file (Listing 7-6). This is the page that is displayed to users outside of Facebook when viewing the external application. This represents the eternal web site that would be making the requests to Facebook on behalf of its users. Visiting this page displays whatever content would be on the external content and executes some logic to determine if the user of the external web site has associated his or her account with a Facebook account.

Listing 7-6: The htdocs/index.php page.

```php
<?php

include_once '../lib/client/facebook.php';
include_once '../lib/AppConfig.class.php';
include_once '../lib/SuperStore.class.php';

// Create a new Facebook client object
$facebook = new Facebook(AppConfig::$api_key, AppConfig::$secret);

$this_app = new SuperStore($facebook);

$has_account = $this_app->has_account();

if ($has_account) {
  $current_user = $this_app->account_id();
  $expiration = $this_app->account_expires();
  $has_expired = $this_app->account_has_expired();
}

?>
<html>
  <head>
    <title>SuperStore 2000</title>
  </head>
  <body>
    <div style="padding: 10px; margin: 10px;">
      <h1>Welcome to Super Store 2000</h1>
<?php if ($has_account) { ?>
<?php if ($has_expired) { ?>
      <p>Oh No! Your Facebook session has expired! Please <a
href="https://login.facebook.com/login.php?v=1.0&api_key=<?= AppConfig::$api_key
?>">log into Facebook</a> before continuing.</p>
<?php } ?>
      <p>It looks like you have associated your Facebook account with Super Store
2000.</p>
<?php } else { ?>
      <p>Do you use Facebook? If you do, you can tie Super Store 2000 with your
Facebook account to update your Facebook profile with cool Super Store 2000
stuff!</p>
      <p><a href="https://login.facebook.com/login.php?v=1.0&api_key=<?=
AppConfig::$api_key ?>">Log into Facebook</a>.</p>
<?php } ?>
      <p>
    </div>
  </body>
</html>
```

The beginning block of PHP code includes several PHP files, and creates a new `Facebook` object and `SuperStore` object. The `has_account` method of the `SuperStore` class is referenced to determine if the viewing user has associated with a Facebook account yet. If the user has done so, you also set some local variables that modify the content displayed to the user.

The body of this page is very simple. You perform several small checks to display different content based on whether or not the user has associated an account and whether or not the session key has expired. If the user has not associated an account yet, you display a link to let the user initiate the process.

The htdocs/callback.php file (Listing 7-7) is the core of the authentication process for this external application. The Facebook Platform references this file when the user has completed the necessary steps to add the external application.

Listing 7-7: The htdocs/callback.php page.

```php
<?php

include_once 'lib/client/facebook.php';
include_once 'lib/AppConfig.class.php';
include_once 'lib/SuperStore.class.php';

// Create a new Facebook client object
$facebook = new Facebook(AppConfig::$api_key, AppConfig::$secret);

$success = false;

$this_app = new SuperStore($facebook);

$has_account = $this_app->has_account();

if (! $current_user) {
  $success = $this_app->tie_account();
}

$current_user = $this_app->account_id();
$expiration = $this_app->account_expires();

?>
<html>
  <head>
    <title>SuperStore 2000</title>
  </head>
  <body>
    <div style="padding: 10px; margin: 10px;">
      <h1>Welcome to Super Store 2000</h1>
<?php if ($success) { ?>
    <p>You have associated your Facebook account with Super Store 2000. <a
href="https://login.facebook.com/login.php?v=1.0&api_key=<?= AppConfig::$api_key
?>">Go to your Facebook profille</a>.</p>
<?php
} else {
  if ($has_account) { // Success is false, there was already an account
?>
```

```
    <p>You have already tied your Super Store 2000 and Facebook accounts. <a
href="#">Go to your Facebook profille</a>.</p>
<?php } else { ?>
    <p>There was an error. Your Super Store 2000 and Facebook accounts were not
tied.</p>
<?php } } ?>
        <p>
      </div>
    </body>
</html>
```

The first few lines include several PHP files and create the `Facebook` and `SuperStore` objects. You also perform a quick check to see if the user has already associated with an account. If the user has not, you call the `tie_account` method to take the `auth_token` passed by the Facebook Platform and retrieve the session information associated with the user of that token. Upon success, you display a message to the user.

The content displayed by this page is very low maintenance. When an account is successfully associated, you let the user know. If the user already had an account associated, you also provide the user with a quick message.

When sending the user to the login page on Facebook, there are several options that can be set using query string parameters:

❑   `popup` — Setting this query string parameter will style the login window differently. It will not contain the usual navigation elements. Additionally, it is styled to best-fit 646 by 438 frames.

❑   `skipcookie` — This query string parameter instructs Facebook to ignore the current logged-in user, if any, and force a user to log in. This can be used to force a clean association, disregarding any users who may have forgotten to log out. If your service or web site can be used through public terminals, setting this option is advised.

❑   `hide_checkbox` — This query string parameter instructs Facebook to hide the "Remember My Information" checkbox that is used to create infinite sessions. This is best suited for external applications that are one-time-use only.

❑   `canvas` — Setting this query string parameter will direct the user to the Canvas page for the application, instead of taking the user directly to the login page.

❑   `next` — When set, this query string parameter is appended to the page that the user is directed to once the user has logged in and granted the application permission. This is used to maintain state during the login process.

The URL that the user is directed to once he or she has taken the necessary steps to add the external application may also have some variation, depending on the initial query parameters set. If the `next` parameter is set, it will also be present on this URL.

This application can be used by pointing your browser directly to the server hosting htdocs/index .php. This represents the external web site that wants to associate its users with Facebook users. Once users initiate the process on the external web site, they are taken through the associate process that includes the htdocs/callback.php page.

Creating Sessions from Desktop Applications

Desktop applications are a variant of external applications and have their own process for authentication. Much like the external application process, this process includes directing a user to the Facebook login page and validating the response with an API method request.

The big difference is in the way `auth` tokens and secrets are handled. Desktop applications create an `auth` token using the `facebook.auth.createtoken` API method and pass that token along with the API key on the login URL, as shown here:

```
https://login.facebook.com/login.php?v=1.0&api_key=[api_key]&auth_token=[auth_token]
```

When the user has followed the URL and completed the necessary steps to log in and add the application (if required), the user is not redirected to a callback URL because desktop applications don't have one. Instead, the user is directed back to the desktop application to finish the process there.

When the user goes back to the desktop application, the application must make an API request to the `facebook.auth.getsession` API method to retrieve the session information required for subsequent API requests. This is where the variation in the session data occurs. In addition to the `session_key`, `expires`, and `uid` fields, the `secret` field is also returned in the response. The `secret` field returned is to be used in place of the standard application secret for all requests with the `session_key`.

The `auth_desktop` example application was included with this chapter to demonstrate the authentication process for desktop applications. With it are three PHP command-line scripts that reference the Facebook Client Library.

Creating this application through the Developers Application is very much like the setup of the "Hello World" example project in Chapter 2, but there are a few changes:

❏ Using the Facebook Developers Application, create a new application with a unique name and URL. For this project, use your initials and **desktop**. When developing this application for this book, I used *ngdesktop* as the name and URL.

❏ When creating the application, under "Application Type," select the "Desktop" option.

The step_one.php file (Listing 7-8) initiates the first step in Desktop Application Authentication. This script sends a request to the `facebook.auth.createtoken` API method and creates the URL that a user should be directed to. This command-line script accepts two arguments: the `api_key` and `secret` for the application.

Listing 7-8: The first step in Desktop Application Authentication.

```php
#!/usr/bin/php
<?php

if (! $argv[0] || ! $argv[1] || ! $argv[2]) {
    print "./step_one.php <api_key> <secret>\n";
    exit();
}

$api_key = $argv[1];
```

```
$secret = $argv[2];

include_once 'lib/client/facebook.php';

$client = new Facebook($api_key, $secret);
$result = $client->api_client->auth_createToken();

print 'Go to http://www.facebook.com/login.php?api_key=' . $api_key .
'&v=1.0&auth_token=' . $result . "\n";

?>
```

Figure 7-2 shows the results.

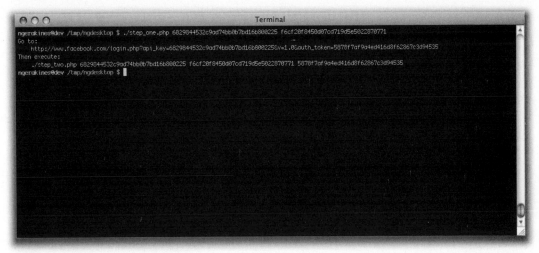

Figure 7-2: The execution of step one.

The current version of the Facebook PHP Client Library does not contain any references to the `facebook.auth.createToken` API method, so you must add it yourself. Thankfully, extending the library is fairly simple.

In the facebookapi_php5_restlib.php class, append the following class method. This is already done for you in the included `auth_desktop` example application.

```php
public function auth_createToken() {
  $result = $this->call_method('facebook.auth.createToken');
  return $result;
}
```

The step_two.php file (Listing 7-9) continues the authentication process by fetching the session information associated with the auth_token created in step_one.php and used by the user to log in and add the application. This script sends a request to the facebook.auth.getSession API method and returns the session information to be used later on. It also proves that the session is valid and executes a FQL query to demonstrate this. This command-line script accepts three arguments: the api_key, secret, and auth_token.

Listing 7-9: The second step in Desktop Application Authentication.

```php
#!/usr/bin/php
<?php

if (! $argv[0] || ! $argv[1] || ! $argv[2] || ! $argv[3]) {
    print "./step_two.php <api_key> <app secret> <auth_token>\n";
    exit();
}

$api_key = $argv[1];
$secret = $argv[2];
$auth_token = $argv[3];

include_once 'lib/client/facebook.php';
include_once 'lib/client/facebook_desktop.php';

$client = new FacebookDesktop($api_key, $secret);
$result = $client->do_get_session($auth_token);

print "Be sure to keep the session key and secret in a safe place!!\n\n";
print "Session: " . $result['session_key'] . "\n";
print "User ID: " . $result['uid'] . "\n";
print "Expires: " . $result['expires'] . "\n";
print "Application Secret: " . $secret . "\n";
print "Session Secret: " . $result['secret'] . "\n\n";

print 'Executing query: SELECT concat(name, " is ", relationship_status) FROM user
WHERE uid = ' . $result['uid'] ."\n\n";

$resp = $client->api_client->fql_query('SELECT concat(name, " is ",
relationship_status) FROM user WHERE uid = ' . $result['uid']);

var_dump($resp);

?>
```

Figure 7-3 shows the results.

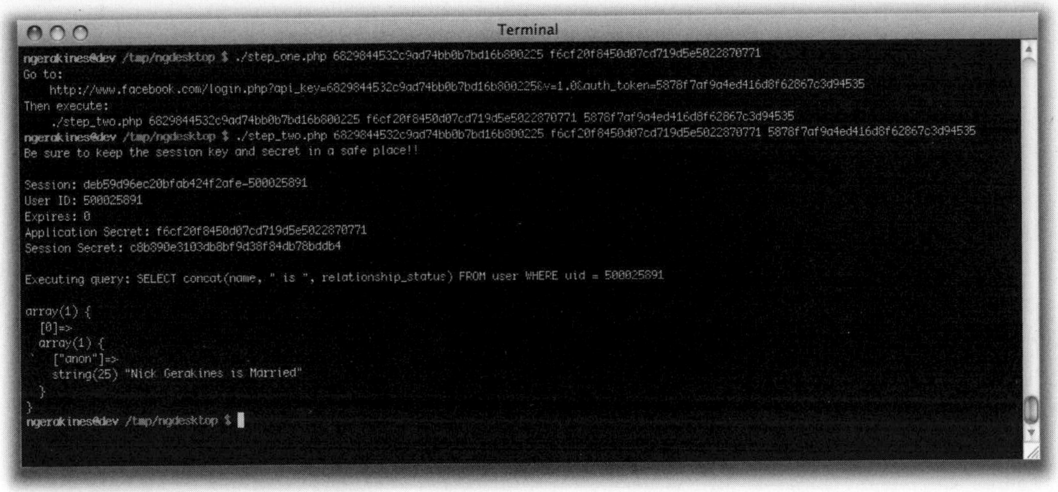

Figure 7-3: The execution of step two.

As you can see in Figures 7-2 and 7-3, the process of creating a session for a user as a desktop application is relatively easy. With some modifications, this process could be adapted to other languages.

Summary

As demonstrated and explained in this chapter, authentication plays a huge part in every aspect of the Facebook Platform. Whether you are verifying that an application request was made through the Canvas or creating signed API requests from a desktop application, the authentication model simply cannot be left out. This chapter continued what was started in pervious chapters with the authentication model and opened the door to external application authentication.

Chapter 8 picks up where this chapter leaves off with external application development. By now, most of the Facebook Platform's core components have been discussed, and you have everything you need to start integrating external web sites and services with Facebook through an external application.

Part II

Building Facebook Applications

Chapter 8: Resources for Developers

Chapter 9: Doing More with Hello World

Chapter 10: External Application Development

Chapter 11: Best Practices

Resources for Developers

8

Before going any further in development, let's stop for a moment and highlight the resources available to Facebook application developers. This chapter reviews the official Developers Application and Developers Web Site provided by Facebook. This chapter will also touch the community-supported wiki and the bug-tracker provided by Facebook.

The key to developing social applications is that the main focus should be (and is always) on the user and community. The Facebook Platform allows developers to tap into the userbase and framework for creating social applications, but without focus on the user, your efforts will be lost.

Through the Discussion Board, official wiki, mailing lists, and blogs, there is a vast amount of knowledge about how to best do things, what to watch for, and what to focus on.

The Developers Application

The base of operations for all Facebook application developers is the official Developers Application. In the Developers Application, you are presented with an interface for creating and managing Facebook applications. This application also provides a means for engaging the Facebook application developer community and managing information about your application. You can find the application at the following URL:

```
www.facebook.com/developers/
```

With a few exceptions, the Developers Application has several of the components that all Facebook applications have. This includes a Discussion Board, Canvas page, and members. The Canvas page hosts several of the services exclusive to the Developers Application, including the "My Applications" page (collectively known as the *application control panel*), a feed of updates from the blog for news and service announcements, and an application stats and metrics page.

My Applications

Outwardly known as "My Applications" (Figure 8-1), this page in the Developers Application is the core of application creation and management. This is where developers go to create new Facebook applications, modify how they operate, and, sadly, delete them. This also includes the management of the application About page.

Figure 8-1: The My Applications page.

At a glance, the "My Applications" page presents developers with a list of the applications they currently have. The link titled "Apply for a key" starts the developer through the process for creating a new application. This process can also be started from the Developers Application.

As shown in Figure 8-2, each Facebook application listed will include links to allow the developer to edit the application's settings and About page settings. There is also a quick reference to the API key and secret key generated by the Facebook Platform. If the application has sent notifications to users, there is also a *spaminess* score displayed. If the application has been submitted to the directory, its acceptance status is displayed on the far right.

Figure 8-2: An application listing on the My Applications page.

Creating an Application

Creating a new application through the Developers Application is very easy. This process has already been covered in depth in Chapter 2 while stepping through the Hello World project. The process is started through the Developers Application using the `editapp.php?new` link, as shown here:

```
http://www.facebook.com/developers/editapp.php?new
```

Figure 8-3 shows the opening screen after clicking the link.

Figure 8-3: The required fields of an application.

As listed in Figure 8-3, when creating a new application within the Facebook Platform, the required fields for an application are few, but important. They include a globally unique Application Name and acceptance of the Facebook Platform Terms of Service.

It's a good idea to read the entire Terms of Service agreement. While it mostly benefits the developer, it is, of course, designed to first protect and serve Facebook, and has several caveats and noticeable terms that could have an impact on your application. You may view the Terms of Service at the following URL:
`www.facebook.com/developers/tos.php`.

In addition to the application name and acceptance of the Terms of Service, there is also an expandable set of "Optional Fields," optional configuration settings for the application, as shown in Figure 8-4. These include the "Callback URL," "Facebook URI," and any additional developers you may want to give access to the application.

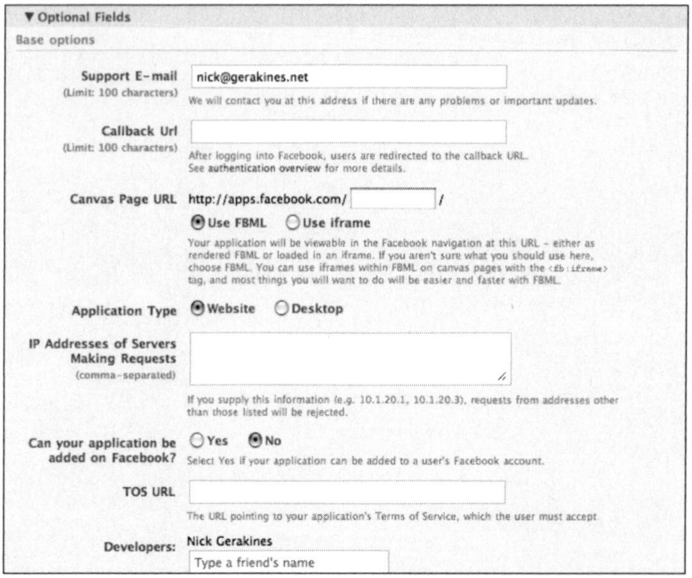

Figure 8-4: The "Optional Fields" of an application's configuration.

Note that there is also a checkbox that states whether or not the application can be added. Checking that field will open up several more configuration sets.

As seen in Figure 8-5, The "Installation Options" allow developers to set various options that dictate how the application will act when a user adds it. This includes the "Post-Add Callback URL," the "Default FBML" that will render in the user's profile file, and so on.

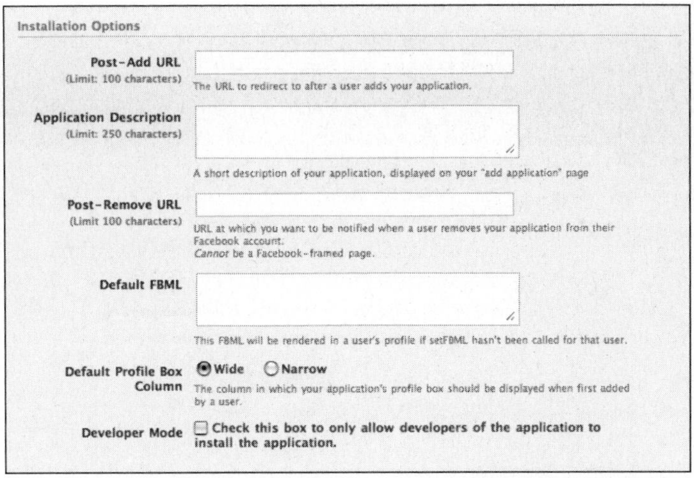

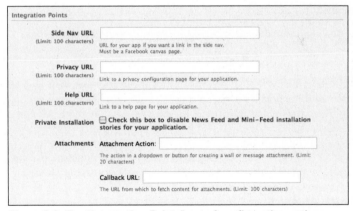

Figure 8-5: The "Installation Options" set of configuration options.

The "Integration Points" set of configuration options shown in Figure 8-6 dictate how the application will integrate with the different components of Facebook. This includes things like the "Help URL" and how attachments are handled by the application.

Figure 8-6: The "Integration Points" set of configuration options.

Deleting an Application

Deleting an application is just as straightforward as creating one. When you follow the "Delete Application" link on the "My Applications" page, you are presented with a confirmation message (Figure 8-7) and, if you choose to continue, the application will be removed from the Facebook Platform.

Figure 8-7: The confirmation dialog displayed when deleting an application.

Removing an application means that all records of that application are lost. The API Key and secret are immediately voided, and the profiles of the users who have added the application are updated to reflect this change. The name and application URL are immediately made available for future applications to use.

Once an application is deleted, there is no way to recover any of the information about it. This includes the users who have installed it, as well as any metrics and statistics about its usage.

Editing the About Page

The About page for an application is one of the first things a user sees before adding an application. The About page for an application consists of a description and optional image of the application, Wall, and discussion board. There are also links to the application's Canvas page (if it has one) and the number of active users for the application.

The About Page Editor allows developers to customize what the users see on the About page. It is composed of two parts: the "Application Info" and the "Picture." This does not include the placement or removal of required elements such as the application About page Wall or discussion board.

As shown in Figure 8-8, the "Application Info" tab consists of the "Description," "Categories," and "Developer Information." There is a two-category limit to the number of categories the application can associate with.

Figure 8-8: Editing the "Application Info" for the application About page.

The "Picture" tab (Figure 8-9) is used to set the image displayed on the application About page.

Figure 8-9: Editing the "Picture" for the application About page.

The Application Directory

The *Application Directory* is a large directory of Facebook applications. After an application has been created and certain requirements are met, the application can be submitted to be approved for entry into the directory, as shown in Figure 8-10.

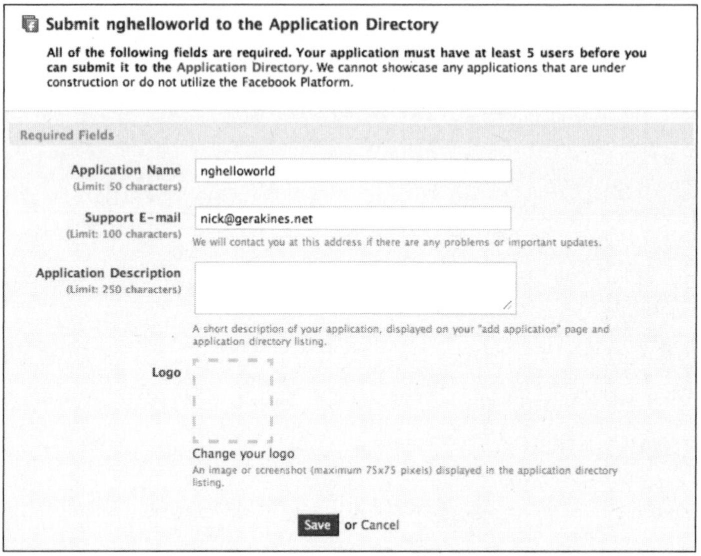

Figure 8-10: Submitting the application for approval.

To be listed in the Application Directory, the application must have at least five users and must be approved by the Facebook staff.

As shown in Figure 8-11, the Application Directory consists of a paginated view of applications listed by category with several filters. Those filters include "Recently Popular," "Most Activity," "Most Active Users," and "Newest." Applications can also be viewed by type, including those used through Facebook, desktop applications, and so on.

Discussion Board

The *Discussion Board* is one of the universal elements found throughout Facebook. The Developer Application's Discussion Board is provided for the development community to encourage communication between developers and Facebook. It has become a hub of information and provides answers to questions that many developers have.

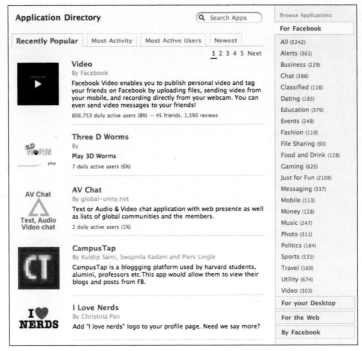

Figure 8-11: The Application Directory in all of its glory.

The Discussion Board is also home to non-development questions and discussion related to the Facebook Platform.

Updates and Service Announcements

On the Developers Application (just beneath the Discussion Board and "My Applications" list) are two sections for Facebook Platform updates and service announcements.

The "Latest News" section is a feed from the Facebook News blog. This blog is the home to Facebook announcements and updates. The majority of its recent posts are directly related to the Facebook Platform and often focus on new features or service changes. You may find this at the following URL:

```
www.facebook.com/news.php?blog=1
```

The "Platform Status" section is a live feed of service announcements for the Facebook Platform. This section contains information about the status of the Facebook Platform, news regarding production changes, and downtime.

Application Stats

The *Application Stats* page shown in Figure 8-12 is a new addition to the Developers Application. The Application Stats page provides a high-level overview of the usage and traffic going to your application from the Facebook Platform.

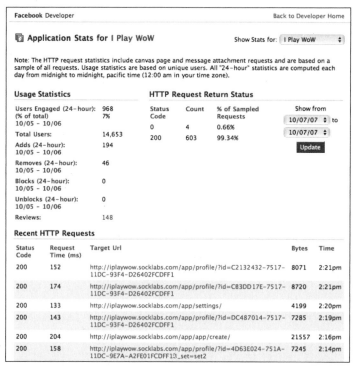

Figure 8-12: An example of the Application Stats page for the I Play WoW Facebook application.

The metrics provided include (but are not limited to) the following:

❑   The total number of users that currently have the application added

❑   The number of users that have engaged the application in the past 24 hours

❑   Recent application page requests

❑   A sample of request status codes

These metrics are calculated at midnight, and go 24 hours back unless stated otherwise.

The Developers Web Site

The Developers Web Site (not to be confused with the Developers Application) is the home to the official documentation, downloads, and tools used to develop on the Facebook Platform. The main purpose of the Developers Web Site is to give developers as much information as possible to engage the Facebook Platform and to start developing.

Documentation

The documentation on the Developers Web Site includes a substantial amount of information on the Facebook Platform API, Facebook Query Language (FQL), and the authentication process. The Developers Web Site does not include documentation on anything that is in beta or testing. You may find the documentation at the following URL:

```
http://developers.facebook.com/documentation.php
```

The official documentation for the Facebook Markup Language (FBML) has been moved to the wiki and will not be covered in this section. Refer to the FBML wiki page at the following URL for more information:

```
http://wiki.developers.facebook.com/index.php/FBML
```

The FQL is outlined and overviewed in great detail here. The FQL documentation also includes the tables, fields, and indexes available.

The authentication process also has a substantial amount of content available on the authentication model. It covers some of the general use cases on authenticating an application.

The documentation also includes several miscellaneous pages:

❑   A list of the link templates to user profiles, group pages, forms to add users as friends, send messages, and so on. You may find it here: `http://developers.facebook.com/documentation.php?v=1.0&doc=other`.

❑   An overview of the information can be stored by third parties using the Facebook Platform. You may find it here: `http://developers.facebook.com/documentation.php?v=1.0&doc=misc`.

Resources

The Resources section of the Developers Web Site is a repository of downloads, including client libraries to the Facebook Platform and example projects. This area also contains a quick overview of the shared components that applications use and interact with.

The PHP Client Library is available on this page. The PHP Client Library contains a set of PHP 4 classes, PHP 5 classes, and the example "footprints" application. The official Java Client Library is also available on this page: `http://developers.facebook.com/resources.php`.

Tools

The tools area of the Developers Web Site contains the API Test Console and the FBML Test Console.

API Test Console

The *API Test Console* shown in Figure 8-13 is one of the quickest ways to validate and test API requests.

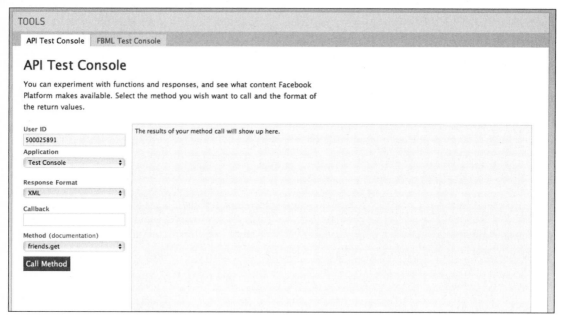

Figure 8-13: The API Test Console.

The API Test Console allows you to submit an API request and select the response format and API method parameters. The available response formats are XML, JSON, and serialized PHP. The application option sets the API key and secret to use when creating the request.

This tool is great for testing FQL and API methods before implementing them in your applications. It can also be used to create response parsers by crafting requests and building them off of the responses.

FBML Test Console

The *FBML Test Console* allows you to craft and preview FBML in a controlled environment. It can apply rules based on several FBML Canvas configurations, including the application Canvas, wide profile column, and feeds.

Wiki

The official development wiki is provided by Facebook for the developer community. With it, developers can collaborate to create documentation and code to be used by other developers to benefit the community. You can find it at the following URL: `http://wiki.developers.facebook.com/index.php`.

The wiki also allows developers and Facebook staff to document the beta and, while testing Facebook Platform features, updating them quickly as they change. The discussion component provided on every wiki page is also used by developers to communicate their thoughts and opinions about particular parts of the Facebook Platform.

Wiki contributors have also gone so far as to add example code, example images, requested feature lists, and extended documentation above and beyond what Facebook provides.

> *It should also be stated that the wiki isn't just for documentation and example code. It has also been used by developers to discuss and develop feature requests, collaborate on application ideas, and organize social events.*

Bug-Tracking

The latest addition to the resources available to developers is the bug-tracking tool. The Facebook Platform team created a Bugzilla installation on which developers may file and track bugs. Developers can also vote on bugs for which they would like to increase the priority. You can find it at the following URL: `http://bugs.developers.facebook.com`.

Test Accounts

Given that most Facebook applications interact directly with users and engage them directly, testing the application plays an important (but difficult) role. Facebook has formalized a process for designating test accounts for developers to use for this purpose.

A *test account* is defined as a fully functional Facebook user account that is "jailed" so as to not interact with other non-test accounts. Users can use Facebook just like anyone else, but can only interact and engage other test accounts. Test accounts are also forbidden to be owners or developers of applications.

Creating a test account is the same as creating a regular Facebook account. Once the account is created, the account must associate with the test environment using the "Become a Platform Application Test Account" as part of the Developers Application. Doing so will jail the account, essentially disassociating itself from the general corpus of Facebook users.

> **Note that this process is not reversible.**

You can find information about a test account here: `www.facebook.com/developers/become_test_account.php`.

The immediate effect of creating a test account is that the account joins the "Facebook Platform Developer Test Accounts" network. Other test accounts are listed there, and developers should be open to adding other test accounts to assist with application testing. Check it out here: www.facebook .com/networks/?nk=838865800.

Summary

The message that Facebook is trying to send to developers is clear: You are not alone and help is available. The amount of effort put into creating a community around developing Facebook applications is impressive.

Developers have several places from which to draw information and communal knowledge. The Developers Application, Developers Web Site, and wiki all include a vast amount of information on the common problems developers face, as well as the best practices for doing things.

Chapter 9 continues the discussion begun in Chapter 2 by taking the Hello World application and enhancing it. In Chapter 9, you will take some of the concepts you've seen in the last few chapters and put them into action. You will also learn about ways to scale and tune your application toward high load performance.

Doing More with Hello World

Chapter 8 took a turn from active development and focused on the resources and tools available to developers. The community behind Facebook application development is growing significantly, and many people have put a lot of time, effort, and energy into documenting their efforts and experiences for public benefit.

This chapter turns back to application development to follow up with the example application from Chapter 2. This chapter will take the application that has been created and enhance its functionality by adding several staple features.

Looking Back

So, what exactly what was done in Chapter 2? Before setting goals, let's first look back at what was done and what needs improvement. When looking at the project as a whole, the real benefit from the work done in Chapter 2 was to create a small framework that can be expanded upon. In Chapter 2, you took a simple idea, and abstracted the structured business logic and templates to make it easier to enhance later.

As stated in the "Outlining the Features" section of Chapter 2, the purpose of the example project provided was to create a small application that allows users to send greetings to the people in their Friends list. While the finished product of Chapter 2 is complete, there was still work to be done to turn it into a viable Facebook application.

The old application had very little interaction with the Facebook Platform. It had a minimal interface and lacked several of the key viral features that are present in the more popular applications today.

Going Forward

One of the major points I'd like to demonstrate in this chapter is that nearly every feature built for users can offer insight into how your users perceive and use your application. Almost every feature can have one or more associated metrics, and ultimately this is for the greater benefit of the developer.

The first milestone is an overhaul of the application's interaction with the Facebook Platform in regard to the user profiles generated. In many ways, the content displayed on the user's Profile page is the first and best way to describe and advertise your application. Through the user's Profile, your applications have the opportunity to become viral, explaining through action what your application does, and why viewing users should add it.

The second milestone is the addition of information tracking through the Post-Add and Post-Remove application events. When applications tie into this portion of the Facebook Platform, this provides huge potential to learn about how users find your application and for how long they use it.

The second milestone leads to the third milestone — the implementation of an invitation system. Application invitations allow your users to advertise and grow your application for you by hand-picking the friends that they think will likely add the application. In the third milestone, you will also engage in referral tracking, allowing you to see when users accept application invitations and from whom.

Preparation

The changes outlined will include some alterations and addition to the application configuration and database. It is also strongly recommended that these enhancements to the application be made in order, because they relate to each other in several ways.

The `AppConfig` class will be using the new `app_home` variable to track the Web root for the application outside the context of the Facebook Platform. Listing 9-1 shows the updated `AppConfig` class.

Listing 9-1: The updated `AppConfig` class.

```
class AppConfig {
  public static $app_name = 'HelloWorld';
  public static $app_url = 'http://apps.facebook.com/nghelloworld/';
  public static $app_home = 'http://fbexample.socklabs.com/nghelloworld/';
  public static $app_id = '18266139880';
  public static $api_key = '69a09711ee2637755f0091ff5b497733';
  public static $secret  = '9d61409757a5ddae385bba8c2a9d37a3';
  public static $db_ip = '127.0.0.1';
  public static $db_user = 'nghelloworld';
  public static $db_pass = 'password';
  public static $db_name = 'nghelloworld';
}
```

The database will also include two new tables to store application invitations and users, as shown in Listing 9-2.

Listing 9-2: The new table schemas for the application.

```
CREATE TABLE users (
  fb_id INT(14) NOT NULL,
  ts_in INT(11) NOT NULL DEFAULT '0',
  ts_out INT(11) NOT NULL DEFAULT '0',
  total_actions INT(11) NOT NULL DEFAULT '0',
  deleted INT(1) NOT NULL DEFAULT '0'
);
CREATE TABLE invites (
  user_from INT(11) NOT NULL,
  user_to INT(11) NOT NULL,
  ts_sent INT(11) NOT NULL DEFAULT '0',
  accepted INT(1) NOT NULL DEFAULT '0'
);
```

Creating Better Profiles

The goal of the first milestone is to improve the performance of profile updates and changes. Originally, the application created a static block of FBML that was posted to the Facebook Platform to render inside of a user's Profile box using the `facebook.profile.setFBML` API method. For many applications, this is a perfectly acceptable way to update user profile content, and it worked well by showing how to systematically set profile content.

There are several reasons why this approach is inefficient:

❏ The implementation made expensive API requests on every profile change. If one or more users are active on the application, there is no pooling to collapse profile changes for a single user into a single request. This can be expensive for both the application and the Facebook Platform.

❏ The application also blurred the roles of the template code and business logic by generating profile content within the `HelloWorld` class that contained the business logic for the application. This makes user profile template changes more difficult to manage and, in some cases, requires that a developer make the changes as opposed to a designer.

❏ Although the user profile content shared several common elements, the application still posts the entire body of a user's profile to the Facebook Platform, not taking advantage of any shared or cached content.

The alternative to the current approach is the use of the `fb:ref` FBML entity. This is a fundamental change in the approach because it transforms user profile changes from a Push to a Pull model. The general idea is that instead of submitting the user's profile content to the Facebook Platform, you instead post an `fb:ref` FBML entity to the profile once, which contains a URL that has the content for that profile. When the profile content changes, you send a command to the Facebook Platform to refresh the content of the user's profile from the designated URL.

The benefits to this approach are clear:

❑ User profiles can have their content set once, and future updates can be made by issuing small requests to the Facebook Platform.

❑ Profile content can be viewed and tested very easily, without issuing complex methods that update the Facebook Platform's profile content for a user.

This process does not replace the `facebook.profile.setFBML` API method, but merely changes its use. You must still set the user profile content to point to a URL. When the content changes, you make subsequent calls to the `facebook.fbml.refreshRefUrl` API method.

To do this, you must make three changes to the application. The first change will be in the `HelloWorld` class in lib/HelloWorld.class.php. Here you cut out all of the code that builds the FBML that was sent with the `facebook.profile.setFBML` API method. You can replace it with a small FBML block that has the `fb:ref` FBML entity that references a URL that the application will host. This fits the cases where you want to update a user's profile. But to set the initial content of the profile, you must introduce a new class method.

In addition to the changes to the `profile_update` method, you will add the `first_time` method to the application class. This method will set the initial FBML that includes the `fb:ref` entity using the `facebook.profile.setFBML` API method, and then immediately call the `facebook.fbml` `.refreshRefUrl` API method to ensure that there is initial content on the user's profile. Listing 9-3 shows the updated `update_profile` and `first_time` methods.

Listing 9-3: The updated `update_profile` and `first_time` methods.

```
function update_profile($user) {
  $url = AppConfig::$app_home . 'profile.php?user=' . $user;
  $this->fbclient->api_client->fbml_refreshRefUrl($url);
  return 1;
}

function first_time($user) {
  $url = AppConfig::$app_home . 'profile.php?user=' . $user;
  $fbml = "<fb:ref url=\"$url\" />";
  $this->fbclient->api_client->profile_setFBML($fbml, $user);
  $this->fbclient->api_client->fbml_refreshRefUrl($url);
  return 1;
}
```

Next, you must add the htdocs/profile.php page to the application. This page is referenced in the `update_profile` method of the `HelloWorld` class and will serve the content used to display a user's profile content.

Much like the other Canvas pages in this project, this PHP file follows a similar behavior. Within the first few lines of code, it includes the required libraries and creates new `Facebook` and `HelloWorld` class objects.

In the business logic, the first thing you want to do is parse out the user ID passed through the user query string parameter. Without this, you cannot display the user-specific profile content. Once you have the ID of the user whose profile you want to display the content of, you continue by calling the get_greetings method to fetch the greetings sent to and from the user. The logic is taken straight out of what you cut from the update_profile method in the HelloWorld class. Listing 9-4 shows the htdocs/profile.php page.

Listing 9-4: The htdocs/profile.php page.

```php
<?php
include_once '../lib/client/facebook.php';
include_once '../lib/AppConfig.class.php';
include_once '../lib/HelloWorld.class.php';

$facebook = new Facebook(AppConfig::$api_key, AppConfig::$secret);
$app = new HelloWorld($facebook);
$user = 0;
if (isset($_GET['user'])) {
  $user = (int) $_GET['user'];
}

$greetings_from = $app->get_greetings('user_from', $user);
$gfromcount = count($greetings_from);
$greetings_to = $app->get_greetings('user_to', $user);
$gtocount = count($greetings_to);
$tomessage = ";
$frommessage = ";
if ($gtocount) {
  $tomessage = "<p><fb:name uid=\"profileowner\" firstnameonly=\"true\"
useyou=\"false\" /> has been waved to $gtocount times.</p>";
} else {
  $tomessage = "<p>No one has waved hello to <fb:name uid=\"profileowner\"
firstnameonly=\"true\" useyou=\"false\" />!</p>";
}
if ($gfromcount) {
  $frommessage = "<p><fb:name uid=\"profileowner\" firstnameonly=\"true\"
useyou=\"false\" /> has waved hello to $gfromcount people.</p>";
} else {
  $frommessage = "<p><fb:name uid=\"profileowner\" firstnameonly=\"true\"
useyou=\"false\" /> has not waved to anyone.</p>";
}
?>
<fb:wide>
<?php echo $frommessage; ?>
<ul>
<?php foreach ($greetings_from as $greeting) { ?>
<fb:if-can-see uid="<?= $user ?>">
<li><fb:name uid="<?= $greeting['user_to'] ?>" useyou="false" /></li>
</fb:if-can-see>
<?php } ?>
</ul>
<?php echo $tomessage; ?>
<ul>
<?php foreach ($greetings_to as $greeting) { ?>
<fb:if-can-see uid="<?= $user ?>">
<li><fb:name uid="<?= $greeting['user_from'] ?>" useyou="false" /></li>
```

(continued)

Listing 9-4 *(continued)*

```
</fb:if-can-see>
<?php } ?>
</ul>
</fb:wide>
<fb:narrow>
<?php echo $frommessage; ?>
<ul>
<?php foreach ($greetings_from as $greeting) { ?>
<fb:if-can-see uid="<?= $user ?>">
<li><fb:name uid="<?= $greeting['user_to'] ?>" useyou="false" /></li>
</fb:if-can-see>
<?php } ?>
</ul>
<?php echo $tomessage; ?>
<ul>
<?php foreach ($greetings_to as $greeting) { ?>
<fb:if-can-see uid="<?= $user ?>">
<li><fb:name uid="<?= $greeting['user_from'] ?>" useyou="false" /></li>
</fb:if-can-see>
<?php } ?>
</ul>
</fb:narrow>
```

> **Developers should remember that this page is not meant to be viewed through the Facebook Canvas. Therefore, you do not perform the usual checks normally done. While it isn't displayed or referenced anywhere within Facebook, it is important to keep in mind that this page is public and could be viewed by anyone.**

The final task for this milestone is to set off an event to update the user's content for the first time. There are two ways to do this, each with its own pros and cons.

One approach is to have a table column with a `bool` indicating that the user's profile content has been initially set. When the `update_profile` method is called, it would do a quick lookup for that value to determine if it needs to set the profile content with the `facebook.profile.setFBML` API method before it issues a `facebook.fbml.refreshRefUrl` API method request.

Another approach is to use the Post-Add callback URL that is called when a user first adds the application. In this case, when the user first adds the application, the user is directed to a Canvas page within your application where you can do any special build-up or initialization actions required.

For this application, let's use the Post-Add callback URL. The main reason is that you can use the Post-Add event for other purposes, hitting two birds with one stone. The other added benefit is that you can forgo the database lookup on every profile change. To do this, you must implement the call to the `first_time` class method.

On the Configuration Options page for the application (found in the Developers Application), there is a setting available titled "Post-Add URL" under the "Installation Options" group of configuration options (Figure 9-1). Set this option to the welcome.php Canvas page and save the changes.

Figure 9-1: The Post-Add configuration field.

This option leads to the addition of the htdocs/welcome.php Canvas page. The Welcome Canvas page will be the first thing that users will see immediately after they have added the application. As mentioned, this is an ideal place to add an introduction and a quick how-to guide on using the application.

Welcome your new users

Take this opportunity to fully explain the application that the user has just added. If the user added the application because of an invitation from another user or from another user's Profile page, he or she might not have a full understanding of what the application does, or how it can be used. Create a quick 60-second guide on the application and include a set of the features, too.

The Welcome page is starting to look very much like the Index page. You create the Facebook and HelloWorld class objects and perform several validation checks on the page request. Once you have confirmed that the request is valid and is coming from Facebook, you call the first_time class method. Listing 9-5 shows the htdocs/welcome.php Canvas page.

Listing 9-5: The htdocs/welcome.php Canvas page.

```php
<?php
include_once '../lib/client/facebook.php';
include_once '../lib/AppConfig.class.php';
include_once '../lib/HelloWorld.class.php';

$facebook = new Facebook(AppConfig::$api_key, AppConfig::$secret);
$facebook->require_frame();
$user = $facebook->require_login();
$facebook->require_add();

$app = new HelloWorld($facebook);
$app->first_time($user);
?>
<fb:dashboard>
<fb:action href="/nghelloworld/">View My Greetings</fb:action>
<fb:action href="/nghelloworld/wave.php">Send a greeting</fb:action>
</fb:dashboard>
<div style="padding: 10px;">
  <h2>Hello <fb:name firstnameonly="true" uid="<?= $user ?>" useyou="false"/>!</h2>
  <p>Welcome to this application!</p>
</div>
```

Event Tracking with Application Events

The previous section introduced the Post-Add application event set by the Facebook Platform whenever a user adds the application. With the Post-Add and Post-Remove application events, it is possible to track application add-and-remove behavior, providing insight into how users find the application and ultimately what influences them to remove the application. The Post-Add and Post-Remove application events are an ideal place to perform an initialization or clean up actions for new or returning users.

In the application configuration through the Developers Application, the "Post-Add URL" and "Post-Remove URL" options are available under the "Installation Options" group of configuration options (Figure 9-2). If you are doing these enhancements in order, you will already have the Post-Add configuration option set, and the Welcome page will already exist.

Figure 9-2: The Post-Add and Post-Remove configuration options.

The Post-Remove configuration has several caveats that affect this implementation. Unlike the Post-Add URL, the Post-Remove URL is called by the Facebook Platform immediately after the user has removed the application. The user is not directed to the page; the page is only called by the Facebook Platform.

The Post-Add configuration option should be set to the welcome.php page as part of the application Canvas. In this example, the application Canvas is at `http://apps.facebook.com/nghelloworld/`. Therefore, the Post-Add URL is set to `http://apps.facebook.com/nghelloworld/welcome.php`. The Post-Remove URL is an external URL from the Facebook Platform's point of view. In the case of this example, the application resides at `http://fbexample.socklabs.com/helloworld/`. Therefore, the Post-Remove URL is set to `http://fbexample.socklabs.com/helloworld/goodbye.php`.

Continuing where we left off in the previous section, the htdocs/welcome.php Canvas page is used to display initial Welcome content to the user and perform any business logic required by the application. In most cases, this isn't necessary, and developers set the Post-Add URL to the main application Canvas page.

The Welcome page already calls the `first_time` method, so you can focus your changes there. There you make two changes to prepare a clean environment for the user, and then continue by marking when the user added the application. This is done by making two SQL calls to the database. The first executes a SQL DELETE statement to delete any records you may have for that user. The second is a SQL INSERT statement that is used to track when the user added the application.

```php
function first_time($user) {
  try {
    $conn = $this->get_db_conn();
    $sql = "DELETE FROM users WHERE fb_id = $user";
    error_log($sql);
    mysql_query($sql, $conn);
  } catch (Exception $e) {
    error_log($e->getMessage());
  }
  try {
    $conn = $this->get_db_conn();
    $sql = "INSERT INTO users SET fb_id = $user, ts_in = UNIX_TIMESTAMP(NOW())";
    error_log($sql);
    mysql_query($sql, $conn);
  } catch (Exception $e) {
    error_log($e->getMessage());
  }
  $url = AppConfig::$app_home . 'profile.php?user=' . $user;
  $fbml = "<fb:ref url=\"$url\" />";
  $this->fbclient->api_client->profile_setFBML($fbml, $user);
  $this->fbclient->api_client->fbml_refreshRefUrl($url);
  return 1;
}
```

To track application removals, you create htdocs/goodbye.php (Listing 9-6). This page is set as the Post-Remove callback URL. The sole purpose of the Goodbye page is to set the date and time that the user removed the application, and also mark the user as deleted for your records. With these small pieces of information, you can gather information about your users, as well as prompt other users to take certain actions based on what you know.

Listing 9-6: The htdocs/goodbye.php Post-Remove Callback page.

```php
<?php
include_once '../lib/client/facebook.php';
include_once '../lib/AppConfig.class.php';
include_once '../lib/HelloWorld.class.php';

$facebook = new Facebook(AppConfig::$api_key, AppConfig::$secret);
$app = new HelloWorld($facebook);
$user = $facebook->require_login();
$app->goodbye($user);

?>
```

There are a few things to remember when working with the Post-Remove callback URL location:

❑ Facebook users are not directed or relocated to the page, nor is the page included in any part of the Facebook Canvas. So, don't bother displaying content.

❑ The Post-Remove callback URL has its request sent to it after the user has removed the application. Thus, the POST parameters will be different.

The goodbye method called by the goodbye.php page will make the necessary changes to the database.

```
function goodbye($user) {
   try {
      $conn = $this->get_db_conn();
      $sql = "UPDATE users SET fb_id = $user, ts_out = UNIX_TIMESTAMP(NOW()),
deleted = 1";
      error_log($sql);
      mysql_query($sql, $conn);
   } catch (Exception $e) {
      error_log($e->getMessage());
   }
   return 1;
}
```

The last metric to track is the total number of actions made by your user. In this application, there is only one type of action: the "wave," or greeting. You track these actions with an integer field on the users table titled total_actions. In this case, when a user waves to another user, you bump the number by one.

```
function wave_hello($user_from, $user_to) {
   try {
      $conn = $this->get_db_conn();
      $sql = "INSERT INTO greetings SET user_from = $user_from, user_to = $user_to,
row_created = UNIX_TIMESTAMP(NOW())";
      error_log($sql);
      mysql_query($sql, $conn);
      $sql = "UPDATE users SET total_actions = total_actions + 1 WHERE fb_id =
$user_from";
      error_log($sql);
      mysql_query($sql, $conn);
   } catch (Exception $e) {
      error_log($e->getMessage());
   }
   try {
      $this->update_profile($user_from);
      $this->update_profile($user_to);
   } catch (Exception $e) {
      error_log($e->getMessage());
   }
   return 1;
}
```

Sending and Tracking Invitations

Application invitations are a big deal for many applications — and with good reason. Application invitations make it possible to let your application grow through its users. Within the Facebook Platform, users can hand-pick and invite their friends.

When the Facebook Platform was first launched, applications used the now-deprecated facebook.notifications.sendRequest API method to send application invitations to and from users on their behalf. Facebook now uses a different flow and process that is much more direct and clean from the Facebook Platform's point of view.

Allowing users to send application invitations requires the `fb:request-form` FBML entity. On its own, that is all that is required, and it works in the most primitive of ways. However, here you want to go a bit further and implement the ability to also track invitations to see how often they are accepted and when. For this, you add a new page to the project and update the previously introduced Welcome page.

The project will include the htdocs/invite.php Canvas page that will be used as the hub of operations for application invitations. Listing 9-7 shows the Invite page.

Listing 9-7: The htdocs/invite.php Canvas page.

```php
<?php
include_once '../lib/client/facebook.php';
include_once '../lib/AppConfig.class.php';
include_once '../lib/HelloWorld.class.php';

$facebook = new Facebook(AppConfig::$api_key, AppConfig::$secret);
$facebook->require_frame();
$user = $facebook->require_login();
$facebook->require_add();
$app = new HelloWorld($facebook);
if ($_GET['ids']) {
  foreach($_GET['ids'] as $key) {
    $app->record_invite($user, $key);
  }
}

$exclude_ids = $facebook->api_client->friends_getAppUsers();
$sent_invites = $app->get_invites($user);
$exclude_ids = array_merge($exclude_ids, $sent_invites);
$referralTracker = urlencode("?referralbyuser=" . $user);
$app_name = AppConfig::$app_name;
$app_key = AppConfig::$api_key;

$invite_fbml = <<<FBML
<fb:name uid="$user" firstnameonly="true" shownetwork="false"/> wants you to add
{$app_name} to receive greetings from <fb:pronoun objective="true"
possessive="false" uid="$user"/>.
<fb:req-choice url="http://www.facebook.com/add.php?api_key={$app_key}&next=
$referralTracker" label="Add {$app_name}" />
FBML;

?>
<fb:request-form type="<?= AppConfig::$app_name ?>" action="invite.php"
content="<?= htmlentities($invite_fbml) ?>" invite="true">
    <fb:multi-friend-selector max="20" actiontext="Invite up to twenty of your
friends." showborder="true" rows="5" exclude_ids="<?= join(',', $exclude_ids); ?>">
</fb:request-form>
```

The Invite page contains much of the same logic that the other applications use to create the necessary objects and perform the required request validity checks. With this Invite page, you can also exclude users from the invitation list. This may include users that have already been invited by this user and those that already have the application added.

On the application Invite page, one of the first things you do is record any invites that you may have just sent. As seen in the `fb:request-form` FBML entity, you set the action of the form to the Invite page, aggregating all aspects of the invite business logic to the self-contained Invite page. When invitations are sent, it posts to itself the IDs of the users you just invited.

```
if ($_GET['ids']) {
  foreach($_GET['ids'] as $key) {
    $app->record_invite($user, $key);
  }
}
```

You then send a request to the `facebook.friends.getAppUsers` API method to build a list of the users to whom you shouldn't send invitations because they have already added the application. You also look up any past invitations from the viewing user and merge that list with the `excluded_ids` list returned by the API call.

```
$exclude_ids = $facebook->api_client->friends_getAppUsers();
$sent_invites = $app->get_invites($user);
$exclude_ids = array_merge($exclude_ids, $sent_invites);
```

The next task is to build the message that the invitees see when they receive the request. This is relatively easy and includes very little FBML. In this block of FBML, you use the `fb:name`, `fb:pronoun`, and `fb:req-choice` FBML entities to display a brief message and provide the user with a way to add the application. The URL set in the `fb:req-choice` entity is the standard application-add URL, but with one difference. You use the `next` query string parameter to include a tracking beacon. When the user follows the application-add URL, the `referralbyuser` parameter will be passed through to the welcome.php page, where you can record that the application add was made because of an invitation sent by a user.

```
$referralTracker = urlencode("?referralbyuser=" . $user);
$app_name = AppConfig::$app_name;
$app_key = AppConfig::$api_key;

$invite_fbml = <<<FBML
<fb:name uid="$user" firstnameonly="true" shownetwork="false"/> wants you to add
{$app_name} to receive greetings from <fb:pronoun objective="true"
possessive="false" uid="$user"/>.
<fb:req-choice
url="http://www.facebook.com/add.php?api_key={$app_key}&next=$referralTracker"
label="Add {$app_name}" />
FBML;
```

Lastly, you get to the content rendered through the application Canvas. The only thing you set to display is the `fb:request-form` FBML entity to render the invitation Canvas widget. Within the request form, you also use the `fb:multi-friend-selector` FBML entity.

```
<fb:request-form type="<?= AppConfig::$app_name ?>" action="invite.php"
content="<?= htmlentities($invite_fbml) ?>" invite="true">
 <fb:multi-friend-selector max="20" actiontext="Invite up to twenty of your
friends." showborder="true" rows="5" exclude_ids="<?= join(',', $exclude_ids); ?>">
</fb:request-form>
```

The `fb:request-form` entity has two required attributes: `type` and `content`. The `type` attribute is used to set the word displayed on the Home page for the request. In most cases, using *invitation* or *request* is best. The `content` attribute is the HTML-encoded content of the request or invitation.

You also set the `action` and `invite` attributes in the example application. The `invite` attribute states that the intent of this form is to send an invitation. This affects the language displayed. The `action` attribute sets the destination when the form is sent, or when the user follows a Skip link.

With the `fb:multi-friend-selector` FBML entity, you set the `max`, `actiontext`, `showborder`, `rows`, and `exclude_ids` attributes. The `max` and `rows` attributes set the maximum number of users that can be selected, as well as the number of rows in which to display the users. The `actiontext` attribute sets the displayed title at the top of the request form. The `showborder` attribute sets or hides a border around the selector. The `exclude_ids` attribute is a comma-separated list of user IDs to represent users who cannot be selected.

Figure 9-3 shows the finished Invite page.

Figure 9-3: The Invite page.

The beauty of the `fb:request-form` entity is that now developers can make inviting users very easy and reduce the amount of code required in their applications. The Facebook Platform presents your users with a clean and easy way to navigate the interface to select multiple friends to invite, and also takes care of processing the invitations.

The next major step is to read the tracking beacon you set as part of the Welcome page. In the Welcome page, you make a single reference to the new `save_referral` method if the `referralbyuser` query string parameter is passed to the Welcome page.

```
$app = new HelloWorld($facebook);
$app->first_time($user);

if ($_GET['referralbyuser']) {
  $app->save_referral($user, $_GET['referralbyuser']);
}
```

You need to add several new methods in the `HelloWorld` class. The first is the `record_invite` method called on the Invite page. This method is used to store the invitations sent to and from users. The main reason you do this is to track how often invitations are accepted, and how concentrated invitations become. *Invitation concentration* is a metric used to track how often one or more members of a group of friends gets invited by one or more of those friends.

There are several side-effects of application-invitation tracking that benefit application developers. First, you get a clear count of how many invitations are sent by any given user and how often invitations are accepted. You can also use this to prevent users from sending many invitations to a select few users, which could harm the application's spam score.

```
function record_invite($user_from, $user_to) {
    try {
      $conn = $this->get_db_conn();
      $sql = "INSERT INTO invites SET user_from = $user_from, user_to = $user_to,
ts_sent = UNIX_TIMESTAMP(NOW()), accepted = 0";
      error_log($sql);
      mysql_query($sql, $conn);
    } catch (Exception $e) {
      error_log($e->getMessage());
    }
    return 1;
  }
```

The `save_referral` method is called on the Welcome page when the tracking beacon is included in the query string of the request, signifying that the application was added because of an invitation sent by a user. This method is composed of a SQL statement to update the invitation sent from the user as per the query string parameter.

```
function save_referral($user, $user_from) {
    try {
      $conn = $this->get_db_conn();
      $sql = "UPDATE invites SET accepted = 1 WHERE user_from = $user_from AND
user_to = $user";
      error_log($sql);
      mysql_query($sql, $conn);
```

```
    } catch (Exception $e) {
      error_log($e->getMessage());
    }
    return 1;
  }
```

The `get_invites` method is called on the Invite page and returns a list of users who have already been invited by the viewing user.

```
function get_invites($user) {
    $conn = $this->get_db_conn();
    $sql = "SELECT user_to FROM invites WHERE user_from = $user";
    error_log($sql);
    $res = mysql_query($sql, $conn);
    $invites = array();
    if (! $res) { return $invites; }
    while ($row = mysql_fetch_assoc($res)) {
      $invites[] = $row['user_to'];
    }
    return $invites;
  }
```

Statistics and Metrics

With the changes you've made to the application, several features have been implemented in a way that is relatively easy to maintain. You have also been exposed to the groundwork for creating new features and learned how simple it is to take a basic application and build it up.

Let's now turn to the metadata and information from the usage of this application. With the addition of the `users` and `invites` table, it is possible to get some simple metrics and usage information. While the cases presented here are very simple, they do provide working examples of how easy it is to create measurables that developers can use and study to improve their applications.

To get a better idea of how these queries work, you want to seed the database with some data, as shown here:

```
INSERT INTO users VALUES
  (12345, 1188676860, 0, 5, 0),
  (12346, 1188680460, 0, 3, 0),
  (12347, 1188684060, 1188684300, 1, 1),
  (12347, 1188687660, 1188687900, 1, 1),
  (12355, 1188763260, 1188770700, 193, 1),
  (12356, 1188766860, 0, 44, 0),
  (12357, 1188770460, 0, 51, 0),
  (12365, 1188849660, 1188930600, 21, 1),
  (12366, 1188853260, 0, 12, 0),
  (12367, 1188856860, 0, 1, 0),
  (12368, 1188849660, 0, 21, 1),
  (12369, 1188853260, 0, 12, 0),
  (12377, 1188943260, 0, 1, 0);
```

Let's start with a simple way to get the total number of users that have added the application.

```
mysql> SELECT COUNT(*) FROM users;
+----------+
| COUNT(*) |
+----------+
|       13 |
+----------+
1 row in set (0.00 sec)
```

Now, let's look at users who have added the application and not removed it at a later point in time.

```
mysql> SELECT COUNT(*) FROM users WHERE deleted = 0;
+----------+
| COUNT(*) |
+----------+
|        8 |
+----------+
1 row in set (0.00 sec)
```

From there, you can build a daily breakdown of the number of times the application was added.

```
mysql> SELECT COUNT(*), DATE(FROM_UNIXTIME(ts_in)) as dt FROM users GROUP BY dt;
+----------+------------+
| COUNT(*) | dt         |
+----------+------------+
|        4 | 2007-09-01 |
|        3 | 2007-09-02 |
|        5 | 2007-09-03 |
|        1 | 2007-09-04 |
+----------+------------+
4 rows in set (0.00 sec)
```

Summary

Chapter 2 closed with a working application that provided a structure and framework that you could grow into something real, something useful. This chapter added several key features to the application.

In Chapter 10, you will build and deploy an external application and expand on your knowledge of how external applications interface with the Facebook Platform.

10

External Application Development

Up to this point, you have been working with Facebook applications that, from a user's point of view, exist completely within Facebook. They are made to use the Facebook Application Canvas and interact with their users in a very direct way. In most cases, profile changes take effect immediately because a user did something on the application through Facebook.

Chapter 9 expanded the features and functionality of the sample project from Chapter 2 — in some ways turning it into a project that could be released into the wild with functionality that is scalable and practical.

This chapter moves into the realm of external application development. The external application model is very different from what you've been doing thus far because an external application is usually a web site or service that interacts with Facebook without the user taking action on Facebook. An example could be an application that updates a user's profile or adds an item to the user's News Feed when he or she buys a book or finishes a project on another web site.

The role that an external application plays on Facebook is often underestimated. There are many web sites and web services available that have the capability to promote their brand and features by integrating their services through the Facebook Platform. Having a simple Profile Box or Mini-Feed entry not only can draw new users, but also provide existing users with new functionality.

Defining the External Application

As stated, an *external application* is a web site or web service that has a mutually beneficial relationship with the Facebook Platform. It can be an online store that wants its shoppers to be able to show off their latest purchases, or a blog that wants to let its users and readers display the posts they are interested in.

An external application can be as simple as a widget on a user's profile, and even go so far as a data-mining service. The point is that almost any web site or service can become an external application.

When comparing an external application to an *internal application*, there are a few things that increase the divide:

❑ External applications do not have a Canvas page. The application Canvas accessed through Facebook is a huge reason to build internal applications. External applications still have access to a limited number of FBML entities through user profile content, the News Feed and Mini-Feed, notifications, and so on.

❑ External applications have a structured and considerably more complex authentication process. As outlined in Chapter 7, the external application authentication model requires several requests and handshakes to authenticate a user. Internal applications have the added bonus of knowing in advance that the viewing user is authenticated and valid.

❑ External applications do not have any user data or information plainly handed to them. For any given request, an internal application can get the viewing user's Facebook User ID, the complete list of his or her friends, flags to determine if the user has or has not granted the application access, and so on. External applications need to, somewhat frequently, make several API methods to get this information.

Creating an External Application

To demonstrate the creation of an external application, you have many options available to you. The discussion in this chapter deviates from the common idea that an external application has one-shot use code. Instead, in this chapter, you will create a bridge between an existing web application and the Facebook Platform.

The example project in this chapter takes a wiki, powered by MediaWiki, to create an external application. In this case, the MediaWiki installation as a whole is the external application, but the two plug-ins developed act as the bridge between the wiki and the Facebook Platform. The first of the two creates a special page on the wiki to allow the wiki visitors to authenticate using their Facebook usernames and passwords.

The second plug-in of the two makes several features available to the user to show the pages that the user has created or edited in the wiki. The authentication plug-in can work on its own, but the integration plug-in requires the first to build the session and user information for its API method requests.

Preparation

To build this application, you must first have a working installation of MediaWiki on which to develop. You also need access to the database that the wiki will use to manage the additional tables required by the application.

MediaWiki

Before you continue, the development of this application requires some advanced knowledge of MediaWiki and its internals. While the general ideas presented are universal, it is strongly recommended that you quickly read and absorb some of the general knowledge about MediaWiki internals and how extensions work. See the following URLs for more information:

```
http://www.MediaWiki.org/wiki/MediaWiki
http://www.MediaWiki.org/wiki/Manual:Extensions
```

This project uses MediaWiki 1.11.0, PHP 5.2.4, and MySQL 5.0.26.

Before writing any code, let's spend some time thoroughly examining what this application should do:

❑   This example project will demonstrate how a Facebook group for DIY Ice Cream can create a wiki to allow its members to participate and share information with each other.

❑   The application will be broken into two separate plug-ins: AuthFacebook and Facebook. Each plug-in will have a SpecialPage as defined by MediaWiki as a page that users can view and interact with, but it will have strict limitations.

❑   The AuthFacebook component of this application will handle both wiki and Facebook authentication. When a user authenticates through Facebook, it will store the authentication information and session information for later use.

❑   The Facebook component hooks into MediaWiki to watch for events that take place when a user edits or creates wiki pages. It also provides a special page that is only accessible when the viewing user has authenticated through Facebook, and provides several options to customize the user experience. This component also makes several API method requests to update and interact with the Facebook Platform on behalf of the user.

Installing MediaWiki

The installation process for MediaWiki is well-documented and relatively easy. This project assumes that the Web root is at /var/www/ngfbwiki.socklabs.com/htdocs/. You should tailor your installation accordingly.

In essence, you want to download the current version of MediaWiki and unpack its contents in a Web root. You must also prepare for the Web-based configuration page (Figure 10-1) and make appropriate files writable by the web server.

```
cd /var/www/ngfbwiki.socklabs.com/
wget http://download.wikimedia.org/mediawiki/1.11/mediawiki-1.11.0.tar.gz
tar xvzf mediawiki-1.11.0.tar.gz
mv mediawiki-1.11.0 htdocs
chmod a+w htdocs/config
```

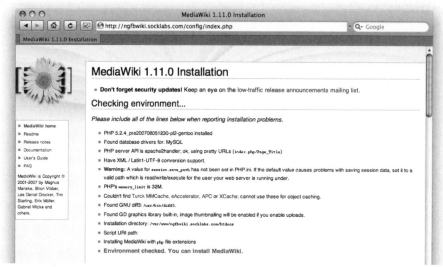

Figure 10-1: The MediaWiki configuration page.

For this project, the wiki name is set to "Do It Yourself Ice Cream." You use the database superuser account to create the tables and grant access. Barring any complications, once the initial settings have been saved, you are instructed to copy the config/LocalSettings.php file to the parent directory.

Although the newly created wiki is operational (Figure 10-2), there are still a few things that must be done before you can develop the application.

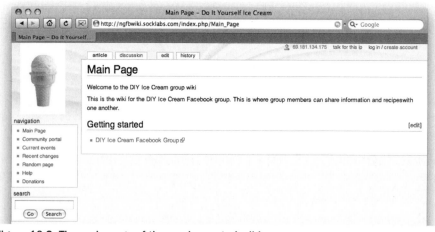

Figure 10-2: The main page of the newly created wiki.

Disabling Anonymous Edits

This wiki is for the members of the DIY Ice Cream Facebook group. To curb spam and abuse, the first thing you must do is to disable anonymous edits to the wiki.

In the LocalSettings.php file in the root directory of the wiki, you must add a single line to set the anonymous group permissions.

```
$wgGroupPermissions['*']['edit'] = false;
$wgGroupPermissions['user']['edit'] = true;
```

Disabling Account Creation

Additionally, you want to disable account creation from the wiki. The only accounts that can be used to authenticate will go through the Facebook Platform authentication process; hence, local accounts are not necessary.

In the LocalSettings.php file in the root directory of the wiki, you must add a single configuration option at the end of the file.

```
$wgGroupPermissions['*']['createaccount'] = false;
```

Removing the Login Link

To discourage users from trying to log into the wiki as local users, you must also remove the anonymous login link visible to non-authenticated users.

In the skins/MonoBook.php file, find the line that iterates through the `personal_urls` array. This array variable contains all of the links that are displayed in the top-right corner of the wiki.

First, find the following code:

```
foreach($this->data['personal_urls'] as $key => $item) {
```

Replace that code with this piece of code:

```
foreach($this->data['personal_urls'] as $key => $item) if ($key != 'anonlogin') {
```

Creating the External Application

The steps to create the application through the Developers Application are very similar to the previous applications described in this book.

1. On the Developers Application, follow the "Set Up a New Application" link to begin the process.

2. On the New Application form (Figure 10-3), assign your application a unique name, and accept the Facebook Platform Terms of Service. In this chapter, the application name is set to "DIY Ice Cream Group Wiki."

3. Leave the Callback URL blank. You will return to this configuration option once you start development of the authentication plug-in component of this project.

4. In the "Base options" group, designate that the application can be added on Facebook.

5. Set the default profile FBML to "This user has not made any edits to the DIY Ice Cream group wiki."

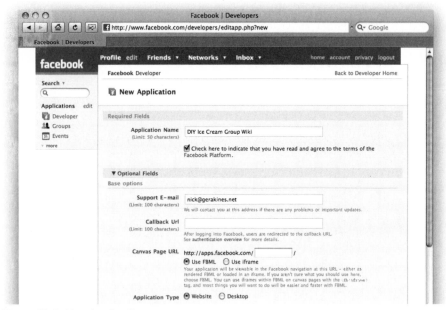

Figure 10-3: New Application page.

Developing the `AuthFacebook` Component

The `AuthFacebook` plug-in component is the first and most important part of this project. The purpose of this MediaWiki plug-in is to allow Facebook users to log in to the wiki using the Facebook authentication process. Through this process, you also store the session information for later use.

In the Web root of the MediaWiki installation, you are interested in the extensions directory. This will be the home of this application. Development starts in the extensions/AuthFacebook directory, where you will create the file AuthFacebook.php. In the extensions/AuthFacebook directory, you also maintain the AuthFacebook.class.php file, which includes the majority of the logic for this plug-in. You also have a copy of the Facebook PHP Library in the root wiki directory under the Facebook Platform Directory.

At this point, you need to prepare the table used by the extension. Through the `mysql` client, create the following table in the database used by the wiki as per the MediaWiki installation:

```
CREATE TABLE user_facebook (
  fb_userid varchar(64) NOT NULL,
  user int(5) unsigned NOT NULL,
  session_key varchar(64) default '',
  session_expires int(11) default '0',
  PRIMARY KEY  (fb_userid),
  UNIQUE KEY user (user)
) ENGINE=MyISAM DEFAULT CHARSET=utf8
extensions/AuthFacebook/AuthFacebook.php
extensions/AuthFacebook/AuthFacebook.class.php
facebook-platform/client/facebook.php
facebook-platform/client/facebook_desktop.php
facebook-platform/client/facebookapi_php5_restlib.php
LocalSettings.php
```

Let's dive right into the plug-in and see what is going on. To understand the code, let's look at it a chunk at a time, beginning with the following code in extensions/AuthFacebookAuthFacebook.php:

```php
<?php
if (!defined('MEDIAWIKI')) {
  echo <<<EOT
To install this extension, put the following line in
LocalSettings.php:require_once("$IP/extensions/AuthFacebook/AuthFacebook.php");
EOT;
  exit(1);
}

require_once("$IP/includes/SpecialPage.php");
require_once("$IP/facebook-platform/client/facebook.php");
require_once("$IP/extensions/AuthFacebook/AuthFacebook.class.php");

define('MEDIAWIKI_AUTHFACEBOOK_VERSION', '0.1');
define('MEDIAWIKI_AUTHFACEBOOK_APIKEY', '385a6b2e60a8249d988663441c92095c');
define('MEDIAWIKI_AUTHFACEBOOK_SECRET', '9904a01fda12369e357453c9906da0a5');
```

The very first code block is meant to prevent direct requests to the page. Immediately after that, several additional PHP files are included and sourced into the component. The next three lines include the definitions of the MediaWiki plug-in version and the API key and secret key as defined by the Facebook Platform.

Next, you need to start laying out the structure of this plug-in. Consider this code:

```php
$wgHideAuthFacebookLoginLink = false;

$wgExtensionCredits['other'][] = array(
  'name' => 'AuthFacebook',
  'version' => MEDIAWIKI_AUTHFACEBOOK_VERSION,
  'author' => 'Nick Gerakines',
  'url' => 'http://www.mediawiki.org/wiki/Extension:AuthFacebook',
```

(continued)

(continued)

```
    'description' => 'Allow wiki users to authenticate using the Facebook Platform
authentication process.'
);

$wgExtensionFunctions[] = 'setupAuthFacebook';

$wgSpecialPages['AuthFacebook'] = 'AuthFacebook';

$wgHooks['PersonalUrls'][] = 'AuthFacebookPersonalUrls';
```

The wgHideAuthFacebookLoginLink variable is used later by the plug-in to determine if the Facebook profile link should be displayed on user pages. The wgExtensionCredits array has a new array pushed onto the end that defines and explains the plug-in. This information is displayed on the Special: Version page. You also tap into the PersonalUrls hook, setting the AuthFacebookPersonalUrls function to be called at that time.

The wgExtensionFunctions variable holds a list of functions called during the initial setup of the plug-in. Plug-ins generally have one function (with no parameters) that is used to initiate the plug-in. The wgSpecialPages contains the list of SpecialPages used by the MediaWiki installation. The map contains a list of classes that will provide Special Page functionality. In this case, you reference the AuthFacebook class as defined in the AuthFacebook.class.php file.

Now, consider this code:

```
function setupAuthFacebook() {
  global $wgMessageCache, $wgOut, $wgRequest, $wgHooks;
  $wgMessageCache->addMessages(array(
    'authfacebooklogin' => 'Login with Facebook',
    'authfacebookrror' => 'AuthFacebook Error',
    'authfacebookerrortext' => 'An error has occured, the site maintainer has been
notified.',
    'authfacebookalreadyloggedin' => 'You are currently logged in as $1.',
    'authfacebooktitle' => 'Facebook Login',
    'authfacebookloggedin' => 'You have logged in as $1.'
  ));
  $action = $wgRequest->getText('action', 'view');
  if ($action == 'view') {
    $title = $wgRequest->getText('title');
    $nt = Title::newFromText($title);
    if ($nt && ($nt->getNamespace() == NS_USER) && strpos($nt->getText(), '/') ===
false) {
      $user = User::newFromName($nt->getText());
      if ($user && $user->getID() != 0) {
        $fb_userid = AuthFacebookGetFBUserID($user);
        if (isset($fb_userid) && strlen($fb_userid) != 0) {
          $url = 'http://www.facebook.com/profile.php?id=' . $fb_userid;
          $disp = htmlspecialchars($url);
          $wgOut->setSubtitle("<span class='subpages'><a
href='$url'>$disp</a></span>");
        }
      }
    }
  }
}
```

The setupAuthFacebook function was appended to the wgExtensionFunctions container and is called by the wiki. In this setup function, you have two goals. The first is to set up any localized variables or messages used by the plug-in. The next is to hook into view of the request and, if it is a user page and the user has authenticated through Facebook, display a link to the profile of that user, as shown in Figure 10-4.

Figure 10-4: The link displayed on the wiki user page of a Facebook user.

Consider the following code:

```
function AuthFacebookGetFBUserID($user) {
  $fb_userid = null;
  if (isset($user) && $user->getId() != 0) {
    global $wgSharedDB, $wgDBprefix;
    if (isset($wgSharedDB)) {
      $tableName = "`${wgSharedDB}`.${wgDBprefix}user_facebook";
    } else {
      $tableName = 'user_facebook';
    }
    $dbr =& wfGetDB( DB_SLAVE );
    $res = $dbr->select(array($tableName),
      array('fb_userid'),
      array('user' => $user->getId()),
      'AuthFacebookGetFBUserID'
    );
    while ($res && $row = $dbr->fetchObject($res)) {
      $fb_userid = $row->fb_userid;
    }
    $dbr->freeResult($res);
  }
  return $fb_userid;
}
```

The AuthFacebookGetFBUserID function is referenced in the setupAuthFacebook function and is used to determine if the user page viewed is associated with a Facebook user. It performs a simple database query based on the User ID of the page viewed and returns a Facebook user ID if there is a match.

Now, look at this code:

```
function AuthFacebookPersonalUrls(&$personal_urls, &$title) {
  global $wgHideAuthFacebookLoginLink, $wgUser, $wgLang;
  if (!$wgHideAuthFacebookLoginLink && $wgUser->getID() == 0) {
    $sk = $wgUser->getSkin();
    $returnto = ($title->getPrefixedUrl() == $wgLang->specialPage( 'Userlogout' ))
? '' : ('returnto=' . $title->getPrefixedURL());
    $personal_urls['authfacebooklogin'] = array(
      'text' => wfMsg('authfacebooklogin'),
      'href' => $sk->makeSpecialUrl( 'AuthFacebook', $returnto ),
      'active' => $title->isSpecial( 'AuthFacebook' )
    );
  }
  return true;
}
```

The `AuthFacebookPersonalUrls` function, as set by the `PersonalUrls` hook, is used to update the links displayed to the wiki viewer in the upper right-hand corner of the page (Figure 10-5). For this application to succeed, it is vital to integrate with MediaWiki as tightly as possible. This is the exact reason that earlier in the chapter you cut out all of the obvious references to the local user login page.

Figure 10-5: The login links created.

The AuthFacebook.class.php file contains all of the structured logic that defines the Special: AuthFacebook page and how it operates. The class itself is a subclass of the `SpecialPage` class as defined in the includes/SpecialPage.php file.

```
<?php
class AuthFacebook extends SpecialPage {

  function AuthFacebook() {
    SpecialPage::SpecialPage("AuthFacebook");
  }
```

In the class constructor, you make a call to the `SpecialPage` class constructor to define the name of the Special Page. See the `SpecialPage` documentation as part of the MediaWiki official wiki for more information on the parameters available to this method.

Now, take a look at this code:

```
function execute($par) {
    global $wgRequest, $wgUser, $wgOut, $wgSessionStarted;
    if (! $wgSessionStarted) {
      $wgUser->SetupSession();
    }

    $this->setHeaders();

    if ($wgUser->getID() != 0) {
```

```
      $this->templateAlreadyLoggedIn();
      return;
    }

    $facebook = new Facebook(MEDIAWIKI_AUTHFACEBOOK_APIKEY,
MEDIAWIKI_AUTHFACEBOOK_SECRET);
    if (! $facebook) {
      $wgOut->errorpage('authfacebookrror', 'authfacebookerrortext');
      return;
    }

    $auth_token = $wgRequest->getText('auth_token');

    if (! $auth_token) {
      $this->templateDefaultPage();
      return;
    }

    try {
      $session_response = $facebook->api_client->auth_getSession($auth_token);
    } catch (Exception $e) {
      $this->templateDefaultPage('There was an error, please refresh the page and
try again.');
      error_log($e);
      return;
    }
    $session_key = $session_response['session_key'];
    $session_expires = $session_response['expires'];
    $fb_userid = $session_response['uid'];

    try {
      $userinfo_response = $facebook->api_client->users_getInfo(array($fb_userid),
array('name'));
    } catch (Exception $e) {
      $this->templateDefaultPage('There was an error, please refresh the page and
try again.');
      error_log($e);
      return;
    }

    $fb_username = $userinfo_response[0]['name'];

    $user = $this->getUserFromFB($fb_userid);

    if (isset($user)) {
      $this->updateUser($fb_userid, $session_key, $session_expires, $fb_username);
    } else {
      # For easy names
      $name = $this->createName($fb_username);
      if ($name) {
        $user = $this->createUser(
          $fb_userid,
          $fb_username,
          $session_key,
          $session_expires
```

(continued)

(continued)

```
                );
            }
        }

        if (! isset($user)) {
            $wgOut->errorpage('authfacebookrror', 'authfacebookerrortext');
        } else {
            $wgUser = $user;
            $wgUser->SetupSession();
            $wgUser->SetCookies();
            wfRunHooks('UserLoginComplete', array(&$wgUser));
            $this->setLoginCookie($fb_userid, $session_expires);
            $this->templateLoggedInPage();
        }
    }
```

The `execute` method is called by MediaWiki when the `AuthFacebook` special page is rendered. This is where the bulk of the code lives and operates. The first few lines of code build a session if it doesn't exist and set any default headers that should be set. You should also try to determine if the viewing user is also logged in, and if so, call the `templateAlreadyLoggedIn` class method and exit. If the viewing user is not logged in, you create a `Facebook` class object and continue. There are two different paths followed, determined by the presence of the `auth_token` query string parameter. If the `auth_token` query string parameter is not present, then you call the `templateDefaultPage` class method and exit. If the parameter is present, then that means that the request has gone through the Facebook authentication process. You must then validate the `auth_token` and fetch any session information associated with it.

If, at any point, the session or user information retrieved from Facebook is invalid, the class displays an error message and prompts the user to restart the process. If the session and user information is valid, then that signals you to log in the user and create an account for that user if it does not already exist.

The `getUserFromFB` class method is called to determine if there is a valid local user account associated with the Facebook user ID via the session information. If the local account does not, in fact, exist, you use the `createName` and subsequent `createUser` class methods to create the local account and store any relevant information (such as the session key and expiration time).

If the local account does exist, you call the `updateUser` class method to update the local information with the most recent and valid session information for later use. Finally, you do an additional check on the user's existence to log the user in, and call the `setLoginCookie` class method to set any cookies that need to be set. You perform the additional check in the edge case where the user is a first-time user and, when created, the creation fails.

Take a look at the following:

```
    private function templateAlreadyLoggedIn() {
        global $wgUser, $wgOut;
        $wgOut->setPageTitle( wfMsg( 'authfacebooktitle' ) );
        $wgOut->setRobotpolicy( 'noindex,nofollow' );
        $wgOut->setArticleRelated( false );
        $wgOut->addWikiText( wfMsg( 'authfacebookalreadyloggedin', $wgUser->getName() ) );
    }
```

The `templateAlreadyLoggedIn` class method is a simple template accessor method that displays a brief message indicating that the user is already logged in. This method uses the localization variables set during the initial setup of the plug-in.

Consider the following code:

```
private function templateDefaultPage($error = null) {
    global $wgUser, $wgOut;
    $wgOut->setPageTitle( wfMsg( 'authfacebooktitle' ) );
    if ($error) {
        $wgOut->addHTML('<table class="messagebox standard-talk" style="border: 2px
solid #000000; background-color: #FFCCCC;"><tr><td align="left" width="100%">' .
$error . '</td></tr></table>');
    }
    $wgOut->addHTML('<p>This wiki uses the Facebook Platform to allow wiki views to
login using their Facebook username and password.</p>');
    $wgOut->addHTML('<p>The login page for local users can be found <a href="/index.
php?title=Special:Userlogin">here</a>, although account creation has been disabled
by the wiki adminstrators.</p>');
    $wgOut->addHTML('<p>To start the authentication process follow the login link
below.</p>');
    $wgOut->addHTML('<p><a href="http://www.facebook.com/login.php?api_key=' .
MEDIAWIKI_AUTHFACEBOOK_APIKEY . '&v=1.0"><img
src="http://static.ak.facebook.com/images/devsite/facebook_login.gif"></a></p>');
    }
```

The `templateDefaultPage` class method renders the content displayed to the viewers of the plug-in page when they are not logged in and the `auth_token` query string parameter is not present. It also takes an `error` parameter and, if present, displays that message to the viewer.

Next, consider this code:

```
private function templateLoggedInPage() {
    global $wgUser, $wgOut;
    $wgOut->setPageTitle( wfMsg( 'authfacebooktitle' ) );
    $wgOut->addHTML(wfMsg( 'authfacebookloggedin', $wgUser->getName() ));
}
```

The `templateLoggedInPage` class method is the last of the template accessor methods used by this class. This method is called after the user has finished the authentication process and is logged in.

Now, let's look at the following:

```
private function setLoginCookie($fb_userid, $session_expires) {
    global $wgCookiePath, $wgCookieDomain, $wgCookieSecure, $wgCookiePrefix;
    global $wgOpenIDCookieExpiration;
    setcookie(
        $wgCookiePrefix . 'AuthFacebook',
        $fb_userid,
        $session_expires,
        $wgCookiePath,
        $wgCookieDomain,
        $wgCookieSecure
    );
}
```

The `setLoginCookie` class method is also called after the user has finished the authentication process. This method sets a cookie with some relevant information.

Next is the following code:

```
private function createName($name) {
    if ($this->isUsernameOK($name)) {
        return $name;
    }
}

private function isUsernameOK($name) {
    global $wgReservedUsernames;
    return (0 == User::idFromName($name) && ! in_array($name,
$wgReservedUsernames));
}
```

The `createName` and `isUsernameOK` class methods are both used when determining if a string qualifies as a valid username. Both methods are used during the user-creation process after a user has authenticated through Facebook and the session and user information has been retrieved.

Consider the following code:

```
private function getUserFromFB($fb_userid) {
    global $wgSharedDB, $wgDBprefix;
    if (isset($wgSharedDB)) {
        $tableName = "`$wgSharedDB`.${wgDBprefix}user_facebook";
    } else {
        $tableName = 'user_facebook';
    }
    $dbr =& wfGetDB( DB_SLAVE );
    $id = $dbr->selectField($tableName, 'user', array(
        'fb_userid' => $fb_userid
    ));
    if ($id) {
        $name = User::whoIs($id);
        return User::newFromName($name);
    } else {
        return NULL;
    }
}
```

The `getUserFromFB` class method is used to retrieve a valid local user based on a Facebook user ID. This information is used by the class immediately after the user has been returned to the AuthFacebook Special Page after going through the Facebook authentication process to determine if the Facebook user has logged into this wiki before. Here it uses the available database helper methods to select the `fb_userid` field from the `user_facebook` table. If a valid ID is returned, it creates a local user object and returns that object.

Now, consider this code:

```
private function createUser($fb_userid, $name, $session_key, $session_expires) {
    global $wgAuth, $wgAllowRealName;
    $user = User::newFromName($name);
    $user->addToDatabase();
    if (!$user->getId()) {
        wfDebug("AuthFacebook: Error adding new user.\n");
    } else {
        $this->insertUser($user, $fb_userid, $session_key, $session_expires);
        $user->setOption('nickname', $name);
        $user->setEmail($fbuid . '@facebook.com');
        if ($wgAllowRealName) {
            $user->setRealName($name);
        }
        $user->saveSettings();
        return $user;
    }
}

private function insertUser($user, $fb_userid, $session_key, $session_expires) {
    global $wgSharedDB, $wgDBname;
    $dbw =& wfGetDB( DB_MASTER );
    if (isset($wgSharedDB)) {
        $dbw->selectDB($wgSharedDB);
    }
    $dbw->insert('user_facebook', array(
        'user' => $user->getId(),
        'fb_userid' => $fb_userid,
        'session_key' => $session_key,
        'session_expires' => $session_expires,
    ));
    if (isset($wgSharedDB)) {
        $dbw->selectDB($wgDBname);
    }
}
```

The createUser and insertUser class methods are used to create local MediaWiki user accounts for Facebook users who have gone through the authentication process for the first time. The createUser class method is directly called by the exec method and creates the actual MediaWiki user account by calling the addToDatabase method. If there were no issues with creating the MediaWiki user account, the insertUser class method is called, which actually stores the association between the Facebook user and the MediaWiki user. The association stored is based on the numeric Facebook user ID and the numeric MediaWiki user ID. It is at this point where you also store the session key and expiration time for later use.

Next up is the following code:

```php
private function updateUser($fb_userid, $session_key, $session_expires,
$fb_username) {
    global $wgSharedDB, $wgDBname;
    $dbw =& wfGetDB( DB_MASTER );
    if (isset($wgSharedDB)) {
      $dbw->selectDB($wgSharedDB);
    }
    $dbw->update(
      'user_facebook',
      array(
        'session_key' => $session_key,
        'session_expires' => $session_expires,
      ),
      array(
        'fb_userid' => $fb_userid
      ),
      'updateUser'
    );
    if (isset($wgSharedDB)) {
      $dbw->selectDB($wgDBname);
    }
}
```

The `updateUser` class method is called by the `exec` method and is used to refresh the locally stored Facebook user to MediaWiki user association information.

With the code for the `AuthFacebook` plug-in written, there is one more step that must be taken to enable the plug-in on the wiki. In the LocalSettings.php file in the root of the MediaWiki installation, there must be a reference to include the plug-in.

```php
require_once("$IP/extensions/AuthFacebook/AuthFacebook.php");
```

Figure 10-6 shows the Special:AuthFacebook page.

Figure 10-6: The Special:AuthFacebook page.

You must also configure the Callback URL option of your Facebook application. Back on the Facebook Developers Application (on the settings and configuration for the application), set the Callback URL to the URL of the Extension you created:

```
http://mywiki.example.com/index.php?title=Special:AuthFacebook
```

Developing the Facebook Component

The Facebook plug-in component is the second part of this project. The purpose of this MediaWiki plug-in is to allow the MediaWiki installation to update the Facebook profile of the authenticated Facebook users when they make any changes to the wiki. This component relies on the existence of the AuthFacebook plug-in.

Much like the AuthFacebook MediaWiki plug-in, this component lives in the Extensions Directory of the Web root. Development starts in the extensions/Facebook directory, where you will create the file Facebook.php. This component will also use the Facebook PHP Library in the root wiki directory in the Facebook Platform Subdirectory.

```
extensions/AuthFacebook/AuthFacebook.php
extensions/AuthFacebook/AuthFacebook.class.php
extensions/Facebook/Facebook.php
facebook-platform/client/facebook.php
facebook-platform/client/facebook_desktop.php
facebook-platform/client/facebookapi_php5_restlib.php
LocalSettings.php
```

The layout and composition of this plug-in are similar to the AuthFacebook plug-in. Let's start the examination with the following code in extensions/Facebook/Facebook.php:

```php
<?php

if (!defined('MEDIAWIKI')) {
    echo <<<EOT
To install this extension, put the following line in
LocalSettings.php:require_once( "$IP/extensions/Facebook/Facebook.php" );
EOT;
    exit(1);
}

require_once("$IP/facebook-platform/client/facebook.php");

define('MEDIAWIKI_FACEBOOK_VERSION', '0.1');
define('MEDIAWIKI_FACEBOOK_APIKEY', '385a6b2e60a8249d988663441c92095c');
define('MEDIAWIKI_FACEBOOK_SECRET', '9904a01fda12369e357453c9906da0a5');
```

The first section of code prevents the plug-in from being called directly by a request. It also includes the required Facebook PHP Library and sets the API key and secret key used by the application.

Now, consider the following:

```
$wgExtensionCredits['other'][] = array(
  'name' => 'Facebook',
  'version' => MEDIAWIKI_FACEBOOK_VERSION,
  'author' => 'Nick Gerakines',
  'url' => 'http://www.mediawiki.org/wiki/Extension:AuthFacebook',
  'description' => 'Allow wiki users to display their wiki edits on their Facebook
user profiles.'
);

$wgHooks['ArticleSaveComplete'][] = array('FacebookNotify');
```

The extension credits are set using the `$wgExtensionCredits` variable. The `$wgHooks` variable is also used to hook into the `ArticleSaveComplete` event that states that an article has been saved by a user. The first element in the array that you set is the name of the function that is called when the event occurs.

Next, take a look at the following:

```
function FacebookNotify(&$article, &$user, &$text, &$summary, &$minoredit,
&$watchthis, &$sectionanchor, &$flags, $revision) {
  global $wgRequest;
  $fbdata = FacebookGetFBUserInfo($user);
  $fb_userid = $fbdata['fb_userid'];
  if (isset($fb_userid) && strlen($fb_userid) != 0) {
    $facebook = new Facebook(MEDIAWIKI_FACEBOOK_APIKEY, MEDIAWIKI_FACEBOOK_SECRET);
    if (! $facebook) {
      return false;
    }
    $facebook->user = $fb_userid;
    $facebook->api_client->session_key = $fbdata['session_key'];
    $article_title = $article->mTitle->getText();
    $article_url = $wgRequest->getRequestURL();
    $total_edits = User::edits($user->getId());
    $subtitle = '<fb:subtitle>Last updated on ' . date("M jS, Y - g\:i a") .
'</fb:subtitle>';
    $profile_content = "<p><fb:name uid=\"$fb_userid\" useyou=\"false\"
firstnameonly=\"true\" /> last updated the wiki page $article_title.</p>";
    $profile_content .= "<p><fb:name uid=\"$fb_userid\" useyou=\"false\"
firstnameonly=\"true\" /> has made $total_edits edits to the wiki.</p>";
    $profile_body = "<fb:wide>$subtitle $profile_content</fb:wide>";
    $profile_body .= "<fb:narrow>$subtitle $profile_content</fb:narrow>";
    try {
      $facebook->api_client->profile_setFBML($profile_body, $fb_userid);
    } catch (Exception $e) {
      error_log($e);
      return false;
    }
  }
  return true;
}
```

The `FacebookNotify` function is called by the wiki during the `ArticleSaveComplete` event when a user creates a new article or edits an existing one. It uses the `$article`, `$user`, `$text`, `$summary`, `$minoredit`, `$watchthis`, `$sectionanchor`, `$flags`, and `$revsion` articles as set by MediaWiki. The first action made by this function is to verify that the user who has made the Save is authenticated through Facebook and has a valid session key. This information is found using the `FacebookGetFBUserInfo` function provided in the plug-in. Once this information is retrieved and a Facebook object created, the profile content is constructed and sent to the Facebook Platform using the `facebook.profile.setFBML` method.

Now, consider the following:

```
function FacebookGetFBUserInfo($user) {
  $vars = array();
  if (isset($user) && $user->getId() != 0) {
    global $wgSharedDB, $wgDBprefix;
    if (isset($wgSharedDB)) {
      $tableName = "`${wgSharedDB}`.${wgDBprefix}user_facebook";
    } else {
      $tableName = 'user_facebook';
    }
    $dbr =& wfGetDB( DB_SLAVE );
    $res = $dbr->select(array($tableName),
      array('fb_userid', 'session_key', 'session_expires'),
      array('user' => $user->getId()),
      'FacebookGetFBUserInfo'
    );
    while ($res && $row = $dbr->fetchObject($res)) {
      $vars['fb_userid'] = $row->fb_userid;
      $vars['session_key'] = $row->session_key;
      $vars['session_expires'] = $row->session_expires;
    }
    $dbr->freeResult($res);
  }
  return $vars;
}
```

The `FacebookGetFBUserInfo` method is called by the `FacebookNotify` method. It takes a MediaWiki user ID and attempts to retrieve the Facebook user ID, session key, and session expiration time as set by the `AuthFacebook` plug-in.

Figure 10-7 shows the results of the profile update.

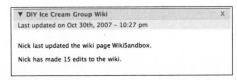

Figure 10-7: The end results of the profile update.

Exercises

This application has come to a close, but there are several things that could be done to extend and enhance its functionality. Take a few minutes to look into the following ideas and consider how they could be implemented:

1. Add group filters to the `AuthFacebook` component. When a user authenticates, the plug-in would make an additional API request to get the groups that the user is a member of, and only allow Facebook users to log in if they are members of a specific group.

2. Add support for Mini-Feed and News Feed updates. In the Facebook component, when a user saves a new article, have an entry made into his or her Mini-Feed listing.

3. Add configuration options to the Facebook component. The Facebook component would have a special page made available to users who are logged in and have gone through the Facebook authentication process. On that page would be options that could be used by the Facebook component to customize the types of profile updates made.

Summary

This chapter examined the idea that almost any web site or technology can bridge its users with the Facebook Platform in the form of an external application. In this chapter's example project, you used a MediaWiki installation to become a hub of information and communication for a niche group of Facebook users.

Chapter 11 recaps what you've learned so far, and begins an examination of the design patterns and best practices developers should consider when developing applications on the Facebook Platform.

11

Best Practices

In the world of software development (as well as many other realms), there are some universal rules. One of them is that there are many ways to do the same thing, and few of them are good. This is especially true when developing applications for the Facebook Platform. Chapter 10 followed this thought by taking a non-traditional web service and creating a Facebook application using some of the simple guidelines outlined throughout the book.

This chapter walks you through several of the strategies used when approaching specific situations and developing features for your applications. This includes example projects that work with automated jobs and protect the privacy of your application users. This chapter also looks at some of the common design patterns seen throughout Facebook and some applications.

Common Goals

Software engineers are problem-solvers. They take an idea, and then model, prototype, and develop an application out of it. Sometimes an issue comes up that stumps them. Developers have a tendency to exhaust all of their resources to solve these problems, which can leave them drained and even turn their attitudes negative about the projects they are working on.

The next few sections work through some of those problematic issues. This discussion addresses two goals. The first is to solve the problems presented. The second is to take what you have learned throughout the book and apply it in practical, working example projects. When looking at the projects involved, keep in mind that these are made to be broken up and applied to your applications as needed.

Creating Automated Jobs

Every so often, a Facebook application must interact with the Facebook Platform on behalf of a user, but without the user initiating the interaction. For this, you need a way to interact with the Facebook Platform in a manner that is detached from the normal modes of operation of the application.

There are two ways to face this problem, and both of them depend heavily on the situation. The first pertains to profile-specific changes. These are when the only interactions made with the Facebook Platform involve updating one or more user profiles.

The second involves API method requests that do more than simple updates to one or more user profiles. This could include writing an entry into a user's News Feed or Mini-Feed, or polling a user's Events or Groups for updates.

I feel that the best way to demonstrate this is with a sample project that provides a service that updates user content on a regular basis. To do this, you will create a small application that reads a feed that updates regularly, and, when it changes, it will post those changes to the user's News Feed through the `facebook.feed.publishStoryToUser` API method, as well as update the users' profile.

Defining the Application

This example application takes the different feeds from The Yahoo Buzz Index (`http://buzz.yahoo.com/`) and provides its users with a way to display those lists on their profiles. It also provides an application Canvas page that lists all of the available lists and allows the user to change the one displayed on his or her profile.

The application gets the information by making HTTP requests to the different feeds and prepares profile content as requested by the Facebook Platform using the `fb:ref` FBML entity set for each type available. This allows you to have a configurable application without having to store any information about the user's choice.

When the page that renders the user's profile content is requested, a query string parameter is called designating one of the available list types provided by The Yahoo Buzz Index, and the proper content is requested and returned.

This application uses the Post-Add Callback URL to find out when a user needs his or her profile content initially set to the default list. In this case, you set the Post-Add Callback URL value to the value of the Callback URL option, and watch for the `installed` query string parameter.

Creating the Application

This application is much like the Hello World project in Chapter 2. The creation of this application follows the same steps.

1. On the Developers Application, create a new application and name it appropriately. In the case of this application, it is named *The Yahoo Buzz Index*, and the Canvas page points to ngbuzzlog.

2. The Callback URL and Post-Add Callback URL options should be set to point to the public location of the htdocs/index.php file.

3. The Side-Nav URL option can also be set to the application Canvas page. In this example, it is set to `http://apps.facebook.com/ngbuzzlog`.

Building the Application

The development of this application is broken into two parts. The first part includes the development of an application that takes several feeds provided by Yahoo and massages the data into a format that can be displayed on a user's profile. It will also include a simple script that can be run as a cron job to update those profiles on a regular basis.

The second half of this project extends the first with database records for each of the users. These records contain the session information required to make API requests on behalf of those users. It stores these data in a way similar to the external application built in Chapter 9.

In the project's htdocs directory are two Canvas pages used to render content to the Facebook Platform. The index.php file will serve the application content directly. The profile.php file is used to return profile content when requested by the Facebook Platform.

In the project's lib directory are three files that include two class libraries and the cron job. The two class libraries include the AppConfig class and the BuzzLog class. The update.php file is the cron job that is called at the command line. The client subdirectory contains the Facebook PHP Class Library.

```
ngbuzzlog/lib/AppConfig.class.php
ngbuzzlog/lib/BuzzLog.class.php
ngbuzzlog/lib/update.php
ngbuzzlog/lib/client/...
```

The BuzzLog class shown in Listing 11-1 contains the core and bulk of the logic for this application. This reduces the complexity of the Canvas page files to simple method calls and provides a single place to focus when developing the internals of the application.

Listing 11-1: The lib/BuzzLog.class.php PHP class.

```php
<?php
class BuzzLog {
  public $fbclient;

  public function __construct($fbclient) {
    $this->fbclient = $fbclient;
  }

  public function update_profile($which = 'buzzover1') {
    $url = AppConfig::$app_home . 'profile.php?which=' . $which;
    $fbml = "<fb:ref url=\"$url\" />";
    $this->fbclient->api_client->profile_setFBML($fbml);
    $this->fbclient->api_client->fbml_refreshRefUrl($url);
    return 1;
  }

  public function get_buzz($list = 'buzzover1') {
    $ch = curl_init();
    curl_setopt($ch, CURLOPT_URL, 'http://buzz.yahoo.com/feeds/' . $list . '.xml');
    curl_setopt($ch, CURLOPT_RETURNTRANSFER, 1);
    $body = curl_exec($ch);
    $matches = array();
```

(continued)

(continued)

```
        preg_match_all("/<title>\d+\.\s+([^<]*)<\/title>/", $body, $matches,
    PREG_SET_ORDER);
        return $matches;
    }

    public function refresh($which = 'buzzover1') {
        $url = AppConfig::$app_home . 'profile.php?which=' . $which;
        $this->fbclient->api_client->fbml_refreshRefUrl($url);
    }

    public function supported_profiles() {
        return array(
            'buzzover1' => 'Overall',
            'buzztv1' => 'TV',
            'buzzmov1' => 'Movies',
            'buzzmus1' => 'Music',
            'buzzgames1' => 'Games',
            'buzzsport1' => 'Sports'
        );
    }


}
?>
```

In the code shown in Listing 11-1, you see that the `update_profile` method takes a Yahoo Buzz Index category and sets profile content to that list for a user. You'll notice that you don't specifically set the user for whom you want to update the profile when calling the Facebook API method. This is because you want it to update the profile content of the user associated with the session key and Facebook application request.

The `get_buzz` method returns a list of the popular search terms for a category according to the Yahoo Buzz Index. This is done by making a very simple `curl` request, and then parsing out the terms using the PHP function `preg_match_all`.

The `refresh` method makes an API request to the Facebook Platform, notifying it that the profile content of an `fb:ref` URL needs to be refreshed.

The `supported_profiles` method returns a simple list of the categories used in this application. It also contains a mapping of the category name and display name.

Let's now look at the htdocs/index.php Canvas page shown in Listing 11-2. This is the application Canvas page and contains the content displayed to the user when accessing the application through Facebook. For this example application, you want to display several of the search term lists, but in a more comprehensive way than on the user profiles.

Listing 11-2: The htdocs/index.php Canvas page.

```php
<?php

include_once '../lib/client/facebook.php';
include_once '../lib/AppConfig.class.php';
include_once '../lib/BuzzLog.class.php';

$facebook = new Facebook(AppConfig::$api_key, AppConfig::$secret);

$facebook->require_frame();

$user = $facebook->require_login();

$facebook->require_add();

$app = new BuzzLog($facebook);

if (isset($_GET['installed'])) {
  $app->update_profile('buzzoverl');
}

if (isset($_GET['switchto'])) {
  $app->update_profile($_GET['switchto']);
}

$overall = $app->get_buzz('buzzoverl');
$tv = $app->get_buzz('buzztvl');
$movies = $app->get_buzz('buzzmovl');
$music = $app->get_buzz('buzzmusl');
$games = $app->get_buzz('buzzgamesl');
$sports = $app->get_buzz('buzzsportl');

$profiles = $app->supported_profiles();

$list_index = array(
 array('What is the internet searching for?', $overall, 'buzzoverl'),
 array('What is the internet searching for on TV?', $tv, 'buzztvl'),
 array('What is the internet searching for at the movies?', $movies, 'buzzmovl'),
 array('What is the internet searching for on the radio?', $music, 'buzzmusl'),
 array('What is the internet searching for that they play?', $games, 'buzzgamesl'),
 array('What is the internet searching for at the arena?', $sports, 'buzzsportl'),
);
?>
<style>
br { clear: both; }
div.wrapper { display:block; float: left; margin-bottom: 1em; padding-left: 2em;
width: 20em; }
</style>
<fb:header>
  What's the buzz, <fb:name firstnameonly="true" uid="<?= $user ?>" useyou="false"
linked="false" />?
</fb:header>
```

(continued)

(continued)

```php
<?php if (isset($_GET['switchto'])) { ?>
<fb:success>
  <fb:message>
    You have switched to the <?= $profiles[$_GET['switchto']] ?> profile
  </fb:message>
</fb:success>
<?php } ?>
<div style="padding-left: 2em;">
<p>What is the internet searching for? Find out with the <a
href="http://buzz.yahoo.com/">Yahoo Buzz Index</a>. Powered by <a
href="http://www.yahoo.com/">Yahoo Search</a>, the Buzz Index categorizes and ranks
search terms to give us a quick snapshot into whats hot on the internet.</p>
<p>This application takes those lists and brings them to your profile.</p>
</div>
<?php
foreach($list_index as $profile) {
?>
 <div class="wrapper">
   <p><?= $profile[0] ?></p>
   <ol>
<?php foreach ($profile[1] as $match) { ?>
     <li><a href="http://search.yahoo.com/search?p=<?= htmlentities($match[1])
?>1&cs=bz&fr=buzz" title="Search for <?= htmlentities($match[1]) ?> on Yahoo!
Search."><?= $match[1] ?></a></li>
<?php } ?>
   </ol>
   <p><a href="<?php echo AppConfig::$app_url ?>?switchto=<?= $profile[2] ?>">Show
this list on my profile.</a></p>
 </div>
<?php
}
?>
<br style="clear: both;" />
```

In the code shown in Listing 11-2, you do very little that could be considered "magical." When the page is loaded, you build a Facebook Client Library object, the application object, and check for several query string parameters before loading the content that is displayed to the user.

The `installed` query string parameter that you check for tells you that the page view is a result of the application being installed (thanks to the Post-Add Callback URL). The `switchto` query string parameter is used to let users configure and set which search term list they would like to display in their profile without the application needing to store any user-specific settings.

The `$profiles` and `$list_index` variables (in conjunction with the `$overall`, `$tv`, `$movies`, `$music`, `$games` and `$sports` variables) are used to display the search term lists to the users.

The htdocs/profile.php file shown in Listing 11-3 is used to return the content that is displayed on the individual user profiles. This page looks for the `which` query string parameter to determine which list it should display.

Listing 11-3: The htdocs/profile.php PHP file.

```php
<?php
include_once '../lib/client/facebook.php';
include_once '../lib/AppConfig.class.php';
include_once '../lib/YahooBuzz.class.php';

$facebook = new Facebook(AppConfig::$api_key, AppConfig::$secret);

$app = new YahooBuzz($facebook);

$which = 'buzzover1';
if (isset($_GET['which'])) {
  $which = $_GET['which'];
}

$profiles = $app->supported_profiles();

$buzz = $app->get_buzz($which);

$long = array_splice($buzz, 0, 10);
$short = array_splice($buzz, 0, 5);
?>
<fb:wide>
  <fb:subtitle seeallurl="<?= AppConfig::$app_home ?>/?ref=profile">
    <?= $profiles[$which] ?>
  </fb:subtitle>
  <div style="padding-left: 3px;">
    <p>This is whats hot right now.</p>
    <ol>
<?php foreach ($long as $match) { ?>
    <li><a href="http://search.yahoo.com/search?p=<?= htmlentities($match[1])
?>1&cs=bz&fr=buzz" title="Search for <?= htmlentities($match[1]) ?> on Yahoo!
Search."><?= $match[1] ?></a></li>
<?php } ?>
    </ol>
    <p><a href="http://buzz.yahoo.com/?ref=facebook_profile">Powered by Yahoo
Search</a>.</p>
  </div>
</fb:wide>
<fb:narrow>
  <fb:subtitle seeallurl="<?= AppConfig::$app_home ?>/?ref=profile">
    <?= $profiles[$which] ?>
  </fb:subtitle>
  <div style="padding-left: 3px;">
    <p>This is whats hot right now.</p>
    <ol>
```

(continued)

(continued)

```php
<?php foreach ($short as $match) { ?>
    <li><a href="http://search.yahoo.com/search?p=<?= htmlentities($match[1])
?>l&cs=bz&fr=buzz" title="Search for <?= htmlentities($match[1]) ?> on Yahoo!
Search."><?= $match[1] ?></a></li>
<?php } ?>
    </ol>
    <p><a href="http://buzz.yahoo.com/?ref=facebook_profile">Powered by Yahoo
Search</a>.</p>
  </div>
</fb:narrow>
```

The key piece of code is the lib/update.php file (Listing 11-4) that actively updates the profile URLs on a regular basis.

Listing 11-4: The lib/updagte.php PHP file.

```php
<?php

include_once 'client/facebook.php';
include_once 'AppConfig.class.php';
include_once 'BuzzLog.class.php';

// Create a new Facebook client object
$facebook = new Facebook(AppConfig::$api_key, AppConfig::$secret);

$facebook->user = AppConfig::$session_info['user'];
$facebook->api_client->session_key = AppConfig::$session_info['session_key'];

$app = new BuzzLog($facebook);

$app->refresh('buzzoverl');
$app->refresh('buzzactl');
$app->refresh('buzzmovl');
$app->refresh('buzzmusl');
$app->refresh('buzzsportl');
$app->refresh('buzztvl');
$app->refresh('buzzgamesl');
```

For each of the search term lists, you call the `refresh` class method. The thing you must overcome is the need for a valid session key and user ID. The `facebook.fbml.refreshRefUrl` API method states that a valid session key must be associated with the request. You can get around this by creating a single infinite session key and storing it in the application configuration class, as shown in Listing 11-5.

Listing 11-5: The lib/AppConfig.class.php PHP class.

```php
class AppConfig {
  public static $app_name = 'ngbuzzlog';
  public static $app_url = 'http://apps.facebook.com/ngbuzzlog/';
  public static $app_home = 'http://fbappps.socklabs.com/ngbuzzlog/';
  public static $app_id = '6082923810';
  public static $api_key = 7d306215bbb25c0605c40096c41586a8;
```

```
public static $secret   = 2fa959d2db491f91659a3473ffaaded9;
public static $session_info = array(
   'session_key' => '95d723b017326fd724195ab-500025891',
   'session_expires' => '0',
   'user' => '500025891'
);
}
```

With the following small change to the local cron daemon, you are done:

```
0 1 * * * php /var/www/fbapps.socklabs.com/lib/update.php
```

And with that, you have a simple model to update dynamic profile content in an offline process.

User-Specific Offline Updates

The previous example works very well and efficiently for simple applications where few updates cover many users. What it doesn't cover is user-specific interactions with the Facebook Platform. To do that, you must make a few changes in the logic of the application.

You must modify the application to store some user metadata in a way similar to the way external applications do.

With the previous example application, consider these changes:

❑ When a user first adds the application (indicated by the installed query string parameter), set the profile content. In addition to that, create a record in the database that stores the list category, session key, session expiration time, and Facebook user ID.

❑ When users change the list that they would like to display (indicated with the switchto query string parameter), update the row with the current session key, session expiration time, and list type.

❑ The scheduled task will require heavy modification to iterate through all of the rows and for each act upon it.

Application Settings and Configuration

Within Facebook, users have a plethora of options, settings, and configuration bits and bobs to customize their experiences. Why should your applications be any different? There are few applications so simple that they cannot accept user input to customize the user's experience. Using several common FBML entities and a few structured objects, you can easily create a page to enhance the user experience.

At the lowest level, the two required components to an application settings page include a Canvas page and a place to store a user's settings and information. It is likely that you'll have some sort of user object that defines users and their attributes. That is probably your best bet, given that a user's settings will seldom be referenced without the rest of the user.

It is also possible to highjack the local session mechanism to store temporary applications specific to a user, but that is beyond the scope of this book.

To demonstrate, let's create the *ngConfigurable* application, which uses several of common elements to create a very simple settings page for the example application.

Creating the Application

This application is much like the Hello World project in Chapter 2. The creation of this application follows the same steps.

1. On the Developers Application, create a New Application and name it appropriately. In the case of this application, it is named *ngConfigurable* and the Canvas page points to ngconfigurable.

2. The Callback URL and Post-Add URL should both be set to the public htdocs/index.php location.

3. The Side-Nav URL option can also be set to the application Canvas page. In this example, it is set to `http://apps.facebook.com/ngconfigurable`.

Additionally, you also need a database and table created to store user information.

```
CREATE TABLE users (
    fb_id INT(14) NOT NULL,
    first_seen INT(11) NOT NULL DEFAULT '0',
    config_profile INT(3) NOT NULL DEFAULT '0',
    config_feed INT(3) NOT NULL DEFAULT '1',
);
```

Building the Application

The development of this application is very simple. There are two Canvas pages that you are concerned with: the default index page and the settings page. The general idea is that when a user first adds the application, the Post-Add Callback URL being set to the default Canvas location will direct the user to the application but also include the `installed` query string parameter. When that parameter is set, you will create a record for that user in the database with various default settings.

For the sake of demonstration, there are only two settings available:

❏ `config_feed` — An integer that represents the type of News Feed entry to be made by this application. A zero value indicates that the user does not want posts made to his or her News Feed.

❏ `config_profile` — An integer representing the type and amount of profile content to display.

The `AppConfig` class contains the API key, secret, and database connection information used. This class can be found throughout the book and will not be covered immediately.

The `Configurable` class shown in Listing 11-6 contains the core and bulk of the logic for this application. This reduces the complexity of the Canvas page files to simple method calls and provides a single place to focus when developing the internals of the application.

Listing 11-6: The lib/Configurable.class.php PHP class.

```php
<?php
class Configurable {

  public $fbclient;

  public function __construct($fbclient) {
    // On creation, set the facebook client
    $this->fbclient = $fbclient;
  }

  function first_time($user) {
    try {
      $conn = $this->get_db_conn();
      $sql = "INSERT INTO users SET fb_id = $user, first_seen =
UNIX_TIMESTAMP(NOW())";
      error_log($sql);
      mysql_query($sql, $conn);
    } catch (Exception $e) {
      error_log($e->getMessage());
    }
    return 1;
  }

  function save_settings($user, $config_profile, $config_feed) {
    try {
      $conn = $this->get_db_conn();
      $sql = "UPDATE users SET config_profile = $config_profile, config_feed =
$config_feed WHERE fb_id = $user";
      error_log($sql);
      mysql_query($sql, $conn);
    } catch (Exception $e) {
      error_log($e->getMessage());
    }
    return 1;
  }

  function get_settings($user) {
    $user_settings = array();
    $conn = $this->get_db_conn();
    $sql = "SELECT config_profile, config_feed FROM users WHERE user = $user";
    error_log($sql);
    $res = mysql_query($sql, $conn);
    if (! $res) { return $user_settings; }
    while ($row = mysql_fetch_assoc($res)) {
      $user_settings = $row;
    }
    return $user_settings;
  }

  function get_db_conn() {
    $conn = mysql_connect(
```

(continued)

(continued)

```
          AppConfig::$db_ip,
          AppConfig::$db_user,
          AppConfig::$db_pass
      );
      if (! $conn) {
          throw new Exception('Error connecting to database: ' . mysql_error());
      }
      $success = mysql_select_db(AppConfig::$db_name, $conn);
      if (! $success) {
          throw new Exception('Error connecting to database: ' . mysql_error());
      }
      return $conn;
    }
  }
  ?>
```

In the code shown in Listing 11-6, the `first_time` method is called on the default index Canvas page when the installed query string parameter is set. This method creates a new user record in the database keyed by the Facebook user ID. It also sets the default configuration values for the user.

The `save_settings` method is called on the settings page when a user has submitted the form to save his or her settings. Its three parameters include the user in question and the two POST variables containing the form data. The `get_settings` method is also called on the settings page and retrieves the settings of a user.

Now, consider the htdocs/index.php Canvas page shown in Listing 11-7. This is the default application Canvas page and, in this example, is primarily used to detect when a user first adds the application.

Listing 11-7: The htdocs/index.php Canvas page.

```
<?php

include_once '../lib/client/facebook.php';
include_once '../lib/AppConfig.class.php';
include_once '../lib/Configurable.class.php';

$facebook = new Facebook(AppConfig::$api_key, AppConfig::$secret);

$facebook->require_frame();

$user = $facebook->require_login();

$facebook->require_add();

$app = new Configurable($facebook);

if (isset($_GET['installed'])) {
  $app->first_time($user);
}

?>
<fb:dashboard>
```

```
<fb:action href="<?php echo AppConfig::$app_url ?>">Home</fb:action>
<fb:action href="<?php echo AppConfig::$app_url ?>">Settings</fb:action>
</fb:dashboard>

<div style="padding: 10px;">
  <h2>Hello <fb:name firstnameonly="true" uid="<?= $user ?>" useyou="false"/>!</h2>
  <p>Isn't it time for bed?</p>
</div>
```

The settings.php Canvas page shown in Listing 11-8 is the focus of this project. This is where you fetch and store the user's settings. You use the fb:editor FBML entity and related FBML entities to create a form with several custom form elements.

Listing 11-8: The settings.php Canvas page.

```php
<?php

include_once '../lib/client/facebook.php';
include_once '../lib/AppConfig.class.php';
include_once '../lib/Configurable.class.php';

// Create a new Facebook client object
$facebook = new Facebook(AppConfig::$api_key, AppConfig::$secret);

// Prevent this page from being viewed outside the context of
// app.facebook.com/appname/
$facebook->require_frame();

// Prevent this page from being viewed without a valid logged in user
// -- NOTE: This does not mean that the logged in user has added the application
$user = $facebook->require_login();

// Require the viewing user to have added the application.
$facebook->require_add();

$app = new Configurable($facebook);

if (isset($_GET['do'])) {
  $app->save_settings($user, $_POST['profile'], $_POST['news_feed']);
}

$user_settings = $app->get_settings($user);

?>
<fb:dashboard>
<fb:action href="/ngconfigurable/">Home</fb:action>
<fb:action href="/ngconfigurable/settings.php">Settings</fb:action>
</fb:dashboard>

<div style="padding: 10px;">
  <h2>Settings</h2>
<?php if ($saved) { ?>
```

(continued)

(continued)

```
      <fb:success>
        <fb:message>Your settings have been saved.</fb:message>
      </fb:success>
<?php } ?>
<fb:editor action="?do=1" labelwidth="200">
  <fb:editor-custom>
  <fb:editor-custom label="Feed Settings">
    <select name="news_feed">
      <option value="0"<?php if ($user_settings['feed'] == 0) { ?>
selected="selected"<?php } ?>>Do not update my News Feed</option>
      <option value="1"<?php if ($user_settings['feed'] == 1) { ?>
selected="selected"<?php } ?>>Update my News Feed</option>
    </select>
  </fb:editor-custom>
  <fb:editor-custom label="Profile Settings">
    <select name="profile">
      <option value="0"<?php if ($user_settings['profile'] == 0) { ?>
selected="selected"<?php } ?>>Show all data</option>
      <option value="1"<?php if ($user_settings['profile'] == 1) { ?>
selected="selected"<?php } ?>>Show only a teaser</option>
    </select>
  </fb:editor-custom>
  <fb:editor-buttonset>
    <fb:editor-button value="Save"/>
    <fb:editor-cancel />
  </fb:editor-buttonset>
</fb:editor>
</div>
```

Figure 11-1 shows the Settings page.

Figure 11-1: The Settings page.

Respecting User Privacy in a Social World

Facebook has gone to great lengths to protect the privacy of users. A multitude of options and privacy settings allow users to customize how much of their information is available. Through the Facebook Platform, you are provided the tools to protect the privacy of your application's users, and should continue to do so. There are several places where your users' privacy can become compromised. One is on Canvas pages where information related to many users is available. This could be a search page or directory of some sort. Another is on Canvas pages where information limited to one user is available. This would include some sort of profile for a user specific to the context of the application.

One of the easiest ways to stamp out privacy leaks is to use available FBML entities. The `if-can-see` and `if-can-see-photo` FBML entities should be used liberally, as they do an excellent job of enforcing user privacy settings and preventing information from being viewed without permission. In most cases, the information will be displayed. However, this will prevent users from viewing users who may have blocked them, which is one of the most important cases.

```
<fb:if-can-see uid="12345" what="profile">
  Check out how cool <fb:name uid="12345" /> is.
  <fb:else>Sorry, no dice.</fb:else>
</fb:if-can-see>
```

Following are some of the cases that should be included in general quality-assurance checks:

❑　A user has blocked one or more users, and those users should not be able to see any information relevant to that user.

❑　A user has set privacy settings such that only his or her friends can see the user's information, including the user's name, networks, and location.

❑　A user has set the privacy of one or more photos and albums so that only the user's friends can see photos that the user owns.

Caveats

Throughout the community, Developers Web Site, wiki, numerous blogs, forums, and so on, there is a vast amount of information available. Every now and then, something important slips through the documentation's cracks and is found on a forum, blog post, or wiki discussion page that can have an impact on the development of your Facebook application.

Callback URLs Are Not to Redirect

When setting one of the Callback URL application settings, ensure that the URL provided does not redirect to another URL. The Facebook Platform does not follow or crawl URLs, and this can lead to confusion in the development and debugging of your application.

The 12-Second Rule

The Facebook Platform has a 12-second time-out when making requests of any kind. This includes requests used to render Canvas content, requests made against any of the Callback URL application settings, requests to fetch or cache images, and also when freshening cached content referenced by the `fb:ref` FBML entity.

Callback URLS Cannot Be Made Using SSL

Your Callback URLs must exist as HTTP, not HTTPS.

Design Patterns

Facebook has a multitude of elements and widgets that are recycled and used throughout Facebook and the Facebook Platform to provide a consistent look and feel. As a developer, you can take advantage of these elements to provide a user interface that integrates with Facebook as closely as possible.

Common Elements

The common elements throughout Facebook include the following:

❑ **Bands of Content Broken into Small Manageable Sections** — For example, on the Home page, on the right side, there are three to five sections that are very focused but live in a single band. In the user profile, the narrow band contains small, managed sections. A group page may have many subsections with relevant content to the group.

❑ **Tabs** — Throughout the site are areas where tabs are used to separate sections and content.

❑ **Dashboards** — Various parts of the site include a "Dashboard" widget that distinguishes separate but related content, and provides an "Add" widget. This easily represents CRUD.

❑ **Horizontal Thumbnails** — Sometimes this includes multiple rows.

❑ **Vertical Line Separated Lists** — See the News Feed, message boards, Walls, and so on, for example. These range from the simple to the more complex.

❑ **Success, Error, and Informational Messages** — These messages are displayed in standard white, light yellow, or light red boxes throughout the site.

❑ **Strictly Styled Forms** — Form elements are rendered in strict table layouts with two columns. The left column identifies the field name and the right column identifies the field by name.

❑ **The Share Button** — The Share button is used throughout Facebook to provide a single visual style to indicate that something can be saved and given to another user.

❑ **Dialog Windows** — Dialog windows are used throughout Facebook for confirmation widgets and user input.

Styles and Colors

Throughout Facebook there are between eight and 12 common colors used.

❑ #0e1f5b

❑ #3b5998 (headers and links)

❑ #7f93bc (the line between Facebook and Links)

❑ #95a5c6

❑ #bdc7d8

❑ #c3cddf

❑ #d8dfea

❑ #f7f7f7

❑   #c4b3c3 (graphs)

❑   #b3cbbc

❑   #67a54b (special buttons, advertising)

The first seven colors are considered core colors and have the heaviest influence throughout Facebook. The last several colors are recent additions and have been seen on the Ads and Pages sections.

Canvas Navigation

This section describes the navigational units.

Tabs

Tabs are used to describe a layout in a very generic way. In your applications, they are constructed with the `fb:tabs` FBML entity. This provides a very simple row of either right- or left-aligned tabs. There are plenty of places within Facebook that use tabs as a navigational unit, including the following:

❑   Tabs provide a very simple and basic interface to indicate multiple sections or places within a larger group or section.

❑   Tab actions can have a right or left alignment.

❑   Tabs can be used as a sub-navigational unit in addition to a dashboard.

❑   Tabs cannot be customized or styled.

Figure 11-2 shows an example of tab usage.

Figure 11-2: An example of a Tabs widget.

Dashboard

The Dashboard widget creates a very clean, styled widget that reserves placement and places emphasis on areas with user input and Help sections. In your application, the dashboard is created with the `fb:dashboard` FBML entity. Following are some common uses:

❑   Provides a very clean display for a CRUD interface.

❑   Automatically displays a title header for the application using it.

❑   Highlights sections for help or knowledge transfer.

❑   Highlights sections of user input with a styled button.

❑   The header displayed cannot be changed.

❑   The style and design cannot be altered.

❑   Actions with long titles can break the clean look of the widget.

Figure 11-3 shows an example of dashboard usage.

Figure 11-3: An example dashboard.

Menus and Lists

Menus and lists are used to cluster navigational links in a clean way. Currently, there are no FBML entities provided to easily create menus or link lists as seen on Facebook. Examples uses include the following:

❑ The side navigational unit that Facebook users can customize with core Facebook components and applications developed on the Facebook Platform

❑ The "Friends" menu as part of the horizontal link list at the top of every Facebook page

Figure 11-4 shows an example of a menu.

Figure 11-4: An example menu.

Wizard

Wizards are selectively used on Facebook. They come into the picture when building multi-step interfaces such as user registration or the creation of an ad campaign or Facebook Page.

Displaying Ads

Displaying advertisements or paid links is a big part of many applications. There are some that do an excellent job at highlighting advertisements, working them into the application.

A simple and easy way to display an advertising banner is through the use of the `fb:iframe` FBML entity. Consider the following example implementation of the `fb:iframe` FBML entity:

```
<hr />
<div style="padding: 5px;">
<center>
<fb:iframe src="http://my.app.domain/ads.html" style="width: 500px; height: 90px;"
frameborder="0" scrolling="0" />
</center>
</div>
```

The contents of ads.html are included in the application through the generated iFrame, and the ads are displayed appropriately.

```html
<html>
<body>
<script type="text/javascript">
    var AdBrite_Title_Color = '0000FF';
    var AdBrite_Text_Color = '000000';
    var AdBrite_Background_Color = 'FFFFFF';
    var AdBrite_Border_Color = 'FFFFFF';
</script>
<span style="white-space:nowrap;">
  <script src="http://ads.adbrite.com/mb/text_group.php?sid=12345&zs=12345"
type="text/javascript"></script>
  <a target="_top"
href="http://www.adbrite.com/mb/commerce/purchase_form.php?opid=12345&afsid=1">
    <img src="http://files.adbrite.com/mb/images/adbrite-your-ad-here-banner.gif"
style="background-color:#FFFFFF" alt="Your Ad Here" width="11" height="60"
border="0" />
  </a>
</span>
</body>
</html>
```

Currently, Facebook has not implemented a way to allow application developers to benefit from the in-house advertising by Facebook.

Developers should be aware that Facebook does display advertisements in the areas outside of the application Canvas.

Using Dialogs Efficiently

Dialogs are an easy way to create interfaces that have little impact on the layout of your application on the application Canvas page. Dialogs can be used to confirm actions or accept user input when interacting with your applications.

To demonstrate how dialogs can be used, let's look at the following dialogs example application. With it, you will create two types of dialogs. The first submits a form and forces a page refresh. The second uses the mock-Ajax code provided by Facebook to fetch content and display it.

Creating the Application

This application is much like the Hello World project in Chapter 2. The creation of this application follows the same steps:

1. On the Developers Application, create a New Application and name it appropriately. In the case of this application, it is named *ngDialogs* and the Canvas page points to ngdialogs.

2. Set the Callback URL appropriately. Setting the Post-Add or Post-Remove configuration options isn't required for this project.

3. The Side-Nav URL option can also be set to the application Canvas page. In this example, it is set to http://apps.facebook.com/ngdialogs.

Building the Application

This application consists of two pages. The first is htdocs/index.php, or the default Canvas page. The index page contains the dialog FBML used to create two dialogs that are activated using an `onclick` event.

```php
<?php

include_once '../lib/client/facebook.php';
include_once '../lib/AppConfig.class.php';

$facebook = new Facebook(AppConfig::$api_key, AppConfig::$secret);

$facebook->require_frame();

$user = $facebook->require_login();

$facebook->require_add();

?>
<fb:header>Dialog Example</fb:header>
<div style="padding: 10px;">
  <h2>Hello <fb:name firstnameonly="true" uid="<?= $user ?>" useyou="false"/>!</h2>
<?php if (isset($_POST['color'])) { ?>
<fb:success><fb:message>Your order for a <?= $_POST['color'] ?> cupcake has been
made.</fb:message></fb:success>
<?php } ?>
  <p><a href="#" clicktoshowdialog="order_dialog">Order a cupcake</a>.</p>
  <p><a href="#" clicktoshowdialog="custom_order_dialog">Order a custom cupcake</a>.</p>
</div>

<fb:dialog id="custom_order_dialog" cancel_button="1">
  <fb:dialog-title>Order a custom cupcake.</fb:dialog-title>
  <fb:dialog-content>
    <p>What color would you like?</p>
    <form id="custom_order_form" method="POST">
      <input type="radio" name="color" value="white" /> White
      <input type="radio" name="color" value="red" /> Red
    </form>
  </fb:dialog-content>
  <fb:dialog-button type="submit" value="Order" form_id="custom_order_form" />
</fb:dialog>

<fb:dialog id="order_dialog">
  <fb:dialog-title>Order a cupcake</fb:dialog-title>
  <fb:dialog-content><form id="order_form">Confirm to place
your order.</form></fb:dialog-content>
  <fb:dialog-button type="submit" value="Order"
clickrewriteurl="http://blog.socklabs.com/fbapps/ngdialogs/htdocs/response.php"
clickrewriteid="order_dialog" clickrewriteform="order_form" />
</fb:dialog>
```

The first block of PHP code creates a Facebook object and verifies the request. In the body of the FBML, you have two links that display the dialogs you defined through the `fb:dialog` FBML entities. Note the `clicktoshowdialog` attributes on the two links. The values of those attributes match the unique IDs given to the dialogs defined later. Figure 11-5 shows the first dialog, and Figure 11-6 shows the response of the first dialog.

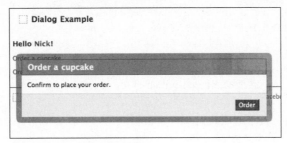

Figure 11-5: The first dialog.

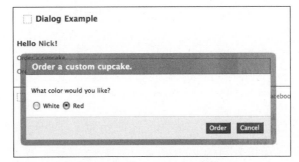

Figure 11-6: The response of the first dialog.

As identified by `custom_order_dialog`, the first dialog you define contains a form for user input and submits that form. It doesn't contain any fancy mock-Ajax calls and is fairly straightforward in implementation.

The second dialog defined acts as a confirmation dialog and does not contain any visible form elements. This dialog uses the `clickrewriteurl`, `clickrewriteid`, and `clickrewriteform` mock-Ajax attributes to submit a form and rewrite the contents of the dialog with the response.

The htdocs/response.php file contains the response displayed by the second dialog defined.

```
<fb:dialogresponse>
  <fb:dialog-title>Order Complete</fb:dialog-title>
  <fb:dialog-content>Your order has been made. Thank you.</fb:dialog-content>
  <fb:dialog-button type="button" value="Close" close_dialog="1" />
</fb:dialogresponse>
```

Figure 11-7 shows this dialog.

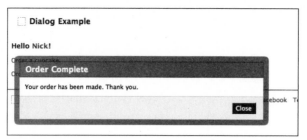

Figure 11-7: The confirmation of the first dialog.

The response contains the `fb:dialogresponse` FBML entity and several child entities that define what content is displayed and how it interacts with the parent dialog.

Defining the dialogs will not display them. Displaying a dialog must be triggered by an event.

Summary

Not every issue is covered in a book, but this discussion did cover some of the basics. This chapter stepped through some of the common goals that developers have when developing applications and features.

PHP File Reference

This appendix provides code listings for the following:

❏   The facebook.php PHP file (Listing A-1)

❏   The facebook_desktop.php PHP file (Listing A-2)

❏   The facebookapi_php5_restlib.php PHP file (Listing A-3)

Listing A-1: The facebook.php PHP file.

```php
<?php
//
// +-------------------------------------------------------------------------
-+
// | Facebook Platform PHP5 client                                          |
// +-------------------------------------------------------------------------
-+
// | Copyright (c) 2007 Facebook, Inc.
|
// | All rights reserved.
|
// |
|
// | Redistribution and use in source and binary forms, with or without
|
// | modification, are permitted provided that the following conditions
|
// | are met:
|
// |
|
// | 1. Redistributions of source code must retain the above copyright
|
// |    notice, this list of conditions and the following disclaimer.
|
```

(continued)

Listing A-1 (continued)

```
// |  2. Redistributions in binary form must reproduce the above copyright     |
// |     notice, this list of conditions and the following disclaimer in the   |
// |     documentation and/or other materials provided with the distribution.  |
// |                                                                            |
// | THIS SOFTWARE IS PROVIDED BY THE AUTHOR ``AS IS'' AND ANY EXPRESS OR       |
// | IMPLIED WARRANTIES, INCLUDING, BUT NOT LIMITED TO, THE IMPLIED WARRANTIES  |
// | OF MERCHANTABILITY AND FITNESS FOR A PARTICULAR PURPOSE ARE DISCLAIMED.    |
// | IN NO EVENT SHALL THE AUTHOR BE LIABLE FOR ANY DIRECT, INDIRECT,           |
// | INCIDENTAL, SPECIAL, EXEMPLARY, OR CONSEQUENTIAL DAMAGES (INCLUDING, BUT   |
// | NOT LIMITED TO, PROCUREMENT OF SUBSTITUTE GOODS OR SERVICES; LOSS OF USE,  |
// | DATA, OR PROFITS; OR BUSINESS INTERRUPTION) HOWEVER CAUSED AND ON ANY      |
// | THEORY OF LIABILITY, WHETHER IN CONTRACT, STRICT LIABILITY, OR TORT        |
// | (INCLUDING NEGLIGENCE OR OTHERWISE) ARISING IN ANY WAY OUT OF THE USE OF   |
// | THIS SOFTWARE, EVEN IF ADVISED OF THE POSSIBILITY OF SUCH DAMAGE.          |
// +----------------------------------------------------------------------------+
// | For help with this library, contact developers-help@facebook.com          |
// +----------------------------------------------------------------------------+
//

include_once 'facebookapi_php5_restlib.php';

class Facebook {
  public $api_client;

  public $api_key;
  public $secret;

  public $fb_params;
  public $user;

  public function __construct($api_key, $secret) {
    $this->api_key    = $api_key;
    $this->secret     = $secret;

    $this->api_client = new FacebookRestClient($api_key, $secret);

    $this->validate_fb_params();
    if (isset($this->fb_params['friends'])) {
      $this->api_client->friends_list = explode(',', $this->fb_params['friends']);
    }
    if (isset($this->fb_params['added'])) {
      $this->api_client->added = $this->fb_params['added'];
    }
  }

  public function validate_fb_params() {
    $this->fb_params = $this->get_valid_fb_params($_POST, 48*3600, 'fb_sig');
    if (!$this->fb_params) {
      $this->fb_params = $this->get_valid_fb_params($_GET, 48*3600, 'fb_sig');
    }
    if ($this->fb_params) {
      // If we got any fb_params passed in at all, then either:
      // - they included an fb_user / fb_session_key, which we should assume to be
correct
```

```
        // - they didn't include an fb_user / fb_session_key, which means the user
doesn't have a
//      valid session and if we want to get one we'll need to use require_login().
(Calling
        //      set_user with null values for user/session_key will work properly.)

// Note that we should *not* use our cookies in this scenario, since they may be
referring to
        // the wrong user.
        $user        = isset($this->fb_params['user'])         ? $this->fb_
params['user'] : null;
        $session_key = isset($this->fb_params['session_key']) ? $this->fb_
params['session_key'] : null;
        $expires     = isset($this->fb_params['expires'])      ? $this->fb_
params['expires'] : null;
        $this->set_user($user, $session_key, $expires);
    } else if (!empty($_COOKIE) && $cookies = $this->get_valid_fb_params($_COOKIE,
null, $this->api_key)) {
        // use $api_key . '_' as a prefix for the cookies in case there are
        // multiple facebook clients on the same domain.
        $this->set_user($cookies['user'], $cookies['session_key']);
    } else if (isset($_GET['auth_token']) && $session = $this->do_get_session($_
GET['auth_token'])) {
        $this->set_user($session['uid'], $session['session_key'],
$session['expires']);
    }

    return !empty($this->fb_params);
  }

  public function do_get_session($auth_token) {
    try {
      return $this->api_client->auth_getSession($auth_token);
    } catch (FacebookRestClientException $e) {
      // API_EC_PARAM means we don't have a logged in user, otherwise who
      // knows what it means, so just throw it.
      if ($e->getCode() != FacebookAPIErrorCodes::API_EC_PARAM) {
        throw $e;
      }
    }
  }

  public function redirect($url) {
    if ($this->in_fb_canvas()) {
      echo '<fb:redirect url="' . $url . '"/>';
    } else if (preg_match('/^https?:\/\/([^\/]*\.)?facebook\.com(:\d+)?/i', $url))
{
      // make sure facebook.com url's load in the full frame so that we don't
      // get a frame within a frame.
      echo "<script type=\"text/javascript\">\ntop.location.href = \"$url\";\n</
script>";
```

(continued)

Listing A-1 *(continued)*

```php
      } else {
        header('Location: ' . $url);
      }
      exit;
    }

  public function in_frame() {
     return isset($this->fb_params['in_canvas']) || isset($this->fb_params['in_
iframe']);
   }
  public function in_fb_canvas() {
     return isset($this->fb_params['in_canvas']);
   }

  public function get_loggedin_user() {
     return $this->user;
   }

  public static function current_url() {
     return 'http://' . $_SERVER['HTTP_HOST'] . $_SERVER['REQUEST_URI'];
   }

  public function require_login() {
    if ($user = $this->get_loggedin_user()) {
      return $user;
    }
    $this->redirect($this->get_login_url(self::current_url(), $this->in_frame()));
   }

  public function require_install() {
    // this was renamed, keeping for compatibility's sake
    return $this->require_add();
   }

  public function require_add() {
    if ($user = $this->get_loggedin_user()) {
      if ($this->fb_params['added']) {
        return $user;
      }
    }
    $this->redirect($this->get_add_url(self::current_url()));
   }

  public function require_frame() {
    if (!$this->in_frame()) {
      $this->redirect($this->get_login_url(self::current_url(), true));
    }
   }

  public static function get_facebook_url($subdomain='www') {
     return 'http://' . $subdomain . '.facebook.com';
   }

  public function get_install_url($next=null) {
```

```php
    // this was renamed, keeping for compatibility's sake
    return $this->get_add_url($next);
}

public function get_add_url($next=null) {
  return self::get_facebook_url().'/add.php?api_key='.$this->api_key .
    ($next ? '&next=' . urlencode($next) : '');
}

public function get_login_url($next, $canvas) {
    return self::get_facebook_url().'/login.php?v=1.0&api_key=' . $this->api_key .
      ($next ? '&next=' . urlencode($next)  : '') .
      ($canvas ? '&canvas' : '');
}

public static function generate_sig($params_array, $secret) {
    $str = '';

    ksort($params_array);
    // Note: make sure that the signature parameter is not already included in
    //        $params_array.
    foreach ($params_array as $k=>$v) {
      $str .= "$k=$v";
    }
    $str .= $secret;

    return md5($str);
}

public function set_user($user, $session_key, $expires=null) {
    if (!$this->in_fb_canvas() && (!isset($_COOKIE[$this->api_key . '_user'])
                                  || $_COOKIE[$this->api_key . '_user'] != $user))
{
      $cookies = array();
      $cookies['user'] = $user;
      $cookies['session_key'] = $session_key;
      $sig = self::generate_sig($cookies, $this->secret);
      foreach ($cookies as $name => $val) {
        setcookie($this->api_key . '_' . $name, $val, (int)$expires);
        $_COOKIE[$this->api_key . '_' . $name] = $val;
      }
      setcookie($this->api_key, $sig, (int)$expires);
      $_COOKIE[$this->api_key] = $sig;
    }
    $this->user = $user;
    $this->api_client->session_key = $session_key;
}

/**
 * Tries to undo the badness of magic quotes as best we can
 * @param      string   $val    Should come directly from $_GET, $_POST, etc.
 * @return     string   val without added slashes
 */
```

(continued)

Listing A-1 *(continued)*

```php
    public static function no_magic_quotes($val) {
      if (get_magic_quotes_gpc()) {
        return stripslashes($val);
      } else {
        return $val;
      }
    }
  }

  public function get_valid_fb_params($params, $timeout=null, $namespace='fb_sig')
  {
    $prefix = $namespace . '_';
    $prefix_len = strlen($prefix);
    $fb_params = array();
    foreach ($params as $name => $val) {
      if (strpos($name, $prefix) === 0) {
        $fb_params[substr($name, $prefix_len)] = self::no_magic_quotes($val);
      }
    }
    if ($timeout && (!isset($fb_params['time']) || time() - $fb_params['time'] >
$timeout)) {
      return array();
    }
    if (!isset($params[$namespace]) || !$this->verify_signature($fb_params,
$params[$namespace])) {
      return array();
    }
    return $fb_params;
  }

  public function verify_signature($fb_params, $expected_sig) {
    return self::generate_sig($fb_params, $this->secret) == $expected_sig;
  }
}

?>
```

Listing A-2: The facebook_desktop.php PHP file.

```php
<?php
//
// +---------------------------------------------------------------------+
// | Facebook Platform PHP5 client                                       |
// +---------------------------------------------------------------------+
// | Copyright (c) 2007 Facebook, Inc.                                   |
// | All rights reserved.                                                |
// |                                                                     |
// | Redistribution and use in source and binary forms, with or without |
// | modification, are permitted provided that the following conditions  |
// | are met:                                                            |
// |                                                                     |
// | 1. Redistributions of source code must retain the above copyright   |
// |    notice, this list of conditions and the following disclaimer.    |
```

```
//  |  2. Redistributions in binary form must reproduce the above copyright   |
//  |     notice, this list of conditions and the following disclaimer in the |
//  |     documentation and/or other materials provided with the distribution.|
//  |                                                                          |
//  |  THIS SOFTWARE IS PROVIDED BY THE AUTHOR ``AS IS'' AND ANY EXPRESS OR    |
//  |  IMPLIED WARRANTIES, INCLUDING, BUT NOT LIMITED TO, THE IMPLIED WARRANTIES |
//  |  OF MERCHANTABILITY AND FITNESS FOR A PARTICULAR PURPOSE ARE DISCLAIMED. |
//  |  IN NO EVENT SHALL THE AUTHOR BE LIABLE FOR ANY DIRECT, INDIRECT,        |
//  |  INCIDENTAL, SPECIAL, EXEMPLARY, OR CONSEQUENTIAL DAMAGES (INCLUDING, BUT |
//  |  NOT LIMITED TO, PROCUREMENT OF SUBSTITUTE GOODS OR SERVICES; LOSS OF USE, |
//  |  DATA, OR PROFITS; OR BUSINESS INTERRUPTION) HOWEVER CAUSED AND ON ANY   |
//  |  THEORY OF LIABILITY, WHETHER IN CONTRACT, STRICT LIABILITY, OR TORT     |
//  |  (INCLUDING NEGLIGENCE OR OTHERWISE) ARISING IN ANY WAY OUT OF THE USE OF |
//  |  THIS SOFTWARE, EVEN IF ADVISED OF THE POSSIBILITY OF SUCH DAMAGE.       |
//  +--------------------------------------------------------------------------+
//  |  For help with this library, contact developers-help@facebook.com        |
//  +--------------------------------------------------------------------------+
//

/**
 *  This class extends and modifies the "Facebook" class to better
 *  suit desktop apps.
 */
class FacebookDesktop extends Facebook {
  // the application secret, which differs from the session secret
  public $app_secret;
  public $verify_sig;

  public function __construct($api_key, $secret) {
    $this->app_secret = $secret;
    $this->verify_sig = false;
    parent::__construct($api_key, $secret);
  }

  public function do_get_session($auth_token) {
    $this->api_client->secret = $this->app_secret;
    $session_info = parent::do_get_session($auth_token);
    if (isset($session_info['secret']) && $session_info['secret']) {
      // store the session secret
      $this->set_session_secret($session_info['secret']);
    }
    return $session_info;
  }

  public function set_session_secret($session_secret) {
    $this->secret = $session_secret;
    $this->api_client->secret = $session_secret;
  }

  public function require_login() {
    if ($this->get_loggedin_user()) {
      try {
        // try a session-based API call to ensure that we have the correct
        // session secret
```

(continued)

Listing A-2 *(continued)*

```php
        $user = $this->api_client->users_getLoggedInUser();

        // now that we have a valid session secret, verify the signature
        $this->verify_sig = true;
        if ($this->validate_fb_params()) {
          return $user;
        } else {
          // validation failed
          return null;
        }
      } catch (FacebookRestClientException $ex) {
        if (isset($_GET['auth_token'])) {
          // if we have an auth_token, use it to establish a session
          $session_info = $this->do_get_session($_GET['auth_token']);
          if ($session_info) {
            return $session_info['uid'];
          }
        }
      }
    }
    // if we get here, we need to redirect the user to log in
    $this->redirect($this->get_login_url(self::current_url(), $this->in_fb_
canvas()));
  }

  public function verify_signature($fb_params, $expected_sig) {
    // we don't want to verify the signature until we have a valid
    // session secret
    if ($this->verify_sig) {
      return parent::verify_signature($fb_params, $expected_sig);
    } else {
      return true;
    }
  }
}
```

Listing A-3: The facebookapi_php5_restlib.php PHP file.

```php
<?php
//
// +---------------------------------------------------------------------+
// | Facebook Platform PHP5 client                                       |
// +---------------------------------------------------------------------+
// | Copyright (c) 2007 Facebook, Inc.                                   |
// | All rights reserved.                                                |
// |                                                                     |
// | Redistribution and use in source and binary forms, with or without |
// | modification, are permitted provided that the following conditions  |
// | are met:                                                            |
// |                                                                     |
// | 1. Redistributions of source code must retain the above copyright   |
// |    notice, this list of conditions and the following disclaimer.    |
```

```php
//   |  2. Redistributions in binary form must reproduce the above copyright     |
//   |     notice, this list of conditions and the following disclaimer in the   |
//   |     documentation and/or other materials provided with the distribution.  |
//   |                                                                            |
//   |  THIS SOFTWARE IS PROVIDED BY THE AUTHOR ``AS IS'' AND ANY EXPRESS OR      |
//   |  IMPLIED WARRANTIES, INCLUDING, BUT NOT LIMITED TO, THE IMPLIED WARRANTIES |
//   |  OF MERCHANTABILITY AND FITNESS FOR A PARTICULAR PURPOSE ARE DISCLAIMED.   |
//   |  IN NO EVENT SHALL THE AUTHOR BE LIABLE FOR ANY DIRECT, INDIRECT,          |
//   |  INCIDENTAL, SPECIAL, EXEMPLARY, OR CONSEQUENTIAL DAMAGES (INCLUDING, BUT  |
//   |  NOT LIMITED TO, PROCUREMENT OF SUBSTITUTE GOODS OR SERVICES; LOSS OF USE, |
//   |  DATA, OR PROFITS; OR BUSINESS INTERRUPTION) HOWEVER CAUSED AND ON ANY     |
//   |  THEORY OF LIABILITY, WHETHER IN CONTRACT, STRICT LIABILITY, OR TORT       |
//   |  (INCLUDING NEGLIGENCE OR OTHERWISE) ARISING IN ANY WAY OUT OF THE USE OF  |
//   |  THIS SOFTWARE, EVEN IF ADVISED OF THE POSSIBILITY OF SUCH DAMAGE.         |
//   +----------------------------------------------------------------------------+
//   |  For help with this library, contact developers-help@facebook.com          |
//   +----------------------------------------------------------------------------+
//

class FacebookRestClient {
  public $secret;
  public $session_key;
  public $api_key;
  public $friends_list; // to save making the friends.get api call, this will get
prepopulated on canvas pages
  public $added;        // to save making the users.isAppAdded api call, this will
get prepopulated on canvas pages
  public $batch_mode;
  private $batch_queue;

  const BATCH_MODE_DEFAULT = 0;
  const BATCH_MODE_SERVER_PARALLEL = 0;
  const BATCH_MODE_SERIAL_ONLY = 2;

  /**
   * Create the client.
   * @param string $session_key if you haven't gotten a session key yet, leave
   *                            this as null and then set it later by just
   *                            directly accessing the $session_key member
   *                            variable.
   */
  public function __construct($api_key, $secret, $session_key=null) {
    $this->secret      = $secret;
    $this->session_key = $session_key;
    $this->api_key     = $api_key;
    $this->batch_mode = FacebookRestClient::BATCH_MODE_DEFAULT;
    $this->last_call_id = 0;
      $this->server_addr  = Facebook::get_facebook_url('api') . '/restserver.php';
    if ($GLOBALS['facebook_config']['debug']) {
      $this->cur_id = 0;
      ?>
<script type="text/javascript">
var types = ['params', 'xml', 'php', 'sxml'];
function getStyle(elem, style) {
```

(continued)

Listing A-3 *(continued)*

```javascript
    if (elem.getStyle) {
      return elem.getStyle(style);
    } else {
      return elem.style[style];
    }
  }
  function setStyle(elem, style, value) {
    if (elem.setStyle) {
      elem.setStyle(style, value);
    } else {
      elem.style[style] = value;
    }
  }
  function toggleDisplay(id, type) {
    for (var i = 0; i < types.length; i++) {
      var t = types[i];
      var pre = document.getElementById(t + id);
      if (pre) {
        if (t != type || getStyle(pre, 'display') == 'block') {
          setStyle(pre, 'display', 'none');
        } else {
          setStyle(pre, 'display', 'block');
        }
      }
    }
    return false;
  }
</script>
<?php
    }
  }


  /**
   * Start a batch operation.
   */
  public function begin_batch() {
    if($this->batch_queue !== null)
    {
      throw new FacebookRestClientException(FacebookAPIErrorCodes::API_EC_BATCH_
ALREADY_STARTED,
      FacebookAPIErrorCodes::$api_error_descriptions[FacebookAPIErrorCodes::API_EC_
BATCH_ALREADY_STARTED]);
    }

    $this->batch_queue = array();
  }

  /*
   * End current batch operation
   */
```

```php
    public function end_batch() {
      if($this->batch_queue === null) {
        throw new FacebookRestClientException(FacebookAPIErrorCodes::API_EC_BATCH_
NOT_STARTED,
          FacebookAPIErrorCodes::$api_error_descriptions[FacebookAPIErrorCodes::API_EC_
BATCH_NOT_STARTED]);
      }

      $this->execute_server_side_batch();

      $this->batch_queue = null;
    }


    private function execute_server_side_batch() {


      $item_count = count($this->batch_queue);
      $method_feed = array();
      foreach($this->batch_queue as $batch_item) {
        $method_feed[] = $this->create_post_string($batch_item['m'], $batch_
item['p']);
      }

      $method_feed_json = json_encode($method_feed);

      $serial_only = $this->batch_mode == FacebookRestClient::BATCH_MODE_SERIAL_ONLY ;
      $params = array('method_feed' => $method_feed_json, 'serial_only' => $serial_
only);

      $xml = $this->post_request('batch.run', $params);

      $result = $this->convert_xml_to_result($xml, 'batch.run', $params);


      if (is_array($result) && isset($result['error_code'])) {
        throw new FacebookRestClientException($result['error_msg'], $result['error_
code']);
      }

      for($i = 0; $i < $item_count; $i++) {
        $batch_item = $this->batch_queue[$i];
        $batch_item_result_xml = $result[$i];
        $batch_item_result = $this->convert_xml_to_result($batch_item_result_xml,
$batch_item['m'], $batch_item['p']);

        if (is_array($batch_item_result) && isset($batch_item_result['error_code']))
{
          throw new FacebookRestClientException($batch_item_result['error_msg'],
$batch_item_result['error_code']);
        }
```

(continued)

Listing A-3 *(continued)*

```php
        $batch_item['r'] = $batch_item_result;
    }
}

/**
 * Returns the session information available after current user logs in.
 * @param string $auth_token the token returned by auth_createToken or
 *   passed back to your callback_url.
 * @return assoc array containing session_key, uid
 */
public function auth_getSession($auth_token) {
    //Check if we are in batch mode
    if($this->batch_queue === null) {
        $result = $this->call_method('facebook.auth.getSession', array('auth_
token'=>$auth_token));
        $this->session_key = $result['session_key'];
        if (isset($result['secret']) && $result['secret']) {
            // desktop apps have a special secret
            $this->secret = $result['secret'];
        }
        return $result;
    } else {

    }
}

/**
 * Returns events according to the filters specified.
 * @param int $uid Optional: User associated with events.
 *   A null parameter will default to the session user.
 * @param array $eids Optional: Filter by these event ids.
 *   A null parameter will get all events for the user.
 * @param int $start_time Optional: Filter with this UTC as lower bound.
 *   A null or zero parameter indicates no lower bound.
 * @param int $end_time Optional: Filter with this UTC as upper bound.
 *   A null or zero parameter indicates no upper bound.
 * @param string $rsvp_status Optional: Only show events where the given uid
 *   has this rsvp status.  This only works if you have specified a value for
 *   $uid.  Values are as in events.getMembers.  Null indicates to ignore
 *   rsvp status when filtering.
 * @return array of events
 */
public function &events_get($uid, $eids, $start_time, $end_time, $rsvp_status) {
    return $this->call_method('facebook.events.get',
        array(
        'uid' => $uid,
        'eids' => $eids,
        'start_time' => $start_time,
        'end_time' => $end_time,
        'rsvp_status' => $rsvp_status));
}

/**
```

```
 * Returns membership list data associated with an event
 * @param int $eid : event id
 * @return assoc array of four membership lists, with keys 'attending',
 * 'unsure', 'declined', and 'not_replied'
 */
public function &events_getMembers($eid) {
  return $this->call_method('facebook.events.getMembers',
    array('eid' => $eid));
}


/**
 * Makes an FQL query.  This is a generalized way of accessing all the data
 * in the API, as an alternative to most of the other method calls.  More
 * info at http://developers.facebook.com/documentation.php?v=1.0&doc=fql
 * @param string $query the query to evaluate
 * @return generalized array representing the results
 */
public function &fql_query($query) {
  return $this->call_method('facebook.fql.query',
    array('query' => $query));
}


public function &feed_publishStoryToUser($title, $body,
                                  $image_1=null, $image_1_link=null,
                                  $image_2=null, $image_2_link=null,
                                  $image_3=null, $image_3_link=null,
                                  $image_4=null, $image_4_link=null) {
  return $this->call_method('facebook.feed.publishStoryToUser',
    array('title' => $title,
          'body' => $body,
          'image_1' => $image_1,
          'image_1_link' => $image_1_link,
          'image_2' => $image_2,
          'image_2_link' => $image_2_link,
          'image_3' => $image_3,
          'image_3_link' => $image_3_link,
          'image_4' => $image_4,
          'image_4_link' => $image_4_link));
}


public function &feed_publishActionOfUser($title, $body,
                                  $image_1=null, $image_1_link=null,
                                  $image_2=null, $image_2_link=null,
                                  $image_3=null, $image_3_link=null,
                                  $image_4=null, $image_4_link=null) {
  return $this->call_method('facebook.feed.publishActionOfUser',
    array('title' => $title,
          'body' => $body,
          'image_1' => $image_1,
          'image_1_link' => $image_1_link,
          'image_2' => $image_2,
          'image_2_link' => $image_2_link,
          'image_3' => $image_3,
```

(continued)

```php
                    'image_3_link' => $image_3_link,
                    'image_4' => $image_4,
                    'image_4_link' => $image_4_link));
    }

    public function &feed_publishTemplatizedAction($title_template, $title_data,
                                                   $body_template, $body_data, $body_
general,
                                                   $image_1=null, $image_1_link=null,
                                                   $image_2=null, $image_2_link=null,
                                                   $image_3=null, $image_3_link=null,
                                                   $image_4=null, $image_4_link=null,
                                                   $target_ids='', $page_actor_
id=null) {
        return $this->call_method('facebook.feed.publishTemplatizedAction',
            array('title_template' => $title_template,
                  'title_data' => $title_data,
                  'body_template' => $body_template,
                  'body_data' => $body_data,
                  'body_general' => $body_general,
                  'image_1' => $image_1,
                  'image_1_link' => $image_1_link,
                  'image_2' => $image_2,
                  'image_2_link' => $image_2_link,
                  'image_3' => $image_3,
                  'image_3_link' => $image_3_link,
                  'image_4' => $image_4,
                  'image_4_link' => $image_4_link,
                  'target_ids' => $target_ids,
                  'page_actor_id' => $page_actor_id));
    }

    /**
     * Returns whether or not pairs of users are friends.
     * Note that the Facebook friend relationship is symmetric.
     * @param array $uids1: array of ids (id_1, id_2,...) of some length X
     * @param array $uids2: array of ids (id_A, id_B,...) of SAME length X
     * @return array of uid pairs with bool, true if pair are friends, e.g.
     *    array( 0 => array('uid1' => id_1, 'uid2' => id_A, 'are_friends' => 1),
     *           1 => array('uid1' => id_2, 'uid2' => id_B, 'are_friends' => 0)
     *           ...)
     */
    public function &friends_areFriends($uids1, $uids2) {
        return $this->call_method('facebook.friends.areFriends',
            array('uids1'=>$uids1, 'uids2'=>$uids2));
    }

    /**
     * Returns the friends of the current session user.
     * @return array of friends
     */
```

```php
public function &friends_get() {
  if (isset($this->friends_list)) {
    return $this->friends_list;
  }
  return $this->call_method('facebook.friends.get', array());
}

/**
 * Returns the friends of the session user, who are also users
 * of the calling application.
 * @return array of friends
 */
public function &friends_getAppUsers() {
  return $this->call_method('facebook.friends.getAppUsers', array());
}

/**
 * Returns groups according to the filters specified.
 * @param int $uid Optional: User associated with groups.
 *   A null parameter will default to the session user.
 * @param array $gids Optional: group ids to query.
 *    A null parameter will get all groups for the user.
 * @return array of groups
 */
public function &groups_get($uid, $gids) {
  return $this->call_method('facebook.groups.get',
      array(
      'uid' => $uid,
      'gids' => $gids));
}

/**
 * Returns the membership list of a group
 * @param int $gid : Group id
 * @return assoc array of four membership lists, with keys
 *   'members', 'admins', 'officers', and 'not_replied'
 */
public function &groups_getMembers($gid) {
  return $this->call_method('facebook.groups.getMembers',
    array('gid' => $gid));
}

/**
 * Returns cookies according to the filters specified.
 * @param int $uid Required: User for which the cookies are needed.
 * @param string $name Optional:
 *    A null parameter will get all cookies for the user.
 * @return array of cookies
 */
public function data_getCookies($uid, $name) {
  return $this->call_method('facebook.data.getCookies',
      array(
      'uid' => $uid,
```

(continued)

```php
                    'name' => $name));
    }

    /**
     * Sets cookies according to the params specified.
     * @param int $uid Required: User for which the cookies are needed.
     * @param string $name Required: name of the cookie
     * @param string $value Optional if expires specified and is in the past
     * @param int$expires Optional
     * @param string $path Optional
     *
     * @return bool
     */
    public function data_setCookie($uid, $name, $value, $expires, $path) {
        return $this->call_method('facebook.data.setCookie',
            array(
            'uid' => $uid,
            'name' => $name,
            'value' => $value,
            'expires' => $expires,
            'path' => $path));
    }

    /**
     * Returns the outstanding notifications for the session user.
     * @return assoc array of
     *  notification count objects for 'messages', 'pokes' and 'shares',
     *  a uid list of 'friend_requests', a gid list of 'group_invites',
     *  and an eid list of 'event_invites'
     */
    public function &notifications_get() {
        return $this->call_method('facebook.notifications.get', array());
    }

    /**
     * Sends a notification to the specified users.
     * @return (nothing)
     */
    public function &notifications_send($to_ids, $notification) {
        return $this->call_method('facebook.notifications.send',
                                array('to_ids' => $to_ids, 'notification' =>
$notification));
    }

    /**
     * Sends an email to the specified user of the application.
     * @param array $recipients : id of the recipients
     * @param string $subject : subject of the email
     * @param string $text : (plain text) body of the email
     * @param string $fbml : fbml markup if you want an html version of the email
     * @return comma separated list of successful recipients
```

```
     */
  public function &notifications_sendEmail($recipients, $subject, $text, $fbml) {
    return $this->call_method('facebook.notifications.sendEmail',
                      array('recipients' => $recipients,
                            'subject' => $subject,
                            'text' => $text,
                            'fbml' => $fbml));
  }

  /**
   * Returns the requested info fields for the requested set of pages
   * @param array $page_ids an array of page ids
   * @param array $fields an array of strings describing the info fields desired
   * @param int $uid   Optionally, limit results to pages of which this user is
a fan.
   * @param string type  limits results to a particular type of page.
   * @return array of pages
   */
  public function &pages_getInfo($page_ids, $fields, $uid, $type) {
    return $this->call_method('facebook.pages.getInfo', array('page_ids' => $page_
ids, 'fields' => $fields, 'uid' => $uid, 'type' => $type));
  }

  /**
   * Returns true if logged in user is an admin for the passed page
   * @param int $page_id target page id
   * @return boolean
   */
  public function &pages_isAdmin($page_id) {
    return $this->call_method('facebook.pages.isAdmin', array('page_id' => $page_
id));
  }

  /**
   * Returns whether or not the page corresponding to the current session object
has the app installed
   * @return boolean
   */
  public function &pages_isAppAdded() {
    if (isset($this->added)) {
      return $this->added;
    }
    return $this->call_method('facebook.pages.isAppAdded', array());
  }

  /**
   * Returns true if logged in user is a fan for the passed page
   * @param int $page_id target page id
   * @param int $uid user to compare.  If empty, the logged in user.
   * @return bool
   */
  public function &pages_isFan($page_id, $uid) {
```

(continued)

287

Listing A-3 *(continued)*

```php
    return $this->call_method('facebook.pages.isFan', array('page_id' => $page_id,
'uid' => $uid));
  }

  /**
   * Returns photos according to the filters specified.
   * @param int $subj_id Optional: Filter by uid of user tagged in the photos.
   * @param int $aid Optional: Filter by an album, as returned by
   *   photos_getAlbums.
   * @param array $pids Optional: Restrict to a list of pids
   * Note that at least one of these parameters needs to be specified, or an
   * error is returned.
   * @return array of photo objects.
   */
  public function &photos_get($subj_id, $aid, $pids) {
    return $this->call_method('facebook.photos.get',
      array('subj_id' => $subj_id, 'aid' => $aid, 'pids' => $pids));
  }

  /**
   * Returns the albums created by the given user.
   * @param int $uid Optional: the uid of the user whose albums you want.
   *    A null value will return the albums of the session user.
   * @param array $aids Optional: a list of aids to restrict the query.
   * Note that at least one of the (uid, aids) parameters must be specified.
   * @returns an array of album objects.
   */
  public function &photos_getAlbums($uid, $aids) {
    return $this->call_method('facebook.photos.getAlbums',
      array('uid' => $uid,
            'aids' => $aids));
  }

  /**
   * Returns the tags on all photos specified.
   * @param string $pids : a list of pids to query
   * @return array of photo tag objects, with include pid, subject uid,
   *   and two floating-point numbers (xcoord, ycoord) for tag pixel location
   */
  public function &photos_getTags($pids) {
    return $this->call_method('facebook.photos.getTags',
      array('pids' => $pids));
  }

  /**
   * Returns the requested info fields for the requested set of users
   * @param array $uids an array of user ids
   * @param array $fields an array of strings describing the info fields desired
   * @return array of users
   */
  public function &users_getInfo($uids, $fields) {
```

```php
    return $this->call_method('facebook.users.getInfo', array('uids' => $uids,
'fields' => $fields));
  }

  /**
   * Returns the user corresponding to the current session object.
   * @return integer uid
   */
  public function &users_getLoggedInUser() {
    return $this->call_method('facebook.users.getLoggedInUser', array());
  }


  /**
   * Returns whether or not the user corresponding to the current session object
has the app installed
   * @return boolean
   */
  public function &users_isAppAdded() {
    if (isset($this->added)) {
      return $this->added;
    }
    return $this->call_method('facebook.users.isAppAdded', array());
  }

  /**
   * Sets the FBML for the profile of the user attached to this session
   * @param    string    $markup         The FBML that describes the profile
presence of this app for the user
   * @param    int       $uid            The user
   * @param    string    $profile        Profile FBML
   * @param    string    $profile_action Profile action FBML
   * @param    string    $mobile_profile Mobile profile FBML
   * @return   array     A list of strings describing any compile errors for the
submitted FBML
   */
  function profile_setFBML($markup, $uid = null, $profile='', $profile_action='',
                      $mobile_profile='') {
    return $this->call_method('facebook.profile.setFBML',
                        array('markup' => $markup,
                        'uid' => $uid,
                        'profile' => $profile,
                        'profile_action' => $profile_action,
                        'mobile_profile' => $mobile_profile));
  }

  public function &profile_getFBML($uid) {
    return $this->call_method('facebook.profile.getFBML', array('uid' => $uid));
  }

  public function &fbml_refreshImgSrc($url) {
```

(continued)

Listing A-3 *(continued)*

```php
      return $this->call_method('facebook.fbml.refreshImgSrc', array('url' => $url));
   }

   public function &fbml_refreshRefUrl($url) {
      return $this->call_method('facebook.fbml.refreshRefUrl', array('url' => $url));
   }

   public function &fbml_setRefHandle($handle, $fbml) {
      return $this->call_method('facebook.fbml.setRefHandle.', array('handle' =>
$handle, 'fbml' => $fbml));
   }

   /**
    * Get all the marketplace categories
    *
    * @return array  A list of category names
    */
   function marketplace_getCategories() {
      return $this->call_method('facebook.marketplace.getCategories', array());
   }

   /**
    * Get all the marketplace subcategories for a particular category
    *
    * @param  category  The category for which we are pulling subcategories
    * @return array      A list of subcategory names
    */
   function marketplace_getSubCategories($category) {
      return $this->call_method('facebook.marketplace.getSubCategories',
array('category' => $category));
   }

   /**
    * Get listings by either listing_id or user
    *
    * @param listing_ids    An array of listing_ids (optional)
    * @param uids           An array of user ids (optional)
    * @return array         The data for matched listings
    */
   function marketplace_getListings($listing_ids, $uids) {
      return $this->call_method('facebook.marketplace.getListings',
array('listing_ids' => $listing_ids, 'uids' => $uids));
   }

   /**
    * Search for Marketplace listings.  All arguments are optional, though at least
    * one must be filled out to retrieve results.
    *
    * @param category      The category in which to search (optional)
    * @param subcategory   The subcategory in which to search (optional)
    * @param query         A query string (optional)
    * @return array         The data for matched listings
    */
```

```php
    */
  function marketplace_search($category, $subcategory, $query) {
    return $this->call_method('facebook.marketplace.search', array('category' =>
$category, 'subcategory' => $subcategory, 'query' => $query));
  }

  /**
   * Remove a listing from Marketplace
   *
   * @param listing_id  The id of the listing to be removed
   * @param status 'SUCCESS', 'NOT_SUCCESS', or 'DEFAULT'
   * @return bool        True on success
   */
  function marketplace_removeListing($listing_id, $status='DEFAULT') {
    return $this->call_method('facebook.marketplace.removeListing',
                        array('listing_id'=>$listing_id,
                              'status'=>$status));
  }

  /**
   * Create/modify a Marketplace listing for the loggedinuser
   *
   * @param int              listing_id  The id of a listing to be modified, 0 for
a new listing.
   * @param show_on_profile  bool        Should we show this listing on the user's
profile
   * @param listing_attrs    array       An array of the listing data
   * @return              int        The listing_id (unchanged if modifying an
existing listing)
   */
  function marketplace_createListing($listing_id, $show_on_profile, $attrs) {
    return $this->call_method('facebook.marketplace.createListing',
                        array('listing_id'=>$listing_id,
                              'show_on_profile'=>$show_on_profile,
                              'listing_attrs'=>json_encode($attrs)));
  }


  ////////////////////////////////////////////////////////////////////////////
  // Data Store API

  /**
   * Set a user preference.
   *
   * @param  pref_id     preference identifier (0-200)
   * @param  value       preferece's value
   * @error
   *    API_EC_DATA_DATABASE_ERROR
   *    API_EC_PARAM
   *    API_EC_DATA_QUOTA_EXCEEDED
   *    API_EC_DATA_UNKNOWN_ERROR
   */
```

(continued)

Listing A-3 *(continued)*

```php
public function &data_setUserPreference($pref_id, $value) {
  return $this->call_method
    ('facebook.data.setUserPreference',
     array('pref_id' => $pref_id,
           'value' => $value));
}

/**
 * Set a user's all preferences for this application.
 *
 * @param  values    preferece values in an associative arrays
 * @param  replace   whether to replace all existing preferences or
 *                   merge into them.
 * @error
 *    API_EC_DATA_DATABASE_ERROR
 *    API_EC_PARAM
 *    API_EC_DATA_QUOTA_EXCEEDED
 *    API_EC_DATA_UNKNOWN_ERROR
 */
public function &data_setUserPreferences($values, $replace = false) {
  return $this->call_method
    ('facebook.data.setUserPreferences',
     array('values' => json_encode($values),
           'replace' => $replace));
}

/**
 * Get a user preference.
 *
 * @param  pref_id    preference identifier (0-200)
 * @return            preference's value
 * @error
 *    API_EC_DATA_DATABASE_ERROR
 *    API_EC_PARAM
 *    API_EC_DATA_QUOTA_EXCEEDED
 *    API_EC_DATA_UNKNOWN_ERROR
 */
public function &data_getUserPreference($pref_id) {
  return $this->call_method
    ('facebook.data.getUserPreference',
     array('pref_id' => $pref_id));
}

/**
 * Get a user preference.
 *
 * @return            preference values
 * @error
 *    API_EC_DATA_DATABASE_ERROR
 *    API_EC_DATA_QUOTA_EXCEEDED
 *    API_EC_DATA_UNKNOWN_ERROR
```

```php
 */
public function &data_getUserPreferences() {
  return $this->call_method
    ('facebook.data.getUserPreferences',
     array());
}

/**
 * Create a new object type.
 *
 * @param  name        object type's name
 * @error
 *    API_EC_DATA_DATABASE_ERROR
 *    API_EC_DATA_OBJECT_ALREADY_EXISTS
 *    API_EC_PARAM
 *    API_EC_PERMISSION
 *    API_EC_DATA_INVALID_OPERATION
 *    API_EC_DATA_QUOTA_EXCEEDED
 *    API_EC_DATA_UNKNOWN_ERROR
 */
public function &data_createObjectType($name) {
  return $this->call_method
    ('facebook.data.createObjectType',
     array('name' => $name));
}

/**
 * Delete an object type.
 *
 * @param  obj_type      object type's name
 * @error
 *    API_EC_DATA_DATABASE_ERROR
 *    API_EC_DATA_OBJECT_NOT_FOUND
 *    API_EC_PARAM
 *    API_EC_PERMISSION
 *    API_EC_DATA_INVALID_OPERATION
 *    API_EC_DATA_QUOTA_EXCEEDED
 *    API_EC_DATA_UNKNOWN_ERROR
 */
public function &data_dropObjectType($obj_type) {
  return $this->call_method
    ('facebook.data.dropObjectType',
     array('obj_type' => $obj_type));
}

/**
 * Rename an object type.
 *
 * @param  obj_type      object type's name
 * @param  new_name      new object type's name
 * @error
 *    API_EC_DATA_DATABASE_ERROR
 *    API_EC_DATA_OBJECT_NOT_FOUND
```

(continued)

Listing A-3 *(continued)*

```php
 *      API_EC_DATA_OBJECT_ALREADY_EXISTS
 *      API_EC_PARAM
 *      API_EC_PERMISSION
 *      API_EC_DATA_INVALID_OPERATION
 *      API_EC_DATA_QUOTA_EXCEEDED
 *      API_EC_DATA_UNKNOWN_ERROR
 */
public function &data_renameObjectType($obj_type, $new_name) {
  return $this->call_method
    ('facebook.data.renameObjectType',
      array('obj_type' => $obj_type,
            'new_name' => $new_name));
}

/**
 * Add a new property to an object type.
 *
 * @param  obj_type      object type's name
 * @param  prop_name     name of the property to add
 * @param  prop_type     1: integer; 2: string; 3: text blob
 * @error
 *      API_EC_DATA_DATABASE_ERROR
 *      API_EC_DATA_OBJECT_ALREADY_EXISTS
 *      API_EC_PARAM
 *      API_EC_PERMISSION
 *      API_EC_DATA_INVALID_OPERATION
 *      API_EC_DATA_QUOTA_EXCEEDED
 *      API_EC_DATA_UNKNOWN_ERROR
 */
public function &data_defineObjectProperty($obj_type, $prop_name, $prop_type) {
  return $this->call_method
    ('facebook.data.defineObjectProperty',
      array('obj_type' => $obj_type,
            'prop_name' => $prop_name,
            'prop_type' => $prop_type));
}

/**
 * Remove a previously defined property from an object type.
 *
 * @param  obj_type      object type's name
 * @param  prop_name     name of the property to remove
 * @error
 *      API_EC_DATA_DATABASE_ERROR
 *      API_EC_DATA_OBJECT_NOT_FOUND
 *      API_EC_PARAM
 *      API_EC_PERMISSION
 *      API_EC_DATA_INVALID_OPERATION
 *      API_EC_DATA_QUOTA_EXCEEDED
 *      API_EC_DATA_UNKNOWN_ERROR
```

```
     */
    public function &data_undefineObjectProperty($obj_type, $prop_name) {
      return $this->call_method
        ('facebook.data.undefineObjectProperty',
          array('obj_type' => $obj_type,
                'prop_name' => $prop_name));
    }

    /**
     * Rename a previously defined property of an object type.
     *
     * @param   obj_type       object type's name
     * @param   prop_name      name of the property to rename
     * @param   new_name       new name to use
     * @error
     *      API_EC_DATA_DATABASE_ERROR
     *      API_EC_DATA_OBJECT_NOT_FOUND
     *      API_EC_DATA_OBJECT_ALREADY_EXISTS
     *      API_EC_PARAM
     *      API_EC_PERMISSION
     *      API_EC_DATA_INVALID_OPERATION
     *      API_EC_DATA_QUOTA_EXCEEDED
     *      API_EC_DATA_UNKNOWN_ERROR
     */
    public function &data_renameObjectProperty($obj_type, $prop_name,
                                               $new_name) {
      return $this->call_method
        ('facebook.data.renameObjectProperty',
          array('obj_type' => $obj_type,
                'prop_name' => $prop_name,
                'new_name' => $new_name));
    }

    /**
     * Retrieve a list of all object types that have defined for the application.
     *
     * @return              a list of object type names
     * @error
     *      API_EC_DATA_DATABASE_ERROR
     *      API_EC_PERMISSION
     *      API_EC_DATA_QUOTA_EXCEEDED
     *      API_EC_DATA_UNKNOWN_ERROR
     */
    public function &data_getObjectTypes() {
      return $this->call_method
        ('facebook.data.getObjectTypes',
          array());
    }

    /**
     * Get definitions of all properties of an object type.
     *
     * @param obj_type        object type's name
```

(continued)

Listing A-3 *(continued)*

```
 * @return               pairs of property name and property types
 * @error
 *     API_EC_DATA_DATABASE_ERROR
 *     API_EC_PARAM
 *     API_EC_PERMISSION
 *     API_EC_DATA_OBJECT_NOT_FOUND
 *     API_EC_DATA_QUOTA_EXCEEDED
 *     API_EC_DATA_UNKNOWN_ERROR
 */
public function &data_getObjectType($obj_type) {
  return $this->call_method
    ('facebook.data.getObjectType',
      array('obj_type' => $obj_type));
}

/**
 * Create a new object.
 *
 * @param  obj_type       object type's name
 * @param  properties     (optional) properties to set initially
 * @return               newly created object's id
 * @error
 *     API_EC_DATA_DATABASE_ERROR
 *     API_EC_PARAM
 *     API_EC_PERMISSION
 *     API_EC_DATA_INVALID_OPERATION
 *     API_EC_DATA_QUOTA_EXCEEDED
 *     API_EC_DATA_UNKNOWN_ERROR
 */
public function &data_createObject($obj_type, $properties = null) {
  return $this->call_method
    ('facebook.data.createObject',
      array('obj_type' => $obj_type,
            'properties' => json_encode($properties)));
}

/**
 * Update an existing object.
 *
 * @param  obj_id         object's id
 * @param  properties     new properties
 * @param  replace        true for replacing existing properties; false for
merging
 * @error
 *     API_EC_DATA_DATABASE_ERROR
 *     API_EC_DATA_OBJECT_NOT_FOUND
 *     API_EC_PARAM
 *     API_EC_PERMISSION
 *     API_EC_DATA_INVALID_OPERATION
 *     API_EC_DATA_QUOTA_EXCEEDED
 *     API_EC_DATA_UNKNOWN_ERROR
```

```
     */
    public function &data_updateObject($obj_id, $properties, $replace = false) {
      return $this->call_method
        ('facebook.data.updateObject',
          array('obj_id' => $obj_id,
                'properties' => json_encode($properties),
                'replace' => $replace));
    }

    /**
     * Delete an existing object.
     *
     * @param  obj_id         object's id
     * @error
     *    API_EC_DATA_DATABASE_ERROR
     *    API_EC_DATA_OBJECT_NOT_FOUND
     *    API_EC_PARAM
     *    API_EC_PERMISSION
     *    API_EC_DATA_INVALID_OPERATION
     *    API_EC_DATA_QUOTA_EXCEEDED
     *    API_EC_DATA_UNKNOWN_ERROR
     */
    public function &data_deleteObject($obj_id) {
      return $this->call_method
        ('facebook.data.deleteObject',
          array('obj_id' => $obj_id));
    }

    /**
     * Delete a list of objects.
     *
     * @param  obj_ids        objects to delete
     * @error
     *    API_EC_DATA_DATABASE_ERROR
     *    API_EC_PARAM
     *    API_EC_PERMISSION
     *    API_EC_DATA_INVALID_OPERATION
     *    API_EC_DATA_QUOTA_EXCEEDED
     *    API_EC_DATA_UNKNOWN_ERROR
     */
    public function &data_deleteObjects($obj_ids) {
      return $this->call_method
        ('facebook.data.deleteObjects',
          array('obj_ids' => json_encode($obj_ids)));
    }

    /**
     * Get a single property value of an object.
     *
     * @param  obj_id         object's id
     * @param  prop_name      individual property's name
     * @return                individual property's value
```

(continued)

Listing A-3 *(continued)*

```
 * @error
 *     API_EC_DATA_DATABASE_ERROR
 *     API_EC_DATA_OBJECT_NOT_FOUND
 *     API_EC_PARAM
 *     API_EC_PERMISSION
 *     API_EC_DATA_INVALID_OPERATION
 *     API_EC_DATA_QUOTA_EXCEEDED
 *     API_EC_DATA_UNKNOWN_ERROR
 */
public function &data_getObjectProperty($obj_id, $prop_name) {
  return $this->call_method
    ('facebook.data.getObjectProperty',
      array('obj_id' => $obj_id,
            'prop_name' => $prop_name));
}

/**
 * Get properties of an object.
 *
 * @param   obj_id       object's id
 * @param   prop_names   (optional) properties to return; null for all.
 * @return               specified properties of an object
 * @error
 *     API_EC_DATA_DATABASE_ERROR
 *     API_EC_DATA_OBJECT_NOT_FOUND
 *     API_EC_PARAM
 *     API_EC_PERMISSION
 *     API_EC_DATA_INVALID_OPERATION
 *     API_EC_DATA_QUOTA_EXCEEDED
 *     API_EC_DATA_UNKNOWN_ERROR
 */
public function &data_getObject($obj_id, $prop_names = null) {
  return $this->call_method
    ('facebook.data.getObject',
      array('obj_id' => $obj_id,
            'prop_names' => json_encode($prop_names)));
}

/**
 * Get properties of a list of objects.
 *
 * @param   obj_ids      object ids
 * @param   prop_names   (optional) properties to return; null for all.
 * @return               specified properties of an object
 * @error
 *     API_EC_DATA_DATABASE_ERROR
 *     API_EC_DATA_OBJECT_NOT_FOUND
 *     API_EC_PARAM
 *     API_EC_PERMISSION
 *     API_EC_DATA_INVALID_OPERATION
 *     API_EC_DATA_QUOTA_EXCEEDED
 *     API_EC_DATA_UNKNOWN_ERROR
```

```php
       */
      public function &data_getObjects($obj_ids, $prop_names = null) {
        return $this->call_method
          ('facebook.data.getObjects',
           array('obj_ids' => json_encode($obj_ids),
                 'prop_names' => json_encode($prop_names)));
      }

      /**
       * Set a single property value of an object.
       *
       * @param   obj_id        object's id
       * @param   prop_name     individual property's name
       * @param   prop_value    new value to set
       * @error
       *     API_EC_DATA_DATABASE_ERROR
       *     API_EC_DATA_OBJECT_NOT_FOUND
       *     API_EC_PARAM
       *     API_EC_PERMISSION
       *     API_EC_DATA_INVALID_OPERATION
       *     API_EC_DATA_QUOTA_EXCEEDED
       *     API_EC_DATA_UNKNOWN_ERROR
       */
      public function &data_setObjectProperty($obj_id, $prop_name,
                                              $prop_value) {
        return $this->call_method
          ('facebook.data.setObjectProperty',
           array('obj_id' => $obj_id,
                 'prop_name' => $prop_name,
                 'prop_value' => $prop_value));
      }

      /**
       * Read hash value by key.
       *
       * @param   obj_type      object type's name
       * @param   key           hash key
       * @param   prop_name     (optional) individual property's name
       * @return                hash value
       * @error
       *     API_EC_DATA_DATABASE_ERROR
       *     API_EC_PARAM
       *     API_EC_PERMISSION
       *     API_EC_DATA_INVALID_OPERATION
       *     API_EC_DATA_QUOTA_EXCEEDED
       *     API_EC_DATA_UNKNOWN_ERROR
       */
      public function &data_getHashValue($obj_type, $key, $prop_name = null) {
        return $this->call_method
          ('facebook.data.getHashValue',
           array('obj_type' => $obj_type,
                 'key' => $key,
```

(continued)

Listing A-3 *(continued)*

```php
                'prop_name' => $prop_name));
   }

   /**
    * Write hash value by key.
    *
    * @param  obj_type       object type's name
    * @param  key            hash key
    * @param  value          hash value
    * @param  prop_name      (optional) individual property's name
    * @error
    *     API_EC_DATA_DATABASE_ERROR
    *     API_EC_PARAM
    *     API_EC_PERMISSION
    *     API_EC_DATA_INVALID_OPERATION
    *     API_EC_DATA_QUOTA_EXCEEDED
    *     API_EC_DATA_UNKNOWN_ERROR
    */
   public function &data_setHashValue($obj_type, $key, $value, $prop_name = null) {
     return $this->call_method
        ('facebook.data.setHashValue',
         array('obj_type' => $obj_type,
               'key' => $key,
               'value' => $value,
               'prop_name' => $prop_name));
   }

   /**
    * Increase a hash value by specified increment atomically.
    *
    * @param  obj_type       object type's name
    * @param  key            hash key
    * @param  prop_name      individual property's name
    * @param  increment      (optional) default is 1
    * @return               incremented hash value
    * @error
    *     API_EC_DATA_DATABASE_ERROR
    *     API_EC_PARAM
    *     API_EC_PERMISSION
    *     API_EC_DATA_INVALID_OPERATION
    *     API_EC_DATA_QUOTA_EXCEEDED
    *     API_EC_DATA_UNKNOWN_ERROR
    */
   public function &data_incHashValue($obj_type, $key, $prop_name, $increment = 1) {
     return $this->call_method
        ('facebook.data.incHashValue',
         array('obj_type' => $obj_type,
               'key' => $key,
               'prop_name' => $prop_name,
               'increment' => $increment));
   }

   /**
```

```php
 * Remove a hash key and its values.
 *
 * @param  obj_type     object type's name
 * @param  key          hash key
 * @error
 *     API_EC_DATA_DATABASE_ERROR
 *     API_EC_PARAM
 *     API_EC_PERMISSION
 *     API_EC_DATA_INVALID_OPERATION
 *     API_EC_DATA_QUOTA_EXCEEDED
 *     API_EC_DATA_UNKNOWN_ERROR
 */
public function &data_removeHashKey($obj_type, $key) {
  return $this->call_method
    ('facebook.data.removeHashKey',
     array('obj_type' => $obj_type,
           'key' => $key));
}


/**
 * Remove hash keys and their values.
 *
 * @param  obj_type     object type's name
 * @param  keys         hash keys
 * @error
 *     API_EC_DATA_DATABASE_ERROR
 *     API_EC_PARAM
 *     API_EC_PERMISSION
 *     API_EC_DATA_INVALID_OPERATION
 *     API_EC_DATA_QUOTA_EXCEEDED
 *     API_EC_DATA_UNKNOWN_ERROR
 */
public function &data_removeHashKeys($obj_type, $keys) {
  return $this->call_method
    ('facebook.data.removeHashKeys',
     array('obj_type' => $obj_type,
           'keys' => json_encode($keys)));
}



/**
 * Define an object association.
 *
 * @param  name         name of this association
 * @param  assoc_type   1: one-way 2: two-way symmetric 3: two-way asymmetric
 * @param  assoc_info1  needed info about first object type
 * @param  assoc_info2  needed info about second object type
 * @param  inverse      (optional) name of reverse association
 * @error
 *     API_EC_DATA_DATABASE_ERROR
 *     API_EC_DATA_OBJECT_ALREADY_EXISTS
 *     API_EC_PARAM
 *     API_EC_PERMISSION
```

(continued)

301

Listing A-3 *(continued)*

```php
 *      API_EC_DATA_INVALID_OPERATION
 *      API_EC_DATA_QUOTA_EXCEEDED
 *      API_EC_DATA_UNKNOWN_ERROR
 */
public function &data_defineAssociation($name, $assoc_type, $assoc_info1,
                                        $assoc_info2, $inverse = null) {
  return $this->call_method
    ('facebook.data.defineAssociation',
     array('name' => $name,
           'assoc_type' => $assoc_type,
           'assoc_info1' => json_encode($assoc_info1),
           'assoc_info2' => json_encode($assoc_info2),
           'inverse' => $inverse));
}

/**
 * Undefine an object association.
 *
 * @param  name        name of this association
 * @error
 *      API_EC_DATA_DATABASE_ERROR
 *      API_EC_DATA_OBJECT_NOT_FOUND
 *      API_EC_PARAM
 *      API_EC_PERMISSION
 *      API_EC_DATA_INVALID_OPERATION
 *      API_EC_DATA_QUOTA_EXCEEDED
 *      API_EC_DATA_UNKNOWN_ERROR
 */
public function &data_undefineAssociation($name) {
  return $this->call_method
    ('facebook.data.undefineAssociation',
     array('name' => $name));
}

/**
 * Rename an object association or aliases.
 *
 * @param  name        name of this association
 * @param  new_name    (optional) new name of this association
 * @param  new_alias1  (optional) new alias for object type 1
 * @param  new_alias2  (optional) new alias for object type 2
 * @error
 *      API_EC_DATA_DATABASE_ERROR
 *      API_EC_DATA_OBJECT_ALREADY_EXISTS
 *      API_EC_DATA_OBJECT_NOT_FOUND
 *      API_EC_PARAM
 *      API_EC_PERMISSION
 *      API_EC_DATA_INVALID_OPERATION
 *      API_EC_DATA_QUOTA_EXCEEDED
 *      API_EC_DATA_UNKNOWN_ERROR
```

```
   */
  public function &data_renameAssociation($name, $new_name, $new_alias1 = null,
                                          $new_alias2 = null) {
    return $this->call_method
      ('facebook.data.renameAssociation',
       array('name' => $name,
             'new_name' => $new_name,
             'new_alias1' => $new_alias1,
             'new_alias2' => $new_alias2));
  }

  /**
   * Get definition of an object association.
   *
   * @param  name          name of this association
   * @return               specified association
   * @error
   *     API_EC_DATA_DATABASE_ERROR
   *     API_EC_DATA_OBJECT_NOT_FOUND
   *     API_EC_PARAM
   *     API_EC_PERMISSION
   *     API_EC_DATA_QUOTA_EXCEEDED
   *     API_EC_DATA_UNKNOWN_ERROR
   */
  public function &data_getAssociationDefinition($name) {
    return $this->call_method
      ('facebook.data.getAssociationDefinition',
       array('name' => $name));
  }

  /**
   * Get definition of all associations.
   *
   * @return               all defined associations
   * @error
   *     API_EC_DATA_DATABASE_ERROR
   *     API_EC_PERMISSION
   *     API_EC_DATA_QUOTA_EXCEEDED
   *     API_EC_DATA_UNKNOWN_ERROR
   */
  public function &data_getAssociationDefinitions() {
    return $this->call_method
      ('facebook.data.getAssociationDefinitions',
       array());
  }

  /**
   * Create or modify an association between two objects.
   *
   * @param  name          name of association
   * @param  obj_id1       id of first object
   * @param  obj_id2       id of second object
   * @param  data          (optional) extra string data to store
```

(continued)

Listing A-3 *(continued)*

```
 * @param  assoc_time  (optional) extra time data; default to creation time
 * @error
 *     API_EC_DATA_DATABASE_ERROR
 *     API_EC_PARAM
 *     API_EC_PERMISSION
 *     API_EC_DATA_INVALID_OPERATION
 *     API_EC_DATA_QUOTA_EXCEEDED
 *     API_EC_DATA_UNKNOWN_ERROR
 */
public function &data_setAssociation($name, $obj_id1, $obj_id2, $data = null,
                                     $assoc_time = null) {
  return $this->call_method
    ('facebook.data.setAssociation',
      array('name' => $name,
            'obj_id1' => $obj_id1,
            'obj_id2' => $obj_id2,
            'data' => $data,
            'assoc_time' => $assoc_time));
}

/**
 * Create or modify associations between objects.
 *
 * @param  assocs       associations to set
 * @param  name         (optional) name of association
 * @error
 *     API_EC_DATA_DATABASE_ERROR
 *     API_EC_PARAM
 *     API_EC_PERMISSION
 *     API_EC_DATA_INVALID_OPERATION
 *     API_EC_DATA_QUOTA_EXCEEDED
 *     API_EC_DATA_UNKNOWN_ERROR
 */
public function &data_setAssociations($assocs, $name = null) {
  return $this->call_method
    ('facebook.data.setAssociations',
      array('assocs' => json_encode($assocs),
            'name' => $name));
}

/**
 * Remove an association between two objects.
 *
 * @param  name         name of association
 * @param  obj_id1      id of first object
 * @param  obj_id2      id of second object
 * @error
 *     API_EC_DATA_DATABASE_ERROR
 *     API_EC_DATA_OBJECT_NOT_FOUND
 *     API_EC_PARAM
 *     API_EC_PERMISSION
 *     API_EC_DATA_QUOTA_EXCEEDED
 *     API_EC_DATA_UNKNOWN_ERROR
```

```php
        */
      public function &data_removeAssociation($name, $obj_id1, $obj_id2) {
        return $this->call_method
          ('facebook.data.removeAssociation',
           array('name' => $name,
                 'obj_id1' => $obj_id1,
                 'obj_id2' => $obj_id2));
      }

      /**
       * Remove associations between objects by specifying pairs of object ids.
       *
       * @param  assocs       associations to remove
       * @param  name         (optional) name of association
       * @error
       *    API_EC_DATA_DATABASE_ERROR
       *    API_EC_DATA_OBJECT_NOT_FOUND
       *    API_EC_PARAM
       *    API_EC_PERMISSION
       *    API_EC_DATA_QUOTA_EXCEEDED
       *    API_EC_DATA_UNKNOWN_ERROR
       */
      public function &data_removeAssociations($assocs, $name = null) {
        return $this->call_method
          ('facebook.data.removeAssociations',
           array('assocs' => json_encode($assocs),
                 'name' => $name));
      }

      /**
       * Remove associations between objects by specifying one object id.
       *
       * @param  name         name of association
       * @param  obj_id       who's association to remove
       * @error
       *    API_EC_DATA_DATABASE_ERROR
       *    API_EC_DATA_OBJECT_NOT_FOUND
       *    API_EC_PARAM
       *    API_EC_PERMISSION
       *    API_EC_DATA_INVALID_OPERATION
       *    API_EC_DATA_QUOTA_EXCEEDED
       *    API_EC_DATA_UNKNOWN_ERROR
       */
      public function &data_removeAssociatedObjects($name, $obj_id) {
        return $this->call_method
          ('facebook.data.removeAssociatedObjects',
           array('name' => $name,
                 'obj_id' => $obj_id));
      }

      /**
       * Retrieve a list of associated objects.
       *
       * @param  name         name of association
```

(continued)

305

```
 * @param  obj_id       who's association to retrieve
 * @param  no_data      only return object ids
 * @return              associated objects
 * @error
 *     API_EC_DATA_DATABASE_ERROR
 *     API_EC_DATA_OBJECT_NOT_FOUND
 *     API_EC_PARAM
 *     API_EC_PERMISSION
 *     API_EC_DATA_INVALID_OPERATION
 *     API_EC_DATA_QUOTA_EXCEEDED
 *     API_EC_DATA_UNKNOWN_ERROR
 */
public function &data_getAssociatedObjects($name, $obj_id, $no_data = true) {
  return $this->call_method
    ('facebook.data.getAssociatedObjects',
      array('name' => $name,
            'obj_id' => $obj_id,
            'no_data' => $no_data));
}

/**
 * Count associated objects.
 *
 * @param  name         name of association
 * @param  obj_id       who's association to retrieve
 * @return              associated object's count
 * @error
 *     API_EC_DATA_DATABASE_ERROR
 *     API_EC_DATA_OBJECT_NOT_FOUND
 *     API_EC_PARAM
 *     API_EC_PERMISSION
 *     API_EC_DATA_INVALID_OPERATION
 *     API_EC_DATA_QUOTA_EXCEEDED
 *     API_EC_DATA_UNKNOWN_ERROR
 */
public function &data_getAssociatedObjectCount($name, $obj_id) {
  return $this->call_method
    ('facebook.data.getAssociatedObjectCount',
      array('name' => $name,
            'obj_id' => $obj_id));
}

/**
 * Get a list of associated object counts.
 *
 * @param  name         name of association
 * @param  obj_ids      whose association to retrieve
 * @return              associated object counts
 * @error
 *     API_EC_DATA_DATABASE_ERROR
 *     API_EC_DATA_OBJECT_NOT_FOUND
```

```
 *      API_EC_PARAM
 *      API_EC_PERMISSION
 *      API_EC_DATA_INVALID_OPERATION
 *      API_EC_DATA_QUOTA_EXCEEDED
 *      API_EC_DATA_UNKNOWN_ERROR
 */
public function &data_getAssociatedObjectCounts($name, $obj_ids) {
  return $this->call_method
    ('facebook.data.getAssociatedObjectCounts',
     array('name' => $name,
           'obj_ids' => json_encode($obj_ids)));
}


/**
 * Find all associations between two objects.
 *
 * @param  obj_id1    id of first object
 * @param  obj_id2    id of second object
 * @param  no_data    only return association names without data
 * @return            all associations between objects
 * @error
 *     API_EC_DATA_DATABASE_ERROR
 *     API_EC_PARAM
 *     API_EC_PERMISSION
 *     API_EC_DATA_QUOTA_EXCEEDED
 *     API_EC_DATA_UNKNOWN_ERROR
 */
public function &data_getAssociations($obj_id1, $obj_id2, $no_data = true) {
  return $this->call_method
    ('facebook.data.getAssociations',
     array('obj_id1' => $obj_id1,
           'obj_id2' => $obj_id2,
           'no_data' => $no_data));
}


/**
 * Get the properties that you have set for an app.
 *
 * @param  properties  list of properties names to fetch
 * @return             a map from property name to value
 */
public function admin_getAppProperties($properties) {
  return json_decode($this->call_method
                    ('facebook.admin.getAppProperties',
                     array('properties' => json_encode($properties))), true);
}


/**
 * Set properties for an app.
 *
 * @param  properties  a map from property names to  values
 * @return             true on success
```

(continued)

```php
    */
   public function admin_setAppProperties($properties) {
     return $this->call_method
       ('facebook.admin.setAppProperties',
        array('properties' => json_encode($properties)));
   }



   /* UTILITY FUNCTIONS */

   public function & call_method($method, $params) {

     //Check if we are in batch mode
     if($this->batch_queue === null) {
       $xml = $this->post_request($method, $params);
       $result = $this->convert_xml_to_result($xml, $method, $params);
       if (is_array($result) && isset($result['error_code'])) {
          throw new FacebookRestClientException($result['error_msg'],
$result['error_code']);
       }
     }
     else {
       $result = null;
       $batch_item = array('m' => $method, 'p' => $params, 'r' => & $result);
       $this->batch_queue[] = $batch_item;
     }

     return $result;
   }

  private function convert_xml_to_result($xml, $method, $params) {
     $sxml = simplexml_load_string($xml);
     $result = self::convert_simplexml_to_array($sxml);


     if ($GLOBALS['facebook_config']['debug']) {
       // output the raw xml and its corresponding php object, for debugging:
       print '<div style="margin: 10px 30px; padding: 5px; border: 2px solid black;
background: gray; color: white; font-size: 12px; font-weight: bold;">';
       $this->cur_id++;
       print $this->cur_id . ': Called ' . $method . ', show ' .
           '<a href=# onclick="return toggleDisplay(' . $this->cur_id . ',
\'params\');">Params</a> | '.
           '<a href=# onclick="return toggleDisplay(' . $this->cur_id . ', \'xml\
');">XML</a> | '.
           '<a href=# onclick="return toggleDisplay(' . $this->cur_id . ', \'sxml\
');">SXML</a> | '.
           '<a href=# onclick="return toggleDisplay(' . $this->cur_id . ', \'php\
');">PHP</a>';
       print '<pre id="params'.$this->cur_id.'" style="display: none;
overflow: auto;">'.print_r($params, true).'</pre>';
```

```php
      print '<pre id="xml'.$this->cur_id.'" style="display: none;
overflow: auto;">'.htmlspecialchars($xml).'</pre>';
      print '<pre id="php'.$this->cur_id.'" style="display: none;
overflow: auto;">'.print_r($result, true).'</pre>';
      print '<pre id="sxml'.$this->cur_id.'" style="display: none;
overflow: auto;">'.print_r($sxml, true).'</pre>';
      print '</div>';
    }
    return $result;
  }



  private function create_post_string($method, $params) {
    $params['method'] = $method;
    $params['session_key'] = $this->session_key;
    $params['api_key'] = $this->api_key;
    $params['call_id'] = microtime(true);
    if ($params['call_id'] <= $this->last_call_id) {
      $params['call_id'] = $this->last_call_id + 0.001;
    }
    $this->last_call_id = $params['call_id'];
    if (!isset($params['v'])) {
      $params['v'] = '1.0';
    }
    $post_params = array();
    foreach ($params as $key => &$val) {
      if (is_array($val)) $val = implode(',', $val);
      $post_params[] = $key.'='.urlencode($val);
    }
    $secret = $this->secret;
    $post_params[] = 'sig='.Facebook::generate_sig($params, $secret);
    return implode('&', $post_params);
  }

  public function post_request($method, $params) {

    $post_string = $this->create_post_string($method, $params);


    if (function_exists('curl_init')) {
      // Use CURL if installed...
      $ch = curl_init();
      curl_setopt($ch, CURLOPT_URL, $this->server_addr);
      curl_setopt($ch, CURLOPT_POSTFIELDS, $post_string);
      curl_setopt($ch, CURLOPT_RETURNTRANSFER, true);
      curl_setopt($ch, CURLOPT_USERAGENT, 'Facebook API PHP5 Client 1.1 (curl) ' .
phpversion());
      $result = curl_exec($ch);
      curl_close($ch);
    } else {
      // Non-CURL based version...
      $context =
        array('http' =>
                array('method' => 'POST',
```

(continued)

```php
                        'header' => 'Content-type: application/x-www-form-urlencoded'."\
r\n".
                        'User-Agent: Facebook API PHP5 Client
1.1 (non-curl) '.phpversion()."\r\n".
                        'Content-length: ' . strlen($post_string),
                        'content' => $post_string));
        $contextid=stream_context_create($context);
        $sock=fopen($this->server_addr, 'r', false, $contextid);
        if ($sock) {
          $result='';
          while (!feof($sock))
            $result.=fgets($sock, 4096);

          fclose($sock);
        }
      }
      return $result;
    }

    public static function convert_simplexml_to_array($sxml) {
      $arr = array();
      if ($sxml) {
        foreach ($sxml as $k => $v) {
          if ($sxml['list']) {
            $arr[] = self::convert_simplexml_to_array($v);
          } else {
            $arr[$k] = self::convert_simplexml_to_array($v);
          }
        }
      }
      if (sizeof($arr) > 0) {
        return $arr;
      } else {
        return (string)$sxml;
      }
    }

}


class FacebookRestClientException extends Exception {
}

// Supporting methods and values------

/**
 * Error codes and descriptions for the Facebook API.
 */

class FacebookAPIErrorCodes {

  const API_EC_SUCCESS = 0;

  /*
```

```
 * GENERAL ERRORS
 */
const API_EC_UNKNOWN = 1;
const API_EC_SERVICE = 2;
const API_EC_METHOD = 3;
const API_EC_TOO_MANY_CALLS = 4;
const API_EC_BAD_IP = 5;

/*
 * PARAMETER ERRORS
 */
const API_EC_PARAM = 100;
const API_EC_PARAM_API_KEY = 101;
const API_EC_PARAM_SESSION_KEY = 102;
const API_EC_PARAM_CALL_ID = 103;
const API_EC_PARAM_SIGNATURE = 104;
const API_EC_PARAM_USER_ID = 110;
const API_EC_PARAM_USER_FIELD = 111;
const API_EC_PARAM_SOCIAL_FIELD = 112;
const API_EC_PARAM_ALBUM_ID = 120;

/*
 * USER PERMISSIONS ERRORS
 */
const API_EC_PERMISSION = 200;
const API_EC_PERMISSION_USER = 210;
const API_EC_PERMISSION_ALBUM = 220;
const API_EC_PERMISSION_PHOTO = 221;

const FQL_EC_PARSER = 601;
const FQL_EC_UNKNOWN_FIELD = 602;
const FQL_EC_UNKNOWN_TABLE = 603;
const FQL_EC_NOT_INDEXABLE = 604;

/**
 * DATA STORE API ERRORS
 */
const API_EC_DATA_UNKNOWN_ERROR = 800;
const API_EC_DATA_INVALID_OPERATION = 801;
const API_EC_DATA_QUOTA_EXCEEDED = 802;
const API_EC_DATA_OBJECT_NOT_FOUND = 803;
const API_EC_DATA_OBJECT_ALREADY_EXISTS = 804;
const API_EC_DATA_DATABASE_ERROR = 805;


/*
 * Batch ERROR
 */
const API_EC_BATCH_ALREADY_STARTED = 900;
const API_EC_BATCH_NOT_STARTED = 901;
const API_EC_BATCH_METHOD_NOT_ALLOWED_IN_BATCH_MODE = 902;

public static $api_error_descriptions = array(
```

(continued)

Listing A-3 *(continued)*

```php
        API_EC_SUCCESS          => 'Success',
        API_EC_UNKNOWN          => 'An unknown error occurred',
        API_EC_SERVICE          => 'Service temporarily unavailable',
        API_EC_METHOD           => 'Unknown method',
        API_EC_TOO_MANY_CALLS   => 'Application request limit reached',
        API_EC_BAD_IP           => 'Unauthorized source IP address',
        API_EC_PARAM            => 'Invalid parameter',
        API_EC_PARAM_API_KEY    => 'Invalid API key',
        API_EC_PARAM_SESSION_KEY => 'Session key invalid or no longer valid',
        API_EC_PARAM_CALL_ID    => 'Call_id must be greater than previous',
        API_EC_PARAM_SIGNATURE  => 'Incorrect signature',
        API_EC_PARAM_USER_ID    => 'Invalid user id',
        API_EC_PARAM_USER_FIELD => 'Invalid user info field',
        API_EC_PARAM_SOCIAL_FIELD => 'Invalid user field',
        API_EC_PARAM_ALBUM_ID   => 'Invalid album id',
        API_EC_PERMISSION       => 'Permissions error',
        API_EC_PERMISSION_USER  => 'User not visible',
        API_EC_PERMISSION_ALBUM => 'Album not visible',
        API_EC_PERMISSION_PHOTO => 'Photo not visible',
        FQL_EC_PARSER           => 'FQL: Parser Error',
        FQL_EC_UNKNOWN_FIELD    => 'FQL: Unknown Field',
        FQL_EC_UNKNOWN_TABLE    => 'FQL: Unknown Table',
        FQL_EC_NOT_INDEXABLE    => 'FQL: Statement not indexable',
        FQL_EC_UNKNOWN_FUNCTION => 'FQL: Attempted to call unknown function',
        FQL_EC_INVALID_PARAM    => 'FQL: Invalid parameter passed in',
        API_EC_DATA_UNKNOWN_ERROR => 'Unknown data store API error',
        API_EC_DATA_INVALID_OPERATION => 'Invalid operation',
        API_EC_DATA_QUOTA_EXCEEDED => 'Data store allowable quota was exceeded',
        API_EC_DATA_OBJECT_NOT_FOUND => 'Specified object cannot be found',
        API_EC_DATA_OBJECT_ALREADY_EXISTS => 'Specified object already exists',
        API_EC_DATA_DATABASE_ERROR => 'A database error occurred. Please try again',
        API_EC_BATCH_ALREADY_STARTED => 'begin_batch already called,
please make sure to call end_batch first',
        API_EC_BATCH_NOT_STARTED => 'end_batch called before start_batch',
        API_EC_BATCH_METHOD_NOT_ALLOWED_IN_BATCH_MODE => 'this method is
not allowed in batch mode',
    );
}

$profile_field_array = array(
    "about_me",
    "activities",
    "affiliations",
    "birthday",
    "books",
    "current_location",
    "education_history",
    "first_name",
    "hometown_location",
    "hs_info",
    "interests",
    "is_app_user",
    "last_name",
```

```
        "meeting_for",
        "meeting_sex",
        "movies",
        "music",
        "name",
        "notes_count",
        "pic",
        "pic_big",
        "pic_small",
        "political",
        "profile_update_time",
        "quotes",
        "relationship_status",
        "religion",
        "sex",
        "significant_other_id",
        "status",
        "timezone",
        "tv",
        "wall_count",
        "work_history");
?>
```

Index

A

Boolean comparisons
  nested, 172
  operators, 172
Boolean flags, 73, 74, 83, 100
Boolean values
  attributes
    fb:friend-selector, 75
    fb:if-is-friends-with-viewer, 61
    fb:iframe, 66
    fb:multi-friend-input, 71
    fb:name, 56, 57
    fb:pronoun, 57, 58
    fb:request-form, 72
    fb:swf, 68
    fb:time, 83
  clear, 139
  show_on_profile, 155
  status_includes_verb, 139
border_color (attribute), 71
br (HTML entity), 48
broadcasting messages
  feeds, 12
  Pages, 14
bugs
  bug-tracker tool, 39, 199, 211
  fb:flv and, 69
Bugzilla installation, 211
building applications
  best practices, 249–270
  developers resources, 199–212
  example applications. See example
    applications
  external application development,
    229–248
building relationships, 19, 20, 24
business network, 25
business relationships, 25
Buzz Index project. See *Yahoo Buzz Index*
BuzzLog class, 251–252

C

cached Include files, 92
Callback URLs, 16
  caveats
    no HTTPS and SSL, 263
    no redirection, 263
  Hello World, 30
  home page, 32. See also htdocs/index.php
  option, 32
callbacks, 6, 7
callbackurl (attribute), 74
Can Your Application Be Added on Facebook?
    (option), 32

candelete (attribute), 74
candidates, presidential. *See* Election '08
canpost (attribute), 73
canvas (query string parameter), 191
Canvas page, 7–8
  default. *See* htdocs/index.php
  mobile, 81
  navigational units, 265–266
  request types, 17
capitalize (attribute), 57, 58
caption (HTML entity), 48
Cascading Style Sheet. *See* CSS
Causes (application), 21–22
caveats
  application development, 263
  Callback URLs
    redirection, 263
    SSL and HTTPS, 263
  FQL queries, 166
  Include files, 92
  12-second rule, 263
cell (value), 60
center (HTML entity), 48
character suffix, 99
cite (HTML entity), 48
class (attribute), 81
clickrewriteform (attribute), 85
clickrewriteid (attribute), 85
clickrewriteurl (attribute), 85
clickthrough (attribute), 85
clicktodisable (attribute), 86
clicktoenable (attribute), 86
clicktoggle (attribute), 84, 85
clicktohide (attribute), 84
clicktoshow (attribute), 84
client libraries, 18. *See also* PHP
  Java, 209
client-side scripting, 87, 89. *See also* FBJS
CMS. *See* content management system
Cocoa, 18
code (HTML entity), 48
ColdFusion, 18
colors/styles (Facebook), 264–265
cols (attribute), 64
comments
  applications and. *See* Honesty Box; Wall
    for entities, 74. *See also* fb:comments
common elements (Facebook), 264
comparison operators (Boolean), 172
comparisons, nested (Boolean), 172
competitive applications, 22
complex data structures
  facebook.users.getInfo, 131–136
  fields with, 173
concat function, 172